W9-ACG-091

Moorings & Metaphors

Moorings & Metaphors

▲▲▲▲▲▲▲▲▲▲▲▲▲▲▲▲▲▲▲▲▲▲▲▲▲▲▲▲▲▲▲▲▲▲

Figures of Culture and Gender in Black Women's Literature

Karla F. C. Holloway

RUTGERS UNIVERSITY PRESS
New Brunswick, New Jersey

Library of Congress Cataloging-in-Publication Data

Holloway, Karla F. C.
    Moorings and metaphors : figures of culture and gender in Black women's litera-
ture / Karla F.C. Holloway.
        p.   cm.
    Includes bibliographical references and index.
    ISBN 0-8135-1745-1 (cloth)   ISBN 0-8135-1746-X (pbk.)
    1. American literature—Afro-American authors—History and criticism.   2. West
African literature (English)—Women authors—History and criticism.   3. Literature, Comparative—American and West African (English)   4. Literature, Comparative—West African (English) and American.   5. Women and literature—United
States—History—20th century.   6. American literature—Women authors—History
and criticism.   7. Women and literature—Africa, West—History—20th century.
8. American literature—20th century—History and criticism.   9. Afro-American
women in literature.   10. Women, Black, in literature.   11. Sex role in literature.   12. Myth in literature.   13. Metaphor.   I. Title.
PS153.N5H65   1992
810.9'9287—dc20   91-16803
                                                                          CIP

British Cataloging-in-Publication information available

*For my sisters, Karen Andrea and Leslie Ellen
and our generations—*

Akili, Ayana, Bem, Aziza, Chinyere, Kelechi, and Chisara

Contents

▲▲▲▲▲▲▲▲▲▲▲▲▲▲▲▲▲▲▲▲▲▲▲▲▲▲▲▲▲▲▲▲▲▲▲▲▲

Acknowledgments

I wish to thank the Rockefeller Foundation and the 1988–89 Rockefeller Humanist-in-Residence Fellowships sponsored through the Center for Research on Women at Duke University and the University of North Carolina at Chapel Hill for providing fellowship support during the research and writing of this book.

The specific support and encouragement of John Bassett, Stephanie Demetrakopoulos, and Henry Louis Gates, Jr., at the beginning of this project assured its completion. The collegial and sisterly support of Lois Rita Helmbold and Wendy Luttrell enriched the time we spent as Rockefeller Humanists, shuttling between the Duke and Chapel Hill offices of the Center for Research on Women. The model of their own scholarly persistence is certainly reflected in the publication of this work. I thank as well Abena Busia and Shari Benstock for their careful reading of this manuscript at critical stages in its evolution.

I am grateful for the wise counsel of colleagues who generously read portions of this manuscript through its various configurations and who encouraged both the idea and my development of it. My gratitude and indebtedness are extended in great measure to two colleagues, Joyce Pettis and Gay Wilentz, not only for their keen critical and scholarly insight, but for their nurturing friendship.

This book benefits from the companionship and support I received from two groups of women: The Friday Night Women—Ida Campbell, Sandra Campbell, Millicent Fauntleroy, Hortense Francis, Faithia Henderson, Anita Miles, Gracie Miller, Barbara Montford, Joyce Pettis, Linda Smith, and Marilyn Welch—whose love of the literature that is the subject of this book and whose joyous Friday night gatherings to talk about these works, in our own especially "serious and sustained" manner, continue to be a major blessing in my life; and the Wintergreen Writers' Collective, whose seasonal gatherings (despite hurricanes and snowstorms) have nurtured many of the thoughts in this text.

I also acknowledge *Black American Literature Forum* and *Callaloo* for permission to reprint portions of this manuscript that originally appeared under their auspices.

At Rutgers University Press, I am especially indebted to Leslie Mitchner for her vision, encouragement, and commitment to this project.

Finally, I thank Russell for his unwavering support and I thank my sister Karen's spirit, whose constant and loving presence remains my only solace.

Moorings & Metaphors

Introduction: Cultural Moorings and Spiritual Metaphors

> bein alive & bein a woman & bein colored is a meta-
> physical dilemma/i havent conquered yet. . . . my
> spirit is too ancient to understand the separation of
> soul and gender.
>
> Ntozake Shange, *for colored girls who have considered
> suicide/when the rainbow is enuf*

This is a book with at least two titles. There is a figurative (and parenthetical) title layered within the given one. It has been a subconscious notation for me as I have researched, written, and thought about this work. The figurative title, *(Cultural) Moorings and (Spiritual) Metaphors,* indicates the two dimensions that most accurately reflect my biases toward critical theory and black women's literature.

"Moorings" marks the starting places of my critical interpretations. It is a word I use to emphasize that mine is a perspective deliberately fixed in a specific place. Its center is where behavior, art, philosophy, and language unite as a cultural expression within an African-American literary tradition. A mooring place has been recovered at the point when an interpretation of literary style and substance, and its formal textures and cultural figurations, specifies certain styles of discourse. My primary argument is that black women's literature reflects its community—the cultural ways of knowing as well as ways of framing that knowledge in language. In this study, I trace figures of language that testify to that cultural mooring place. These are inversive, recursive and sometimes even subversive structures that layer the black text and give it a dimension only accessible when its cultural context is acknowledged.

The second parenthetical notation within my title is probably the more unwieldy of the two. As a means of grasping this more spiritual figuration of the way I discuss metaphors, consider the citation of my epigraph to this introduction. My reflection on the dilemma that Ntozake Shange's lady in yellow presents suggests that the creative vision of black women writers makes "bein a woman and bein colored" defy any dissembling of their spiritual unity.[1] It is through the ancient spirituality of this literature that the unity of soul and gender is not challenged but is recovered and celebrated. Within this spirituality, the recovered metaphor that articulates the relationship between soul and gender is the metaphor of the goddess/ancestor. I focus on this subjective metaphor to illustrate the importance of cultural, spiritual, and metaphysical places in both African and African-American women's writing. Contemporary African-American women writers whose work focuses on the recovery of an ancestral figure often use this figuration as an enabling metaphor in their literary revisioning of cultural mythologies. In a similar fashion, twentieth-century West African writers use the goddess figure to represent the dimension of spirituality that is so important to women's characterizations within their texts.[2] My effort, to articulate a relationship between the essence and the place of the goddess in West African literature, constructs a thesis that bridges the goddess with the ancestral figure in African-American women's writing. I believe that far from being a coincidental selection of metaphor, the ancestral presence in contemporary African-American women's writing reconstructs an imaginative, cultural (re)membrance of a dimension of West African spirituality, and that the spiritual place of this subjective figuration is fixed into the structures of the text's language. African women writers' choice of a goddess (sometimes a lady of the lake) as a metaphor connected to women's characterizations, behaviors, and ways of saying is a dimension of this same spirituality. The emphasis that is a discrete pattern in West African women's writing, and that is shared by these authors across the boundaries of cultures and countries, preserves the presence of ancestors and deities within a synchronous realm. Both traditions represent an imaginative and creative selectivity and reflect African and African-American writers' interest in symbolically representing, through the screen of language, the cultural dimensions of women's experiences. The bridge that is achieved between the West African writer and the African-American writer emphasizes the ways in which cultural and spiritual mythologies are a substantive aspect of literary traditions.

The significance these authors place on an articulation of the relationship between soul and gender is revealed through the choices of their textual languages. As an example of these choices, I discuss the ways that language reveals metaphorical dimensions of cultural ways of saying. I explore those repeated textual structures that not only illustrate the call and response strategies and traditions of the black text but also reveal recursive strategies in women's symbolic language.[3] This book illustrates the effect of a textual language that is mythic in its proportion and its intent. It also suggests the ways in which cultural metaphors point to an organization of textual reality rather than to individual instances of minimally related symbols within a text.

Ethnicity, Ethics, and Gender ▲

A basic question of this text concerns the difference that identifies black women's literature as a discrete tradition. In order to begin the argument of the black text's theory, this issue of difference must be addressed. The categories of literature in this study presume intertextual relationships between ethnicity, gender, and literature.

In discriminatory societies, where decisions of privilege are made and are determined by factors external to one's intrinsic capabilities or character, all modes of discrimination are linked. When color and ethnicity matter, they take precedence over stratifications of economics or politics. In 1895, D. G. Ritchie argued that "the idea of equality has grown out of the idea of privilege." Ritchie's conclusion echoed the sentiments of Jefferson Davis's proclamation made thirty years earlier on the "eve of the civil war," that "one of the reconciling features of the existence [of black slavery] is the fact that it raises white men to the same general level, that it dignifies and exalts every white man by the presence of a lower race."[4] I need not catalogue here the history of Euro-American racism; but I want to underscore that racism and its consequential commodification of human lives were European constructs, exported to the African continent and the Americas not only by the slave trade, but by colonialism. The same empire that claimed an economic justification for slavery in the Americas, claimed an economic right to the colonial administration of Africa. My point in stressing the European source of cultural racism is to argue that the shared ethic that lay at the root of the ethnic outrages of colonialism and slavery was one further dimension of the cultural intertext of black women's experiences in West Africa and the Americas.

The discipline within prejudice—by this I mean its rigidity, its reach, and its inclusiveness—is the source of its vitality. Because sexism does not separate itself from the ethics of racism, the relationship between gender and ethnicity follows established stratifications within society. Foucault's suggestion that the *bodies* of individuals are vulnerable to the operations of power helps to clarify the notion that as long as bodies are distinguished in political and social systems in terms of ethnicity and gender, these bodies can be even more carefully distinguished (the aim of prejudice is finer and finer forms of distinction) by another level of bias. In light of this claim, "blackwoman" can be conceived of as a category in the same way that "black" and "woman" are social categories.

The sociophysiological features of bias argue for an acknowledgment of the association between society and health (it can make you sick); society and mortality (it can kill you); society and maternity (it can kill your children); society and psyche (it can lay waste to your spirit). Given the concentration on literary themes of illness (physical and spiritual), death, infanticide, suicide, and psychic fracture in literature by these authors, it is ingenuous to downplay either the gendered or cultural identity of the group. However, and this point is critical to my theoretical position in this text, *neither the internal text nor the frame of theory should be understood as if a mirror of society.* If we expect a reflection, we should anticipate the biases of a historical document or the reductive focus of a sociological tract. Women lose power in social structures and are diminished or absented from historical records. Social structures most certainly do identify (name) the authors, but my argument concerns the imaginative language within their texts. Here, a common ground of verbal lore and the expressiveness within the creative word that "black-women" share cross-culturally mediate black women's literary styles, substantive linguistic strategies, and textual theses.

My argument calls for a recursive acknowledgment of Barbara Smith's 1977 argument ("Toward a Black Feminist Criticism") that the "politics of sex as well as the politics of race and class are crucially interlocking factors in the works of Black women writers." For some, Smith's call for an intersection between writers' and critics' "use of Black women's language and cultural experiences" defeated her argument. Although I read of no creative writers who took her to task for this assertion of what one critic has called a "monolithic" black female language (the phrase is McDowell's), the critical community worried mightily over the possibility that this might exclude them.[5] What if they were not black, could they write convincingly about black women's literature? What if they were black and middle class? What if they wrote like white people? What is writing like white people? What if they were not black "enough"? What would be the criteria for membership in the "interpretive community?" Although there is surely a valid forum for this dimension of the argument, it reveals how easily we are sidetracked from the text. The production of criticism of the black text has been almost as noteworthy an enterprise as the text itself and for this reason, the presentation is conflicted. The authors of criticism have experienced as much scrutiny as their textual subjects. The authors and their work have been politically disassembled and reassembled as the representative point of view in critical anthologies of feminist criticism, collected into so-called "definitive" anthologies, and scattered through professional journals. It is my sense that the subject of the critical enterprise, the black woman's text and its language, has been shortchanged by this highly charged battle for space. Both object and subject are politically enmeshed and victimized by the divisive dialectic about race, class, culture, and gender.[6]

I suggest we return to Smith's argument for a reflexive consideration of black language that has a "miraculously rich coalescing of form and content [that] takes their writing far beyond the confines of white/male literary structures."[7] I suggest we consider whether or not she was right, and that we separate from this consideration our concerns over the membership, color, class, and gender of the interpretive community. I suggest we place this examination into a focused and fair forum.

Attention to the language of black women's writing is not absent from published criticism, but acknowledging its presence has not meant clarifying its nature. Mary Helen Washington postulated the existence of a "specific language" of black women writers in her introduction to *Midnight Birds*. Hortense Spillers suggests a "politics of intimacy" in the "*grammar* of male and female relationships," a grammar that may lead to a discovery of how "woman-freedom, or its negation, is tied to the *assertions of myth, or ways of saying things*" (emphasis added). The critical work that uses black women's literature as its subject is consistently focused and refined. Its examinations of text are often luminous and significant for our developing understanding of this tradition. However, critical proclamations about textual language are acknowledged but not explored. Dianne Sadoff proposes that black women writers' "ambivalence about matrilineage" is coupled, somehow, with "her link to an oral as well as a written tradition." Mae Gwendolyn Henderson identifies Barbara Christian's reference to a "creative dialogue" in the ways black women speak as a Bakhtinian *dialogic of differences* based on a complicated subjectivity. Bakhtin's references seem appropriate for this criticism, especially if we shift them towards the dimensions of race, gender, and culture that are the issues in black women's literature. I believe that his vocabulary can provide a useful construct from which to begin a critical dialogue. Yet Bakhtin's discourse implies a consideration of language and identity that is assumed in the black woman's text without being specified in the critical project.[8]

Theorizing about the linguistic construction of black women's literature necessarily requires acknowledging the intimate relationship between the cultural and ethnic distinctiveness of this work and gender. The texts of black women are different from literature by black men. My argument is that the area of their distinctiveness lies between the spoken text and the expressive text—between voice and vision. Literature by black males does attest to the differences of race and gender and does inscribe this dialogic of difference and identity within the hermeneutic systems of their texts. However, where the place of complexity is extraterritorial for black women writers, texts by black males often isolate the word, circumscribe its territory, and subordinate its voice to expressive behaviors. The province of the word for black women commands a perspective that does not isolate it from its community source. Black male writers' texts claim the power of creative authorship but do not seem to share the word with the reader, or among the characters, or within narrative structures of the text. Instead, the word is carefully controlled and its power is meagerly shared. Black women writers seem to concentrate on shared ways of saying, black males concentrate on individual ways of behaving.

Although the innervision of the word is the figurative goal of black literature in general, its articulation frames the gendered difference. The word identifies dissembled characters and their fractured behaviors in literature by black males. In Chinua Achebe's *Things Fall Apart,* the earth goddess, Ani, is a significant textual presence. However, the male character's relationship with this goddess is characterized by sacrilegeous behaviors against Her. He kills a man during a funeral, beats his wife during a ritual time of peace preceding the planting of yam, and finally kills himself, adding to his series of offenses against the earth.[9] In such work, protagonists sever spiritual intimacy by outrageous behaviors that divide and endanger communities. Soyinka's *Season of Anomy* endangers a priestess (Iriyise) who has shifted away from her gin-drinking goddess and city-woman image.[10] Iriyise is kidnapped by a Cartel whose Western association and materialistic motivation force a holocaust on the villagers. Although Iriyise is rescued, she loses her spiritual essence. At the novel's end she is wasted and unconscious, raped by the horrors she endured during her incarceration. The text's detailed explication of catastrophic tragedies centers this work. Language and voice are secondary to the visual collocation of scenes where macabre violence and dreadful images of death prevail. The visions in this book, "the territor[ies] of hell" silence the pages' words and overshadow the villagers' voices with the ghastly portraits of victims.

From similarly grim images of violence in Richard Wright to similarly silent texts of contemporary black male authors, vision retains its privilege over voice. Although we may see ancestral figures lurking through this literature, Ben Franklin, the ancestor who comes to accompany Mamie Franklin's last days in Al Young's *Seduction by Light,* is hardly the resonant generational figure we find in black women's texts.[11] This book achieves its sardonic and expressive humor by remaining on the surface of every told story. Mamie's voice does control the narrative, but she so overloads it with detail that we learn nothing substantive about the stories within her life. For example, on one of the occasions when Mamie is visited by spirits (her dead husband accompanied by Ben Franklin), Mamie's narrative voice instructs the reader:

> *Picture* yourself. *Picture* how it would feel to be slidin away from your own body. . . . Then after you walk around a little bit and notice can't anybody see it's you, . . . you get shook up. . . .
> "Burley? I said. "Is that you?"
> "Yes," he said, "but it's somebody with me. . . .
> "Ben?" I asked finally, comin right on out with it. "Ben, is that you?"
> The minute I said it, *the whole picture* started fallin back in place . . . almost *like if you were to run a movie.* (Emphasis added.)[12]

The depth of spiritual history is absent from this novel. This is not a weakness—the novel gains a great deal of its energy from its Hollywood setting. Superficiality is a part of its strategy; yet it is detail without substance. These texts have words and use them to emphasize their representative (pictorial) and reflective potentials; but they do not claim the dimensions of voice.

Richard Perry's *Montgomery's Children* has striking (and sometimes puzzling) similarities to Toni Morrison's *Song of Solomon.* However, when Perry's character flies, he ascends over a town, above a steeple and beyond a chasm, but we get no sense of his movement through time, myth, and dimension. Like the characters in West African novels by males, Perry's Norman tries (mostly unsuccessfully) to avoid the paralysis that accompanies evil: "He needed to be above it all. He'd had a close call; he'd been in the presence of evil, and it had left him shaken and feeling unclean. How hard it was to keep faith in the midst of forces that worked to hold you down . . . You could not steal the ability to fly." [13] Evil is an omnipresent, earth-bound presence in black males' texts—whether in the lack of name and kinship that threaten the father and son in Ernest Gaines's *In My Father's House,* or in the "experiment in pain" that literally and figuratively isolates Modin in Ayi Kwei Armah's *Why Are We So Blest?* [14] In Armah's novel, Modin and a white girl (Aimee) both volunteer for a psychological experiment on the thresholds of pain (his is very low, hers is quite high). At the novel's end, Aimee watches as Modin's penis is cut off in a graphic and disabling scene indicative of the impotency and loss that characterize this novel.

Because of the images they sketch, the words in these texts fix us into a sometimes horrific and challenging present. Although the past may be recalled to the story, although ancestors and goddesses may filter through the visual screens, the dominant mediums of the text are behavior and act—sometimes to the extent that voice is intentionally silenced so that image can claim all of our attention.

As an example, consider Soyinka's *The Interpreters.* Sekoni's death in this novel, another in a series of graphic and violent moments, is preceded by his stuttered assertion that (in life) "there is no dddirection . . . bbbridges dddon't jjjust gggo from hhere to ththere; a bridge also faces backward." His stuttering symbolizes the impotent word. His own lack of direction (Soyinka calls his head "short-sighted") disables him in a world where Europeans and Africans struggle for domain on a land one has lost and the other can never totally repossess. [15] Similarly dispossessed is Leroi Jones's Roi (*The System of Dante's Hell*) whose quest for his cultural and sexual self begins in the "deepest part of hell." Jones's novel does not hesitate to point out the link between gender and culture. Roi cannot find his black self until he finds his male self. Even if his maleness is an expressive homosexuality, it is his legitimate source. He is traumatized because he had been running, "against [his] own sources . . . in terror, from [his] deepest responses and insights." [16] Jones (Imamu Baraka) articulates the trauma of cultures in contact and articulates the subordinate role of voice in tracing the traditions of gendered spaces in male writers' texts.

Although James Baldwin does bridge the past and the present in a novel like *Go Tell It on the Mountain,* this work illustrates the significantly contrastive strategies of the black male writer.[17] Baldwin bridges epochs, with language as stunning and evocative as any in literature; but his is not the language of memory, it is the language of the insistent present. His strategy is not recursive and, in a characteristic he shares with his gender, his methodology is not revision. Instead, the text is stative. Repetition would be redundant to the visual imagery that overloads our sensory responses. Revision would allow us an alternative path to the text's thesis, but writers like Baldwin insist on directing the reader quite specifically, with little or no wandering, through the specified symbolic network. Whatever collage of symbols there is, it constantly dissembles in order to express their distinct meanings within the text. In Baldwin's work, images of sexuality and religion are mixed but distinguishable. Urban blight and religious sin are clearly the figural levels of this text and its thesis. There is complexity, but ambiguity is not the goal of these writers' works. The visceral metaphor that Baldwin's literature shares with black male writers in Africa and America images the nature of evil. In *The Fire Next Time* Baldwin wrote of his fear. He was "afraid of the evil within me and afraid of the evil without."[18]

In *The Chaneysville Incident,* David Bradley comes closest to the narrative strategies that I identify within the black woman's text.[19] But his character's recovery of history, accomplished so that he might insert the untold story of his ancestor's role in the suicidal incident at Chaneysville, is an effort of "imaginative completion . . . of the fictional reconstruction of the unfinished story-line of history."[20] Although there is an oral "mode" in this story, place and event take precedence in the text. John Washington is a historian whose effort is to make the story he researches about his own past fit into the historic schema he trusts. So even though he eventually burns his note cards, the dimensions of time and place within this novel embrace the imaginative words into their service. The thesis in this text indicates that history can be made right, absences can be filled with black American presences, untold stories can become a part of the record. The visual dimensions of this story struggle to make the historical text real—to reconstruct, renew, and make things whole. Bradley's work depends, as the historical reclamation of his character John Washington depends, on appearance: "it came to me how strange *it would all look* to someone else. . . . I wondered if she would understand *when she saw* the smoke go rising" (emphasis added).[21]

The massive emotional purges in black males' literature, the activity attached to those emotions, their passions, and the behaviors that accompany them focus their works on "acting out" even while distancing the authorial and the narrative response (voices) from the emotional and spiritual pressure within the text. In contrast, a collective "speaking out" by all the voices gathered within the text, authorial, narrative, characters, and even the implicated reader, is the responsive strategy in black women's literature.

Language as Cultural Intertext ▲

Moorings and Metaphors is an extended discussion of the kinds of theoretical considerations that emerge with a critical reading of black women writers' imaginative textual languages. A careful attention to the cultural sources of that language and its spiritual configurations is a necessary complement of the theory.

Although the theory I explore reflects some consideration of contemporary modes of critical inquiry, my intent is to extend the frames of traditional methodologies, *not* to replicate them. It is important to clarify that the (conscripted) vocabulary of Western critical theorists is an intentional strategy of my process in this book. However, even though the vocabulary of Western critical theorists performs a useful structural function for this work, the semantic shifts that these words undergo as they are appropriated and contextualized within the literature of African and African-American writers has created its own kind of critical process. This secondary enterprise performs a critical (as well as lexical) function in its claim of theoretical space. It affirms my sense that race has a cultural presence in the fiction of this tradition. The "essential" difference of my work is, I believe, my insistence that there is a textual place where language and voice are reconstructed by black women writers as categories of cultural and gendered essence. The operative place of race within my theoretical argument is within the *fictive* places of black women's literature. Here, in these imaginative realms, race becomes the ultimate signifier as it plays within the imaginative domains of fictional language.

Even with these considerations of vocabulary and structure in mind, it has been most important to my theoretical process that my primary organization reflects the three contextual perspectives—revision, (re)membrance, and recursion—that extend from my consideration of the imaginative dimensions of the language within this literature.

All of the work I consider is literature in English. Written by black women in Africa and America, this is a literature that crosses the linguistic and cultural histories of (at least) three continents and reflects the multiple linguistic and cultural frames of these continents. An Afrocentric critical posture, whether a discussion of the African writer who writes in English or of the African-American author, replaces the European center of ideology and metaphor as it affirms the multicultural implications of the chosen language of the text. It is this (perhaps) curious complicity between the vocabulary of the West and the visions within this literature that underscores the unique task of definition that the theorist of black literature must accomplish. The history of West African and African-American women is bio-geographical (the phrase is Ngugi's)—a concept that suggests that the imaginative literature of these women may be a significant source of cultural continuity. The literary/linguistic figurations of metaphor, in this case the imagery of the goddess/ ancestor, facilitate my focus on the nature of this connection and my exploration of the literary commonalities between cultures separated by history.

I have (almost completely) restricted my exploration to literature by contemporary black writers because at no other time in the history of this literature have the imaginative and creative dimensions of their language been so fully and gracefully extensive, so rich, and so very elegant. Further, contemporary texts by black women writers emphasize with uncompromising clarity the critical relationship between character and voice.

I collect the discussions within this book into two major divisions. Part one, "A Figurative Theory," gathers the various theoretical configurations that articulate the cultural and gendered spaces within this literature.

A discussion of some of the current ways of understanding the theoretical enterprise is the subject of my first chapter—"A Critical Consideration of Voice, Gender, and Culture." It is in this chapter that I introduce the three frames—*revision, (re)membrance* and *recursion*—that organize the relationship between meaning, voice and community. In chapter one, I discuss my recovery of the culturally related figures of an ancestral presence and a goddess as a dimension of the intertextual, shared traditions in African and African-American women writers' texts.

Chapter two is a personal reflection on the kinds of decisions that must be made and challenged when articulating the relationship between text and theory. It focuses on the literary traditions that have historically marginalized the texts and authors that are the subject of this book and addresses the source of the reconstructed theory that grounds contemporary criticism of black women's literature. This chapter is a commentary on the issues I raise in this introduction as well as on the interpretive community that has chosen black literature as its subject.

My next two chapters examine recursive structures in literature and language, and consider literary figurations and textual language with a focus on metaphor. My discussion is framed by the three textual features introduced in chapter one. Each is relevant to textual organization. In the case of *revision*, the narrative is propelled towards inversion—a restructuring of traditional (i.e. Western) modes of organization. *(Re)membrance*—spelled with the parenthetical (re) to emphasize the bodying suggested by "membrance" as well as the restorative aspect of the prefix—acknowledges a spiritual point of origin that for these works was oral and poetic at a time when oracy and poetry were not distinct modes of expression but were intimately linked. In addition, a *(re)membered* text privileges ways of organization that support the processes of memory as an accurate and appropriate means towards figuring one's history. In this way, those black and female voices that have been excluded from Western historiography tell and (re)member their own stories using their own means of recovering these experiences. The focus of a *recursive* text is to layer ways of memory and discourse and the mythic figures within language and culture until each is folded into the other. Recursion is a generative activity

that depends on a succession of events. Multiplied texts have
figurative dimensions that continually reflect other, deeper dimensions. Their language and their imaginative visions suggest
a certain depth of memory that black women's textual strategies
are designed to acknowledge.

Chapters three and four concentrate on recursion as a way of
retaining an idea of repetition even if there is no visible repetition of words or phrases in the sentence. Literary recursion, the
subject of chapter three, focuses on the metaphorical dimensions of the text. It is a figurative and symbolic signal that the
reflective, backwards glance of the recursive process is significant to the strategies of revision and (re)membrance. Linguistic
inversions (like dialect and redundancy) signal recursion. Chapter four explains how a relationship between memory and experience is encouraged through linguistic recursion.

"Mythologies," chapter five, is an exploration of how these
texts shift the traditional explanation of myth to one that includes a sustained, mythic level of language instead of myth
merely as context and story. Cultural patterns in language embrace both the text and its tradition, rather than merely a particular moment within the story or a certain and clearly
circumscribed way of using language. Although I affirm that it
is within the texts of black women that the most lucid indicators
of preserved, cultural meanings (myth) can be found, my claim
does not alienate mythic literature to black women writers.
However, women's texts do indicate how the expressive aspect
in the voice of mythologies of the non-Western world is an intimate aspect of the narrative voice within the text. Instead of the
external events and objective phenomena that dominate the
texts of black male writers, an intensely internal and self-
reflexive perspective identifies the work of black women writers.
In this chapter, I discuss how this view of mythology privileges
memory.

Part two of this work is "An Intertextual Study" of literature
by contemporary black women writers in West Africa and
America. The theoretical frames of part one are critical to my
readings of selected texts in this tradition.

Chapters six and seven discuss in detail the ancestral metaphor of African-American writers' texts and the goddess metaphors within West African writers' texts, explaining how the

metaphor is a creative vision within both the cultured and the gendered spheres of these texts. Although the discussion of these chapters considers several different works from contemporary women writers of these traditions, my focus is on the ideas of metaphor and mediation and their legislation of shared textual themes like birth, wholeness, spirit, community, and voice. The revision of the word and its creative regeneration are the foci of my discussions of contemporary literature by African and African-American women writers. The oral traditions that define the patterns of storytelling, arrangements of text, and the significance of voice as reconstructed memory are culturally specific and gendered features of this literature. The metaphorical and mediative presences of the goddess and ancestors center my critical enterprise in these chapters.

Chapter eight, "Spirituals and Praisesongs: Telling Testimonies," explores the intertextual, bicultural frames that this kind of theory makes possible. Using Flora Nwapa's *Efuru* and Toni Morrison's *Beloved* as touchstones, I put to use the kinds of interpretive decisions that come from a consideration of features like *recursion, revision,* and *(re)membrance.* This chapter clarifies the roles of the cultural and gendered traditions as they emerge in the spiritual regions of these writers' works.

In a manner that illustrates the process of a recursive text, the subject and method of my final chapter are a commentary on my first. In this way I mean to illustrate how a consideration of words is a circular consideration. To return to the figurative sources as they appear within the texts of this tradition is to begin the critical process again and to anticipate that it will recover itself, again and again, through this consistent reflection of the cyclic nature of the critical enterprise.

Part 1

A Figurative Theory

1

▲▲▲▲▲▲▲▲▲▲▲▲▲▲▲▲▲▲▲▲▲▲▲▲▲▲▲▲▲▲▲▲▲▲▲▲▲▲▲

A Critical Consideration of Voice, Gender, and Culture

> There were always the prophets—necromancers whose folk tales and sermons defied the conventions of plot, conflict, causality and motivation.
>
> Ishmael Reed, "Can a Metronome Know the Thunder or Summon a God?"

In *Sassafrass, Cypress and Indigo,* Ntozake Shange weaves the various textures of words found in recipes, journal entries, narrative streams, poetry, and letters into the pages of her novel in ways that make each one of her carefully chosen words translucent.[1] A consequence of Shange's style is that her text resonates with the sounds from these voices as much as it envisions the collection of her words. Shange's stylistic device clearly designates the importance of the oral origins of her text. In addition, the history within her words and their connection to gendered and cultural sources are as important an emphasis. Indigo is described as a child/woman "with a moon falling from her mouth . . . a consort of the spirits." Her name claims her relationship with darkness and the sky. Indigo embodies the dark colors of blood, the deep colors of the sea, and the depth of the midnight sky. Hers is an ancient fertility—"I've got earth blood, filled up with the Geechees long gone, and the sea." Indigo is, as a child with the "south" in her, left at the end of this book with the creative legacy of her ancestral mentor, a midwife who assures that the community will have the appropriate creative accompaniment of Indigo's ancient talents.[2]

The reclamation of women's voice is the critical accomplishment of contemporary literature by black women writers in America and Africa. Their return to the word as a generative source—a source of textual power that both structures story and absorbs its cultural legacy—is a return to the power of the word itself. It is a recovery of text through the literary and linguistic activity of recursion—a refocusing of meaning back to the semantic and syntactic structures that have assured the unity between meaning and source.

In this critical turn toward language there is a potential to recover a cultural bridge between black women writers of West Africa and America. Certainly, there are important differences in the literary subjects and styles among women of West Africa and African-American women writers. This is a given dimension of the contemporary political, cultural, and social differences between them. The colonial history of West Africa has yoked the indigenous politics of the community, forcing the language and structures of European cultures and politics onto a continent without regard to or interest in the indigenous cultural communities. The social structures of European governments rescinded centuries-old patterns of life and complicated the economic and religious lives of the communities. For African women and men, loss characterized the colonial era. For black Africans who became a powerless majority in their own country, a set of circumstances different from black Africans who lost their nation, their majority, and their power within the system of Euro-American slavery emerged. In societies that are both racist and sexist, bias is a distinction of culture *as well as of gender.* All that was buried in colonial Africa—language, religion, political independence, economic policy—was lost by enslaved Africans. Retrieval for Africans means an overthrow of power and a reinvestment in self-determination. For the African-American, retrieval is not possible. Instead, recovery means an act of spiritual memory rather than physical possession.

There is, however, a compelling historical reason to explore the potential for commonalities among these writers. The cultural history that links black writers in America also calls for an acknowledgment of the West African sources of that history. It is this perspective that allows for an exploration of the intertextual, shared images and patterns among writers with a common cultural history to emerge in the midst of the acknowledged differences between them. The result is an activity that explores how particular manipulations of words and specific ways of arranging meaning can call attention to gender in culture. Attention to the ways that black women writers arrange meaning and specify figures of language circumscribes another way of gathering that cultural community of writers. The gathering makes even more specific the detail of their intimate connection.

I do not propose any one discrete critical theory of black women's texts as establishing "the" system by which critics might interpret texts within the black women writers' tradition. This reduction simplifies the complex cultural presence in this literature. Instead, a theoretical exploration can establish a dialogue between theorists of language and literature. The dialogue would bridge the speculations of language and literary theorists concerning black language patterns and figures in black literature. Linguists argue that there are recoverable aspects of language in the dialects of the diaspora—patterns in its organizations and systems of meanings—that reflect their shared West African history.[3] I suggest we look at this literary language in terms of the patterns in/of some of its imaginative figures. Scholarship on linguistic patterns within languages of the diaspora can then be related to literary criticism that explores an African female aesthetic (such as the work of Carol Boyce Davies). Such an enterprise would emphasize a potential common cultural ground for language patterns and a literary aesthetic.

There is another, and perhaps more problematic, dimension to this exploration of language and literature within the framework of its cultured and gendered sources. Lawrence Lipking articulates a perspective of the "desperation" he notes in feminist criticism that accounts for the absence of women in the "precious imposing bastions of literary theory." Lipking suggests that the efforts of feminist criticism to show how "women fit in" (to Marxism, semiology, Lacanian, post-structuralist, and deconstructive theory) is necessary because feminist critics "acknowledge no mothers."[4] There are no women, Lipking laments, at the center of feminist thought. Instead, feminist criticism is marked by an insistence on definitions that put "Adam and Marx" at their critical centers. My argument for an Afrocentric interpretive model for black women's literature is an argument that acknowledges both a spiritual *and* a physical mother at its center. The spiritual presence of the ancestor and the figural representation of the goddess in literature by black women writers is the centering imagery of *Moorings and Metaphors.*

Because of the accompanying vocabulary of what some might be persuaded to label as white, male, and Western theoretical jargon, I think it important to call attention to the generative nature of a transformational project like this one. I use these linguistic terms quite intentionally because within transforma-tional-generative theory language is understood to have at least two levels of meaning—one having to do with performance, and the other with comprehension. Surface structures of lan-guage—in this case the lexicon of traditional (white, male and Western) theory are semantically meager in comparison to the linguistic deep structures they represent. In these (deeper) places, the sounds and sense of culture and experience generate transformations of the arrangement and semantic categories within the linguistic surface structures. I view my project in a similar way. Henry Louis Gates, Jr. also acknowledges this trans-formational potential when he notes that in theorizing the black text, "the critic, by definition, transforms the theory."[5] My deci-sion to acknowledge both a metaphorical as well as a metaphys-ical presence at the center of my own work is a way to call attention to the generative potential within an Afrocentric theo-retical perspective. My objective is to gather together figures of language, myth, and literary imagery in a creative recovery of an original cultural and gendered intimacy.

Careful and cogent discussions of such thematic issues as class and community, character and nature have invigorated the pubished criticism of black women's texts. I believe there also has been a more subtle, and sometimes puzzling tendency to avoid an imaginative and theoretical coalescence concerning what we have learned about black women's texts—their lan-guage, the nature of their literary discourse, and the cultural mythologies that identify them.[6]

A parallel consequence of specifying non-Western cultural

metaphors that are a dimension of this literature is the acknowledgment of this as a literature only barely escaped from the hegemony of Western critical ideology. Naming a source outside of this tradition forces the nominative activity to be creative as well as definitive. As an example, consider the epigraph I have chosen for this chapter. Ishmael Reed specifies "conventionality, causality and motivation" as features likely to be subverted in the "necromancy" of the black text. Reed reminds us of the true history in black letters.[7] It has been consistently nonconventional; its causality has more often than not indicted the ideological base of the West; and its motivation has been to assert the voice and to affirm the humanity that the Western world has conspired to suppress and deny. Interestingly enough, the discussion of this literature within a canon that barely acknowledged its existence and would distract the critical audience away from its complexity (and towards a so-called more "universal" model) has been a process of both affirmation and denial. Most critics of African-American literature, aware of the opposition between the (traditionally black and Third World) subject of the literature under discussion and the (traditionally white and Western) audience for whom that discussion was intended, generally found it safer to affirm the difference of the text without the parallel acknowledgment that the white and Western world was predisposed to undervalue this literature or, even worse, to place it into a sociological frame that would somehow explain to them what they know as the "black man's burden." An essential loss of critical substance occurs in this failed acknowledgment. The dialectic between the critical audience and the text is diminished. A result of this subjective/objective fragmentation is theoretical invisibility or silence.

Traditionally, the differential relationship between a critical theory of literature and its critical audience substantiates a dialectic. However, the perverse consequence of a failed relationship between black literature's critical theory and the canonically chauvinistic Western academy has been the dislocation of the West as the center that frames meanings and inscribes values. In the context of the African-American literary tradition, the displacement has a bi-textual effect. It dissolves the hegemony of Western ideology and affirms the occupation of the necromancers—the creative crafters of the word—within the black literary tradition. Their contemporary and historical work persistently dislocates the superstitions of Western ideologies. The metaphors that identify black traditions of literary theory are those that reach outside of Western history for their source.

This is a selection underscored by Reed's shift from prophet to necromancer in the citation. Necromancy and magic are decidedly and historically not mainstream (i.e. Western). When Benvenuto Cellini's sixteenth-century Sicilian priest donned his necromancer's robe, also called a "wizard's robe" in *The Autobiography,* the priest/necromancer/wizard tried to recruit young Cellini to "consecrate a book" not because of his excellence in Latin (he could have found "plenty of good Latinists") but because of Cellini's "firm soul." It was not, therefore, Cellini's classical sensibilities that would liberate the magic from the book, but his spiritual resolve.[8] Spiritual creativity is at the center of the tradition that Reed embraces when he chooses the folktale tellers and sermon deliverers as the tradition's early sources of necromancy. African-American history and African history document that the tellers were women and their stories and songs were the oral archives of their culture.[9]

Revision, the first of three perspectives that organizes this book, represents a gathering of the ways a culture organizes language, the privilege given to particular speakers, and the association between language, voice, and the physical presence of the speaker. Indicative of this gathering are works by black women writers that illustrate what Ishmael Reed calls "an oral . . . talking book" and what Gates calls the "speakerly text."[10] These works revise the parameters of speech and the dimensions of voice in ways that force a critical attention to the intertextual nature of this revision. Reed's purpose is not to characterize the work of black women writers in this instance (indeed, Reed's characterizations of black women writers have often been quite vicious), and Gates cites both Ishmael Reed and Zora Neale Hurston as authors of speakerly texts. I claim revision and the processes of transformation and generation as my theoretical methodology (not only in my citation of Ishmael Reed, but in reference to the language and vocabulary of contemporary critical inquiry) and as the substantive context of the black woman's text. My use of revision as a gender-specific instance foregrounds gendered spheres of knowledge—women's ways of framing and keeping that knowledge in the place of the representation of the "speaking black voice."[11]

The second perspective that organizes this book is (re)membrance. It focuses on the ways that memory is culturally inscribed. Generally, this kind of inscription is assigned to the genre of myth. The mythic dimensions within these works stress the intimacy between myth and cultural memory. In them, the spoken text retains a figurative intimacy to the mythic text. Memory is a tactile path toward cultural recovery. When we complicate this value with the destabilizing activities of traditional historiography, we are forced to acknowledge the distinct versions of memory that myth, as an a priori oral text, recovers. These are works that claim the texts of spoken memory as their source and whose narrative strategy honors the cultural memories within the word. The literary category of myth has traditionally been credited as a source of creative, that is, imaginative activity and a point of genesis of original meanings. An important question to my study is to determine what happens when the connection between creativity and genesis is used as literary method.

The recovery of myth is linked to the emergence of textual complexity. Both myth and memory acknowledge a linguistic/cultural community as the source of the imaginative text of recovered meaning. Attention to the innervision of the word—its approximation of consciousness—is a way of understanding the literary revision of the mythic principle in black women writers' texts. By assuming this perspective, my intention is to stress the use of myth in black women writers' texts as a vehicle for aligning real and imaginative events in both the present and the past and for dissolving the temporal and spatial bridges between them. Within this framework, myth complicates language and imagery. It is a dynamic entity that (re)members community, connects it to the voices from which it has been severed, and forces it out of the silence prescribed by a scriptocentric historicism. Gates's theory that the "two-toned, double-voiced metaphor of the black text's antecedent" is "central to the full explication of the canonical black text" establishes a critical relationship, a mooring, between the spoken texts of myth and the (re)membered consciousness within the literate word.[12]

Recursion is the third perspective that organizes my discussion. Its concerns address the concepts of complexity, layering, and the multiplied text. Black writers' textual voices are layered within the narrative and linguistic structures of both the text itself and the characterization within the text. This layering creates a ritualized, recursive structure that identifies imagery and language particular to the black woman's literary tradition. The ritualistic process of repetition and reflexiveness becomes a linguistic metaphor equal in intent, I believe, to the metaphorical Esu, who, in Gates's critical argument, stands for the critical activity of interpretation and signifyin(g) in the black literary tradition.[13]

Women's Ways of Saying ▲

In ways that emphasize these three perspectives, the extended discussions in *Moorings and Metaphors* refine, develop, practice, and explore each perspective as a discrete feature in black women's literature. A woman-centered principle grounds these works and emphasizes the cultural representation of language. What connects language and creativity is that for women, biologically confronted with the possibility of creation, motherhood embraced or denied is unique to her sense of self.

Black women writers nurture the spoken word within their texts. The intersections between voice, language, and gender underscore the ways in which black women's writing is different from the feminist text. (My effort to distinguish between them is illustrated in my use of the term "woman-centered" to describe these texts.) The integration of gender and ethnicity is critical to the representation of cultures of West Africa and the diaspora. Western feminists are not likely to see themselves mirrored in the black woman's text. Julia Kristeva, for example, argues that symbolic coherence is the achievement of a "mother tongue."[14] This relational vision of maternity and language is not the vision within black women's texts. Although Kristeva's poetic language is expressively chaotic in its gestation, and although this destabilizing and unconscious chaos is an important dimension of the black woman's text, Kristeva's "mother tongue" lacks ownership. This lack of specificity distinguishes this feminist reconstruction from that of the black woman writer for whom possession of the word is a cultural and gendered legacy.

In reference to the English language text, criticism has to acknowledge that literacy, creative and otherwise, has a basic and troubled association with freedom in black America. In colonized Africa, children have been whipped and beaten for using tribal languages in colonial schools. For black people on both continents, the English language has a context of abuse and dehumanization. Black women's biological experience with maternity—pregnancy, birth, and lactation—has a similar association with peril. Certainly there are few more dismal images in literature than Sethe's mournful, angry, and pitiful litany that recalled how "those boys came in there and took my milk. . . . Held me down and took it. . . . And they took my milk. . . . And they took my milk!" [15] Toni Morrison's character in *Beloved,* an escaped slave, repeats those words until they rock her into a memory of her pain and loss. This is simply not the experience of white women's literature. As much as women's studies may claim (what are essentialist) commonalities of women's experiences, the truth is that in racist societies, race and gender stratification are constructs of cultural demarcations. My point is that when black women writers imaginatively engage this English language in their texts, the sociocultural history in these words requires the processes of revision. Otherwise, the history of these words would be so repressive that any form of creativity with them would be impossible. Ownership of the creative word means making these words work in cultural and gendered ways that undermine the hegemony of the West.

Hélène Cixous may problematize "the literal connection between female biology and the kind of writing this 'ink' produces," but the "violence" which has separated women from "white ink," from "writing the body" is not like Sethe's loss of her milk, or black women's loss of their tribal languages and their spheres of power. [16]

Mary Poovey argues that a debate over whether or not women speak like Luce Irigaray imagines (a discourse of which women would be the object or the subject) is not the point of the feminist project. I want to expand Poovey's notion to include the argument of this text as well. Poovey writes that "the endeavor is to imagine some organization of fantasy, language, and reality other than one based on identity and binary oppositions, which is currently the dominant mode.[17]

The language of the black woman's text is "acknowledged power" as Barbara Christian suggests in an essay on African women writers. Christian stresses the significance in claiming a linguistic articulation beyond oracy. She writes that "articulation occurs . . . when African women themselves [gained] access to the pen." Christian's discussion shortchanges the relevance of their possession and creation of an oral tradition in framing that literate articulation. Still, its focus on colonialism as a system that contributed to "a prescribed fate of [literary] . . . silence" appropriately identifies the source of their silence as an external construct, foreign to their indigenous cultural behavior.[18] Although it is certainly "access to the pen" that erases this kind of silence, it is spoken language that is metaphorically embraced as the vehicle of this creative power.

Alice Walker's Celie recognizes the survival that language promises as she refuses the silence she is ordered to maintain ("Don't tell nobody" she is warned by Mr.) and chooses to "tell" by writing her soul out of its hiding place. In this novel, Walker signifies upon her subject as her own writing structures the written narrative of Celie's eventual liberation. Celie addresses some of her letters to God—a symbolic address to her spiritual self. However, in a recursive acknowledgment of the voice within and without the text, both Celie and Alice Walker create, tell, and talk back. Celie defies Mr. in the insistence of maintaining her voice. Considering the storm of protest this novel has engendered from a legion of black male critics, it is obvious that Alice Walker has talked back as well.[19] She and Celie both assert their creative rights of gender. Indeed, Walker's deceptively elliptical dedication of this book "To the Spirit / Without whose assistance / Neither this book / Nor I / Would have been / Written" is not an ellipsis at all, but a warning of the linguistic recursion that will frame her story. Because the reader knows, along with Celie and Walker, that this is really a spoken text and that writing is a way to preserve a voice that was threatened, warned, and silenced, *The Color Purple* is actually a long signifying tale.

Motherhood as "membrance," a phrase I use to suggest its physiological and visceral relationship to femaleness, is central to African women writers. It is a theme that not only asserts the ability to create life, but a principle that emerges as central to feminine *potentia* in religion, politics, economics and social spheres. It enlarges the simple biological principle to engage these others. In an essay on this subject in Igbo writers, Carol Boyce Davies calls the African woman writer's interest in motherhood a "preoccupation" that is distinctly "African feminism."[20] Asserting the critical role of motherhood to female identity is an important distinction from Euro-American feminist ideology. It takes the issue of physiological reproduction further than social consequences because it assertively includes this physiology in a woman's sense of self. The preoccupation Davies has noted parallels the linguistic power that also preoccupies Walker's fiction and essays. The complications inherent in motherhood as both a physiological and a metaphysical construct identify a unique bridge between African-American and African women writers.

As an example, consider the significance of the umbilicus between language and creation for Nigerian writer Buchi Emecheta. This emphasis is clear as her character Nnu Ego (*The Joys of Motherhood*) laments, "How will I talk to a woman with no children?" In contrast, works by African-American women writers often recognize, then sever this symbolic umbilicus, underscoring the tragedy endemic to such separation. Toni Morrison's Pecola (*The Bluest Eye*) is raped into silence, bears a dead baby, and sacrifices her spirit to illusion and madness. In her Pulitzer Prize winning novel, Morrison's title character, Beloved, appears as a spirit daughter, only to become a succubus to the mother who is victimized by mother-love. Hurston's Janie (*Their Eyes Were Watching God*) is a "born orator," but her poetry is stifled by her husband Jody. In consequence, Janie must learn to direct her language inward, eventually recovering her soul. Only at the novel's end is she sufficiently empowered to call in her soul to see her poetic light and subvert the tragedy silence portends by a birthing of her poetic self.[21]

Davies suggests that several concerns unique to African women and revealed in their literature may, especially in comparative studies of African and African-American women writers, reveal "an overall female aesthetic." In a critical theory that links acts of language to activation of character, the issues of motherhood and self gain significance as we look at them within the organization of language. Davies's codicil to her discussion notes that Euro-American critical frameworks are inadequate for framing such analyses or structuring such comparative studies because, among other things, in the "critical criteria of the literary establishment which is European and male dominated, many of these African female forms are dismissed as weaknesses."[22] In other words, the very items that can define the theory are the items easily dismissed by Western cultures. This is an especially insidious dismissal when we examine how pervasive the loss of orature is in Western pedagogy. Historical frames, political and legal processes, and education and psychology are all dependent on scripted performances that can be undermined by any insertion of the spoken word.

Textual attention to the devices of language reifies the primary and feminine principle of language. Spiritual rediscovery, loss, and acknowledgment are structural devices in the arrangement of text and the telling of story in black women writers' works. Such attentiveness and testimony are evidence of specific principles of textual organization. It is important not to lose sight of the cultured and gendered contexts within these fictive encounters because discovering context may also mean recovering consciousness. This can lead as well to a critical recovery of cultural organization and patterns of memory and telling.

The kinds of theoretical processes that I want to emphasize in this book depend on acknowledging the way in which a specific collection of linguistic structures is able to function as a bridge to a collection of metaphorical structures. We might recall Hegel's expressed doubt that there was a consciousness (or a culture) that one could associate with the African imagination. In Hegel's view, the absence of a "contemplation of . . . objectivity" suggested that awareness of an objective self was not among the characteristics of the African's (mental) life.[23] The privilege and value that Hegel extended to the objective consciousness—the enterprise of a successfully individuated subject—is typical of the focus of Euro-American thought. Within these parameters, any kind of collective, even a metaphorical one, loses value when viewed as an alternative to the subject's willingness to objectify its experience. In this comparison, a collective consciousness—the enterprise of a successfully collaborative group of subjects—is not a commodity of significant value. Ironically, it is the subordination of the opposition between the subject and the object that is a hallmark within the black woman's text. This literature reconstructs the schismatic pair by insisting upon the collaborative nature of the enterprise—the communication between between author and character, reader and text (subject and object)—a clear challenge to the Western (Hegelian) notion of their polarity. Their complicity restores not an ideology, but an oracular and primal text—myth.

Memories within the Word ▲

Myth vitalizes language, giving it a presence outside of the interpretive mode and forcing its significance to a level where the community's shared meanings are the basis of its understandings and interactions with both the spiritual and the physical worlds. Myth is neither one of these worlds; it is both of them. In its ways of recursive signification, it is the perfect vehicle for methodology. Signifying is a black trope—a verbal acknowledgment of the call with a subtle but certain articulation of an implied and responsive thesis. Similarly, mythologizing is a recognition and an articulation of an implicit, cultural memory. Gabriel Setiloane notes how, "in their myth about the 'genesis' of things, it is significant that Africans invariably teach that the first appearance of people was as a group in company . . . it is as a community that they came."[24] The unity indigenous to such mythology is reflected in a community's emulation of that unity within its own linguistic traditions. Examples of such unity are explicit in African oral literature, where, as in the folktales of the diaspora, there is obeisance to audience—a linguistic bridge from the metaphorical structures in the story to the collected audience of listeners. Such bridges between the storytellers and the listeners reorganize the (visually) separated subjects and objects back into a metaphorical group that has been collected by words and maintains (even underscores) the community of the storyteller, the listeners, and the story text. Illustrations of these gatherings flourish in contemporary African and African-American literatures and in African and African-American oral narratives. The structure of *The Color Purple,* for example, indicates a contemporary vision of this community. In the oral traditions of Hausa, storytelling is both formal and formulaic.

There is a consistent structure that introduces story in Hausa, an exchange between the storyteller and the audience. Hurston's records of African-American folktales (*Mules and Men*) set up similar rituals that collect the community of listener, teller, and text.[25] In both the African tradition and the African-American literary (re)membrance of this tradition, the "call" to community meets a "response" from a gathering—a coming together that reflects both the physical and psychological significance of the collective community, linked by story and traditions.

The traditions of myth are also echoed in the literature of the diaspora. Toni Morrison's Shadrack (*Sula*) gathers the community to celebrate the myth of his own making, Suicide Day, the day that at first metaphorically explicates and then literalizes the community's plight. In a similar acknowledgment of a community's involvement in myth, Buchi Emecheta complicates the destruction of the village of Shavi in her novel, *The Rape of Shavi* with the story of a river goddess (Ogene) whom the villagers revere but ignore as they ignore other emblems of their culture. Communal betrayal of myth, memory (tradition), and meaning is intertwined with Emecheta's story of rape. It is significant that the corruption (rape) by Western values in Shavi is layered within the story of a village girl who is raped by one of the Westerners who have invaded her village. The biological legacy of this girl and the cultural legacy of her community are both sacrificial victims in the Emecheta work.[26]

For black women, telling is an activity complicated by a history that in addition to being dominated by a masculine ethic is told in terms that support this ethic. Perhaps it is this reason that makes the tale a black woman writer tells, just in its being voiced, reflect an urge towards a metaphysical definition of one's self. Jean Miller looked for a language to describe women's metaethics as organized around principles of "affiliations and relationships," her point being that even the language of psychology was inappropriate to determine the parameters of women's sense of themselves.[27] Similarly, a critical theory that acknowledges the roles of culture and gender must acknowledge that its thesis is ironically framed by the invisibility of women's writing in traditional theories of literature. Traditional

criticisms often work to disable the female and cultural voice
rather than to reveal the distinct articulation of those voices.

Mary Poovey proposes that what she terms "materialist feminists" recognize:

> that "woman" is currently both a position within a domi-
> nant, binary symbolic order *and* that that position is arbi-
> trarily [and falsely] unified. On the other hand, we need to
> remember that there *are* concrete historical women whose
> differences reveal the inadequacy of this unified category
> in the present and the past. The multiple positions real
> women occupy—the positions dictated by race . . . class . . .
> or sexual preference—should alert us to the inadequacy of
> binary logic and unitary selves.[28]

A decentered ethic also shifts the place of logic from one that
emphasizes a binary argument (between polar opposites) to one
that seems more circular, and more woman-centered. A unitary,
individuated self specifically contradicts an idea of the communal self—a presence which I will argue is articulated in the
characterizations within black women's writing.

Complexity, multiple presences, and cyclic rather than linear
principles are definitive aspects of the works of black women
writers. In this sense, telling as a complication of history is also
a (re)membrance and a revision of history both in its mythic and
its gender-specific dimensions. For example, telling in the form
of a goddess's prophecy is an important feature of Flora Nwapa's *Efuru*. Nwapa's title character becomes a priestess of the
goddess of the lake, a "symbolic acceptance of self," writes Carol
Davies, who claims that such acceptance is a positive note because it includes the realization that her "existence was not totally defined by her motherhood."[29] However, her existence
does become enmeshed with a creatrix, and the imagery of the
goddess she worships is woven into Efuru's own imagery and
the narrative structures of the text.[30] The pronominal reference
(marked here with an [*]) in a passage Davies also cites, is, I
think, deliberately obscured. Because the fertility of both the
goddess and Efuru are lamented here, creativity is mythically
extended past the physical to metaphysical spirituality—the

realm of true creative possibility: "Efuru slept soundly that night. She dreamt of the woman of the lake, her beauty, her long hair, and her riches. She had lived for ages at the bottom of the lake. She was as old as the lake itself. . . . She gave women beauty and wealth but she had no child. She[*] had never experienced the joy of motherhood."[31] The recursive nature of the ambiguous "she," that points both to the goddess and Efuru, is an example of the figurative depths of black women's written language. Even if the characters' generative powers fluctuate, are abandoned, raped, or redefined, the language sustains its generative powers.

The new mythology of women who have discovered their inner nature encompasses the spiritual metaphor of a revisioned goddess. Women's voices in the community collect, articulate, and culturally reconstruct myths. They are the "acts" of language that Toni Cade Bambara calls "spirit-force . . . energizer[s]."[32] The unifying character of mythology and women's voices and literature by black women creates its own community. Not accidentally, the conceptual link between such belonging and being is a thematic structure shared in the fiction of these writers who acknowledge the feminine voice as a creative act. This conversion is sustained through the gender of their literary community and through the cultural (re)memory of a collective female community ultimately responsible for its own vitality. Toni Morrison's Milkman (*Song of Solomon*) is reunited with this community through women's voices that haunt him at his birth, taunt him through his childhood, eventually embrace him (like his Aunt Pilate's singing), and finally enfold him into the very fabric of the myth he must discover *is* his life. Carrying such knowledge, he can give it away. " 'You want my life?' Milkman was not shouting now. 'You need it? Here.' "[33] Enabled by the myth acknowledged, Milkman uses Pilate's life force, epitomized in the ancient community she and Circe represent, to determine his own.

An example of the metaphorical complexity of linguistic recursion is found within the silenced artistry of Gwendolyn Brooks's Maud Martha, whose frustrated creativity disallows the possibility of creating even a "good Maud Martha." "The bit of art that could not come from any other" is at the center of the "raging silence" that shouts for recognition in this novel.[34]

Maud's gifts are words (like Pilate's are song). Mary Helen Washington has written that Maud craves words because they are "elaborate, immutable and sacred" expressions of her own "shimmering form."[35] The compacted rage of her silence is evidenced in the recursive structural complex of the text itself, whose shortened chapters ("vignettes," Washington labels them) echo and enact her rage.

Affirming that the creative, spoken word, concretized within the text, is the source of women's power, Hurston writes that her character Janie almost missed her actualization because "she didn't read books, so she didn't know that she was the world."[36] I am convinced that this curious aside in Hurston's text is a subtle indication of the reader's implicit involvement in Janie's story, and of the importance of this collaborative community of author, character, and reader in black women writers' texts. At the novel's end, in much the same way that Celie thanks the trees and stars and god and everybody, Janie, too, collects her universe, "pulls in her horizon like a great fish-net . . . from around the waist of the world and drape[s] it over her shoulder."[37]

Taking advantage of the creative potential that the reclamation of the word promises, black women writers' texts make linguistic rituals in recursive, metaphoric layers that structure meaning and voice into a complex that eventually implicates the primal, mythic, and female community of its source. This community is an imaginative reconstruction of the figurative lives of women of the African diaspora. Their confusion of voices multiplies the depths of language: some of it silenced, some loud and hateful. Others are like the voice of Ursa Corregidora, Gayl Jones's character, whose bluesy, poetic prose defines the antithetical nature of her soul and her own crisis.[38] Although we see these women as mulatto or dark, tall or "pressed small," it is what we hear of them that connects the reader to the structure of the textual unity and pulls us into their lives as we are pulled into the fabrics of their stories. Beyond their visual symbology, their activation within the story is their call to look at what they say or how they are silenced and to add the judgments that come from such analysis to their characters. We must understand both facets of Nnu Ego's voicelessness—the internal silence that comes from a psychological bonding to another's motherhood and the external silence forced from a system that decides, without significant contribution from its female communities, how motherhood shall be valued.

Later chapters in *Moorings and Metaphors* discuss another important layering that I will note briefly here. The narrative voice within the texts is not only the voice of the author and storyteller, but it is intricately woven into the fabric of textual structures. Sometimes, the threads of narrative voice echo a character's soul. In Hurston, narrator and character often exchange tone and poetry.[39] "Certainty of reference" is suspended as the black text speaks both to and of itself—just as Nwapa's Efuru, who is pledged to the goddess, talks both to herself and of her goddess.[40] They are spiritually and linguistically inseparable. In such a speakerly text, the vital, active power of language is not only retained, but is a device of their construction. The communal construction of the black text shares linguistic power—investing itself, its structures, its characters and its events with the same creative power in the process of making itself a reflection of its community. Black women authors' manipulation of that creative power makes such textualizing a specifically female vitalization. When Barbara Johnson reads Zora Neale Hurston, she writes of her consciousness of Hurston's "foregrounding" the "complex dynamism" of differential interactions between the seeming oppositions in her texts.[41] The interaction of language, culture, community, and women's voice is a widening gyre in literature by black women writers. It collects a universe of black voices and coils them into each other until the center reflects the dark, rich, fertile, and, yes, ambivalent collage of women whose voices have both complicated the story and dared to tell it.

The Oracular Text ▲

Oracular, a word that characterizes the contemporary work of black women writers, comes from a classic text of the early twentieth century—Jean Toomer's *Cane*.[42] Toomer's novel foregrounds a narrative voice that chronicles the experiences of women's fracturing experiences within African-American communities. The primary difference between Toomer's work and the texts of black women writers is in the presumed role of the narrative voice. The carefully maintained distance between narrative and text distinguishes Toomer's style, and I would argue the style of black male writers, from women's texts. The voice in women's texts claims intimate knowledge and ownership of all narrative dimensions. However, I do not find it at all contradictory that the word that specifies a theoretical context for black women's writing introduces one of the most complex works in American literature written by a black male. Toomer's use of "oracular" does promise a text predicated on voices. However, although the density of his text depends on our understanding the exchanges between word and act, it is the terrifying present that dominates Toomer's work—an interpretation borne out in a review of the insistent visual elements within *Cane*. For example, how the smoke appears and curls and caresses the scenes in "Karintha" is described in a language as lingering and as tactile as the scene itself. Appearance and behavior are important thematic emphases achieved through the techniques of language in texts by black male writers.

The organizing principle of *Moorings and Metaphors* is that the oracular texts of black women writers replace an emphasis on appearance with consciousness and on behavior with memory. These are works that reflect an inner speech. The inner voice mediates the critical vision in black women writers' works. Rather than the dominant mode of storytelling, vision and act are proffered as ways toward memory, and memory is recovered through language. Recall, for example, the closing passage referred to earlier from *Their Eyes Were Watching God*. In the final scene of the novel (which, because it is in a recursive text, is also the first scene of the novel) Janie sits surrounded by her memories of Tea Cake, their days on the muck, and her learning to live as a woman. It is not the visual imagery of sunlight and shadow that crisscrosses the room where she sits that concludes (and also begins) her story; it is her *call* to her soul to "come in and see" that is the final word of the story. Black women's writing is oracular because it is incantatory. Repetition, recursion, and (re)membrance are its goals because these are activities directed inwards: the oracles we consult are ourselves.

I want to close this chapter with a suggestion of a way to reconsider one of the words in its opening epigraph—"necromancy." Surely the texts we use are evidence of our necromancy.

This is a perfect word for a creative and imaginative retelling. Its medieval Latin origin is *nigromantia*—black magic—and although the *Oxford English Dictionary* claims that this is a noun of unknown origin, I strongly suspect that its mystery lies in its non-Western origins. Scholarship becomes "unknown" when the geography leaves the West. *Moorings and Metaphors* is an effort at naming, placing, and specifying—three critical features of the incantatory word in the numinous literatures of black women writers.

2

▲▲▲▲▲▲▲▲▲▲▲▲▲▲▲▲▲▲▲▲▲▲▲▲▲▲▲▲▲▲▲▲▲▲▲▲▲▲▲

The Novel Politics of
Literary Interpretation

> The novel is Europe's creation; its discoveries, though
> made in various languages, belong to the whole of
> Europe. . . . NOVEL (European) . . . a historic entity
> that will go on to expand its territory beyond geo-
> graphic Europe. In the richness of its forms, the . . .
> intensity of its evolution and its social role, the Euro-
> pean novel (like European music) has no equal in any
> other civilization.
>
> Milan Kundera, *The Art of the Novel*
>
> The danger . . . literary ideology poses is the act of
> consecration, and—of course excommunication.
>
> Wole Soyinka, *Myth, Literature, and the African World*

The canonical debates of contemporary criticism have forced a
more careful attention to critical commentary like that by Milan
Kundera, who argues for what amounts to a hierarchy among
world literatures. Kundera insists that the definitions of "Sixty-
three Words" (the glossary that is his final chapter of *The Art of
the Novel*), compose only what he calls a "personal dictionary"
for his novels—the result of his experiences with translators
who have forced him to "think about every one of [his] words."[1]
However, it does not seem so personal a list. It is, in fact, a list
that supports the cultural/critical hierarchies that fuel the contemporary canonical debates. Here, his definition of "Novel (European)," far from being cultural metaphor, assumes
an authoritative and exclusive posture. Works by Third World

novelists in Africa and America are marginalized by his subordinating definition.

The excerpt I cite from Kundera's "personal dictionary" claims that even after translation and extension, the loftiness of the European novel is unreachable, no matter what its legacy may eventually include. The contemporary critic and theorist of black literature finds little room within such a rubric for common literary ground. Little wonder then that the result of the hegemony in European sociocultural systems that have dominated our critical glossaries has been an underscoring of the decidedly political dimensions of our critical dialogues. We have been forced to acknowledge the ways in which the literary canon has become an elitist protectorate.

A contemporary consideration of an answer to the question "For whom do we write?" must consider as well that implicit in any attention to the object of this query is a parallel attentiveness to the subjective "we" and to the nature of this thing "we" are writing about. It is a consideration that forces us to acknowledge the ways in which the spherical world of criticism and text has come to have sides.

My effort in this book is to practice a kind of critical inquiry that recognizes the cultural complexity and gender specificity of African and African-American women writers' texts. It is an effort that in one sense embraces Kwame Appiah's assertion that "the point at which to address the older canons is not by challenging their criteria: it is by challenging the very idea of the canon . . . that there is some recoverable notion of purely literary value that . . . explains why [some texts are classics and others] are not."[2] Yet, where Appiah sees an intrinsic error in arguing for literature as a "repository of racial or gendered experience," I see a literature with a refractive purpose. It does not gather together as much as it imaginatively alters the course of our ideas concerning experiences that are (for example) cultural or gendered. In the space created by this interpretive/refractive moment, the twin ideas "older canons" and "older canonical critics" are challenged.

The works of African and African-American writers that I consider have forced me to set aside forms of inquiry and critical definitions that would subordinate their imaginative substance. If the language used to discuss literature does not engage and encourage a dialogue among the cultures of the texts, the critics who interpret them, and the readers who engage them, then the literary critic can only be writing, as Gates suggests, primarily for *other* critics of literature. If these others have excommunicated the critics, literatures, and readers that do not articulate a European ethic and consecrate an exclusively European ideology, then the critical dialogue of the twentieth century is but a masque.

Unfortunately, the potential for such silencing is not difficult to imagine. Reagan-era Secretary of Education William Bennett's call for a return to a basic (and classical) curriculum made it clear that the basic curriculum he heralded did not include the Third World as its subject—only as its object. If we write for critics who believe that an author's race, sex, politics, religion, or ethnic origin are intrusions upon the processes of critical judgment rather than participants in imaginative acts, then we had better understand that here there would be little opportunity to secure a place for dialogue and only a cramped space for an exchange between writers and readers. The whole construct of the participant text—engagement between the community of words represented in its voices and ours—is nullified in the face of criticism that claims to be politically disinterested. The political interests of cultural criticism explicity extend from its assertion of its place in critical inquiry. Although others must take on the responsibility of articulating the form of politics that emerges from such an assertive insertion, it is important to explain that the interpretive effort itself does not gain its identity through this effort. Politics extends as a result of the inquiry— as one of its facets (a sort of Ooankalian tentacle, to use an image from Octavia Butler's *Adulthood Rites*);[3] but it does not define the nature of the criticism itself nor does it predict the interpretive result. Even Appiah, who resists the notions of essentialist criticism, recognizes the fragmentation implicit in the critical process when he writes that although "hegemony sets the framework [of a dominant system of concepts] it does not need to be so totalizing as to enforce consensus."[4]

The tumultuous canonical debates of the 1980s have succeeded in revitalizing the words within the literary text in an acknowledgment of their potential to remind us, as readers, that there is diversity enough in the text to locate and specify

the interpretive community reflected in the textual organization. The privilege assumed by this community, indeed its very
membership, establishes the contemporary debate. Stanley Fish
argues that "the assumption that an interpretive community is
monolithic and is therefore a new kind of object in relation to
which the problem of interpretation is not resolved but merely
reinscribed . . . must be challenged."[5] However, the actual challenge seems to revolve as much around the membership of the
community (there is certainly evidence of vehement debate on
this point) as it concerns the textual diversity that the community will gather together to interpret. Because of the two-sided
nature of the canonical argument, literary criticism as practiced
by theorists of Third World and minority texts has had the interesting side effect of calling attention to texts that by their authorship alone testify in support of the assertion that critical
theory is no longer one monolithic consecration of Euro-
American and male critical theorists. Yet, that which critics of
Third World and minority texts discuss, at least for Milan Kundera, is merely an echo of a European god. We are compelled
to assess the critical implications of such a granite-like standard
because of its potential to undermine the object of our inquiry—the text.

I suspect that here we have a premise much like the one posed
by Bakhtin as he faced the need to define dialogical relationships between linguistic styles and social dialects that belong to
the study of the *word,* even though "they fall outside the province of its purely linguistic study."[6] In this distanced province,
historical, cultural, and gendered frames collect around the
word. For some of us who write criticism and read it, these
frames are quite naturally contradictory—they confront as well
as consecrate literary ideologies, encouraging the dialogue that
should define our enterprise. Yet, perhaps quite perversely,
they also characterize the "we" who write as a deconstructed
Other, consecrating the alterity that, by its very nature, negates
the polarity implicit in the pairing of text and reader. This is a
definitive act for the texts of the African diaspora.

The activity of the canonical debate, the movement of text
from a study of the word to the construction of a relationship
between elements within and outside of the text, is certainly an
activity of political gerrymandering—defining the districts
from which we legislate our politics. In addition, this debate has

a role in determining the membership of the interpretive community. Historically, the drawing of lines has been a process of redlining (like Kundera's European borders)—an exclusive excommunication that my epigraph from Soyinka's text warns is the inherent danger of ideology. The entombment of criticism within these redlined districts of Euro-American frames comes as much from what we have decided constructs the canon as it comes from what we have determined is our relationship to it. Such retrenchment behind the lines has been a safe haven that allowed critical language to retain a sort of ethnic purity and to celebrate a prescribed community of critics who need not even have talked to each other to discover that they were alike in their decisions of what was the nature of the beautiful and the sublime, what civilizations were human and therefore could lay claim to both a culture as well as a historical reality, and who was permitted to make these decisions. The lines of demarcation were clearly European and male, and clearly excluded the texts of the Third World and women writers from the literary discussions of beauty or sublimity. I would argue that there was no real debate—no voicing of the "dialogical relationships that . . . belong to the study of the word." No actual polemic exists outside of complexity. What reigns instead is an exclusive and simplistic standard, like Kundera's, that closes the text's authorship as well as encloses its readers. This means that the words we use as literary critics, established as they are by our academic glossaries, are dormant and monologic until they are uttered—voiced into being. It is at the point of utterance where these critical lexica deepen—weighted by both the activity within the text and the engagement of the reader. The assumption of their dialogic structure is quite natural and reflects, at this point, an ideology more akin to the Bakhtinian *ideologija,* an "'idea system' [that is] determined socially [and] that . . . possesses semiotic value," rather than that which Caryl Emerson notes is the "unfortunate" suggestion of ideology, a word that in English "suggests something inflexible and propagandistic."[7]

The dynamic rehearsal of critical theory should certainly inspire a liberation rather than an enclosure of ideas. There is, in the critical discussions of the form(s) of the novel, practical evidence of the connection that Bakhtin makes between the construct of the word with the conception of the idea. It is an association that emphasizes how the idea "resembles the word [in its wanting] to be heard, understood, and 'answered' by other voices."[8] Sociohistorical or cultural diversity is claimed when our critical language embraces not only the cultural histories within the words of the text and the social dialectic assumed by their gendered authorship, but when that language reveals how the nuance in our critical words about textual words is our own form of sociohistorical utterance. In this book, I use such terms as "shift" and "translucence" and "reflexive reflection" in ways that encourage their embracing a cultural perspective of critical inquiry. Our voiced critical texts (and glossaries) acknowledge both Other texts and Other textual theorists. It is within this articulation that the Other gains a dimension for the critic of black literature that asserts both its political facet and the necessary multiplying of vision that is definitive for literary criticism of the black text. Here, in a reference that reminds the canonical critic of the definitive potential of the black text to speak both to itself and to answer itself, is reified Bakhtin's notion that the idea must be "answered by other voices." The text's double vision, its basis in orature and the task of the Other, is clarified within this conversational revision.[9]

Françoise Lionnet draws our attention to the voices of these Other literatures using *métissage,* a concept that underscores what she sees as the "heteronomous identities [of] postcolonial subjects." In her explanation of her use of *métissage* as an aesthetic concept, Lionnet notes that she is able to bring together "biology and history, anthropology and philosophy, linguistics and literature" in a reading practice that brings out "the inferential nature of a particular set of texts." This construction of a "set of texts" underscores her sense that an understanding of postcolonial cultures through the literary expression of these women writers is at least a possibility. Although Lionnet's attention is focused on autobiography, *métissage* is a concept that speaks to the imaginative literatures of postcolonial women writers as well. These writers share the critical dimensions of discrete metaphorical strategies, the figurative narrative complexity outlined in the concluding chapters of this work. The imaginative literatures of postcolonial women seem to be an intensive aspect of the "intertextual weaving or mé-tissage of styles" in the "emancipatory metaphors" of women's autobiographies.[10] I believe there is a compelling relationship between the figurative dimensions of the multiplied text and the cultural dimensions of *métissage*.

Reflexive Reflection ▲

The kinds of generative processes that are of most concern to the thesis of this book have experienced a swell of figurative and imaginative attention in the past decade. They metaphorically echo from assertions like that of Toni Morrison's Sula, who argued that she did not want to make any children, she wanted only to make herself. Once this felt soul becomes Sula's closest companion (her best friend Nel, whom "she had clung to . . . as the closest thing to both an other and a self," is estranged from her), a certain realm of spiritual intimacy is achieved. However, a sometimes dangerous freedom that accompanies such closeness is a constant feature of Sula's characterization. Her independent lifestyle is consumptive—"What's burning in me is mine!" she argues at the same time that she threatens to "split this town in two and everything in it before I'll let you [her grandmother] put it out!"[11] Her threat echoes the episode of her mother's death by fire and foreshadows her own. Sula's death is feverish, as if her soul is both generating and being consumed by flames. Seeing one's own soul equates self-love with self-knowledge. This becomes a dangerous liaison in some works of contemporary black women writers. Kimberly Benston offers us a historical perspective on this liaison in recalling the scene from Ellison's *Invisible Man* where "the rest of the text" is obscured once this kind of intimacy and sight are conflated: "I walked struck by the merging fluidity of forms seen through the lenses. Could this be the way the world appeared? . . . 'For now we see as through a glass darkly but then—but then—' I couldn't remember the rest of the text."[12]

Benston cites this episode to illustrate how the union of body and language is like effacement—erasure of the Other as it is consumed by the Self. "The scene rises from the voiced," he notes of the moment in *The Color Purple* when Celie and Shug face each other and call their names. (Remember that when Nel finally calls Sula's name in *Sula* it is years too late for her acknowledgment of the Other.) Following his notion that the "topos of facing" renders a "theory and praxis of reading," Benston argues that "the subjects of black literature cannot form themselves in freedom from ideology, those subjects can create culture by engaging ideology in awareness of the positions from which they speak."[13] Benston's "topos of facing" is akin to the spiritual mooring place offered by black women writers.

Toni Ansa's *Baby of the Family* has its first moment of physical connection to a spiritual place when the infant in a photograph of her father's dead sister attempts to pull the protagonist, Lena, into its frame.[14] Lena, herself a child when this happens, remembers that "it looked like the baby's eyes were looking directly at her" and that "a voice inside the room or inside her head" compelled her to climb up to where the photograph was mounted over her grandmother's bed. Once she was near the picture, "two small hands with yellowed lace at the wrists . . . grasped Lena's own small hands, and began pulling her . . . through the frame . . . as if it were an open window." It is significant that her own voice was thwarted in this event. One scream resulted in "no sound" and her "second terrified scream was muffled in the warm soft lap of what seemed like yards of rotting old lace" (38, 39). This contact with her ancestor is critically placed in a circumstance where voice and mirror (the framed glass of the ancestral portrait) collide but do not intersect. From the portrait, the child's eyes seem to follow little Lena around her grandmother's room (the only "old-fashioned" room in the house). These eyes, that attempt to fix Lena's gaze, become her contact with the past; but she is unable to offer the voice that would be a critical and saving mediator for this traumatic event. Following this episode, Ansa writes of another gaze in a glass that is as startling a moment for Lena. This time, however, there is no trauma. "Whenever she looked into the car's rear-view she smiled at her reflection. But this time when she caught sight of herself, she was shocked by the image. . . . For the first time she saw eyes that were obviously connected to a soul. . . . she saw that she was REAL!" (55). On this occasion, Lena's voice does inscribe the event. This time she knew that "it would be okay to tell" and her assertion to her mother and brothers that she was real could happen because "she saw her spirit look back at her in the mirror" (55, 56).

The final spiritual encounter of this novel is lengthy and significantly includes a spiritual dialogue. Although Lena's meeting on the beach with Rachel, the ghost of a slave woman, is frightening, she is able to articulate this fear—"Lady, I'm scared of you"—and eventually talk with the ghost about her past. It is a question and answer (call and response) session of great import because Rachel's past is also Lena's. Through this discourse Lena is assured that she belongs anywhere on earth she wants to—even in the spiritual places that house the spirit Rachel. Ansa writes of sight and voice in a way that encourages sight to cross traditional and credible boundaries and extend itself through time and across the mirrored spaces of the soul. Lena is a baby born with a veil. The consequence of the mystical powers associated with this gift is her own "second sight."

This same kind of densely textured imagery is clearly emphasized in Alice Walker's *The Temple of My Familiar*.[15] When Suwelo gazes at a series of photographs, he realizes that as different as the women in the pictures look, and as many decades as they encompass, they are all Miss Lissie, the goddess/ancestor of this text. Miss Lissie's timeless characterization enables her to bridge the fragmented cultures of women who have been scattered in the diaspora. Towards the novel's end, Suwelo faces his own ancestry in acknowledging his spiritual kinship to Miss Lissie. It is her voice (Miss Lissie leaves him a tape) that prompts his (re)memory. "Remember the last time you stood over them," Miss Lissie has suggested to him (400). Her persistent urging enables him to (re)member the episode of his parents' tragic death in a way that encourages Suwelo to forgive his father. Walker writes that he is "too tired to keep watch over the door of his heart" (403). With this memory, his kinship to Miss Lissie is complete and Suwelo "realizes one of the reasons he was born; one of his functions in assisting Creation in this life" (412). It is a scene reminiscent of the final moments in Morrison's *Song of Solomon*. Milkman sings for his dying Aunt Pilate the ancient song that she had sung when he was born. In a similar fashion, Suwelo passes on Miss Lissie's voice to Mr. Hal who "could always see Lissie" despite the changes of many generations of living and despite her spiritual masks. Sight and voice— seeing through a glass, albeit darkly, seem to be the way to effacement and effacement seems to be the way to internalize (by erasure) the Other. The text that Ellison's Invisible Man forgets is (re)membered in contemporary black women writers' works.

Miss Lissie is not the only ancestral mediator in contemporary fiction by black women writers. It is Circe's story that directs

Milkman in Morrison's *Song of Solomon,* just as the ghostly Rachel guides Lena in Ansa's *Baby of the Family.* Anyanwu's numinous bravery assures survival of her ancestors regardless of the fact that their lifetimes (and hers) are scattered across three centuries and despite their living in Africa, New England, or Louisiana in Octavia Butler's *The Wild Seed.* These are all telling and ancient women. Sometimes their presence is ambivalent and mythical, but their insistent survival is always linked to their ability to tell their own stories and to secure their generational continuity. Consequently, they assure that their spoken narratives make their way into that scriptocentric West. So, when Nigerian writers Buchi Emecheta and Flora Nwapa, for example, write of their books *as* their children, the reappearance of these metaphors of creation and reflection, voice and sight, are not surprising. Emecheta writes in her autobiography (*Head Above Water*) that she does not see her own face when she looks in a mirror but she sees her aunt's. This aunt (called "Big Mother") is a most significant relative for the young Buchi because of the way she celebrated her relationship with her niece by telling the story of Buchi's birth at a time when she was surrounded by all of the village children. Emecheta's bond with Big Mother is consequently one that joins the face that she sees in the mirror to the voice that tells of her own birth. The contrapuntal exchange between the storyteller-aunt (who establishes Buchi's ancestry by asking "Who is our mother come back from Agbogo?"), Buchi (who responds "It's me"), and all her "little relatives sitting on the sand at Otinkpu" (who shout "It's her! It's her!"), gathers the community into a generational ritual that places the text in the midst of its own community of the author (who is responsible for its generation) and the reader (who is responsible for its name).[16]

The reflective mirror of these creative acts is certainly inclusive, but it just as often mirrors contradiction. Although the mirrored image promises some dimension of sight, this vision is not always restorative. In Morrison's *Song of Solomon,* Hagar sees a "tiny part of her face reflected in [a] mirror," which prompts a revelation of sorts—"No wonder, she said at last. . . . No wonder. No wonder. . . . Look at how I look."[17] This episode not only invites the reader to look with her, but its repetitive structure calls attention to the vision within the vision that Hagar must see in the pieces of mirror. Celie's lack of self-love in Walker's *The Color Purple* allows her to see no one in the glass, nothing other than her "naked self." Her experience with reflection allows her only a "face to face" confrontation with her body. There is no depth because nothing of her spirit is revealed in what she sees. In this episode she cannot even imagine what it is that Shug loves about her because she is frozen by the images of her outer body—her hair, her dark skin, and her nose and lips.[18] In a reference to this scene, Kimberly Benston writes that the consequence of Celie's failed sight is that she is "locked in a binary dynamic of reflection with no possibility of exchange . . . a parody of the Lacanian '*stade du miroir*,' seeing in the body-wholly-body . . . not an enviably whole 'Other' but a figure stripped of any sign of defining coherence."[19]

These kinds of metaphorical moorings, so persistent in the contemporary literature of black women writers, argue my theoretical perspective. The conflation of the ancestor and goddess is a persistent figurative praxis in the texts of these writers. The spiritual and cultural dimensions of their presences underscore a relationship between gender and race achieved through discrete cultural ways of saying, the voices that connect black women writers of West Africa and America. Terry Eagleton, who argues that culture need not "argue its way to political relevance" because "questions of the human subject" are not distinct from "questions of political struggle" seems to anticipate the relationship between the cultural moorings of these textual subjects and the spiritual metaphors that articulate their struggles.[20] Whether or not this struggle is political or poetic, and whether or not these subjects are image or reflection, contemporary literary theory must anticipate both of them in its critical interpretations of the texts of black women writers.

Community, Ethics, and Identity ▲

> In any case the novel itself was an outgrowth from earlier traditions of oral tales and of epic poetic narratives like those of Homer's . . . or those of Liyongo in Swahili literature. . . . The African novel as an extended narrative in written form had antecedents in African oral literature.
>
> Ngugi wa Thiong'o, *Decolonizing the Mind*

If we were to accept Kundera's districts, the African novel should restrict its dialogue to itself because, although the "Novel (European)" is destined to expand its boundaries, it would nonetheless retain its nonpareil status. If, however, the purpose of its differentiation, its distinctiveness, is to label its derivations as secondary—qualitatively less than the original—then the identity of that gloss fades, diminished in the face of the act of differentiation. Here, a point like Jacques Derrida's assertion that identity is dissembled by "the necessity of alterity, reference beyond to another" is especially appropriate.[21] The historically racist and sexist structuration that this brand of differentiation supports is no longer a simple matter of the categorization of a literary term; it is an issue of identity.

The critical dilemma posed by Kundera's ethnocentrism is that his sixty-three words function exactly as they were designed to, to end possibility, to enclose the frames of words and his texts and to force them, without any question of exteriority or figuration, to fulfill a simplistically interior and literal purpose. However, within the more expansive vision of the "literary canon," we can view the loss of the word "novel" as a loss of its metaphorical stature. Perhaps it is Ngugi's note in *Decolonizing the Mind* that best illustrates the divisiveness in a definition like Kundera's. Ngugi claims that "the social or even national basis of the origins of an important discovery or any invention is not necessarily a determinant of the use to which it can be put by its inheritors" and further that the "crucial question is not that of the racial, national, or class origins of the novel, but that of its development and the uses to which it is continually being put" (68, 69). His commentary sustains a metaphorical decolonization of the genre and allows a multitude of other voices (including, ironically, Kundera's) to enter African fiction. The argument that is the result of Ngugi's literary decolonization— a dialogue concerning which language is the "appropriate 'fiction language'"—culminates in a celebration of the potential for the African novel to encourage a "real dialogue between the literatures, languages and cultures of . . . different nationalities" (85). Such dynamism is absolutely antithetical to the closure implicit in the hierarchical superiority of Kundera's European novel. Ngugi's anticipation of a dialogue does not represent a politicization of the lexicon of critical language even though it is a political assertion that the lexicon of the canon is a cultural metaphor. He affirms the sociocultural legitimacy of critical dialects and asserts his legitimate membership in the interpretive community. Curiously, but illustrative of the shift in critical vocabulary when it includes the Third World, Ngugi's membership pulls the interpretation of this term (community) away from its exclusive and privileged connotations. He shifts it towards an(Other) (and I would argue a Third World) interpretation that emphasizes both the exterior and interior nature of community.[22]

Even after the critical vision has been emended to include a worldview enriched by considerations of how gender and ethnicity affect literature and literary criticism, the neocolonial postulates of a Euro-American hierarchy can still manage to assert themselves. Rand Bishop makes this issue central to his discussion of African literature and criticism. Bishop writes:

> the criticism of [their] literature was being based on the assumption that, because it employed European languages, African literature in French and English were . . . branches of French and English literature, and that one need only apply the underlying principles of Western literary criticism in assessing the new literature. Thus, Chinua Achebe found himself the grand-nephew of Joseph Conrad, and the mark of T. S. Eliot and Gerard Manley Hopkins was ferreted out in many African poets.[23]

In an indication of how such ethnocentrism can subvert the text from itself, Bishop notes how "the oral tradition was seen *merely* as a precursor to writing . . . that the African tradition, when it did develop, would perforce develop along the lines of the Western tradition since it was clearly behind in its evolution" (emphasis added).[24] This assumption illustrates why it is imperative that the premises of criticism be liberated from the narrow theoretical focus of a consecrated ideology and that theories of criticism indigenous to the literature they discuss supplant any theory of critical inquiry that would deny the activity of dialogue.[25] Christopher Miller illustrates the consequences of canonical ethnocentrism in his note considering Georg Gugelberger's initial "disappointment" with African literature's failure to support what Gugelberger could identify as a "politically progressive attitude." Miller writes that Westerners "too often expect third world literatures to respond to our hopes and concerns, to liberate *us,* when in fact they may be answering their own questions instead of ours."[26]

The very being of the novel represents both question and answer for Toni Morrison, who acknowledges this collective perspective when she asserts that her own work is created for a *community* of people who need it. There is clearly a non-Western ethic operating in such a definition and the parameters of her canon are certainly not ambivalent for Morrison:

> If anything I do, in the way of writing novels . . . isn't about the village or the community or about you, then it is not about anything. I am not interested in indulging myself in some private, closed exercise of my imagination . . . which is to say yes, the work must be political. It seems to me that . . . you ought to be able to make it unquestionably political and irrevocably beautiful at the same time.[27]

Ironically, the gestures of exclusion are creative gestures that formulate, probably unintentionally and certainly contrary to its intent, their own extremes. This creative activity has therefore been (quite correctly) perceived as a process of canonical politicization because its essence extends from the choosing of sides, the definition of districts, and the naming of processes. Joan Kelly wrote that the "doubled vision of feminist theory," was a vantage point that would identify a new "social and political position with regard to patriarchy."[28] Kelly's "doubled vision" or Elaine Showalter's interpretation of women's double-voiced discourse is different only in degree from the historical position of the black text and its critic. I would identify the canon of black literature as one already specified by the dialogic relationships in (and between) self and text, voice and vision as well as the dialogic complexity (complexion?) of an(Other). Such complexity demands a shift in usage if not in significance. It is within the latter parameter where the political ideologies of the critical language within our literary canons have come to have definition.

This brings me to a final point. It is not the (external) lexicon of literary criticism that identifies the politics of critical inquiry.

Were this true, Kundera would need no gloss for "Novel (European)." Instead, the internal semantic shifts that this lexicon experiences as it is manipulated by the various theorists who appropriate it in their critical discussions clarify the dimensions of canonical politics. Derrida notes that the "designation 'novel' ... does not, in whole or in part, take part in the corpus whose denomination it imports. . . . It gathers together the corpus, and at the same time . . . keeps it from closing."[29]

Although novels reflect the communities who author them, their territory is both geographic and spiritual. It is important to maintain the distinction that "naming" (or definition) claims as a metaphorical activity of the literary theorist. As metaphor, naming specifies the various dimensions of the interpretive community rather than identifies an enclosed vocabulary for that community. It seems to me that when the process of naming is an activity of a community formed as a result of a dialogic relationship between the world and the word, then the nature of that naming process has shifted from a naming of the discourse of criticism to naming *as discourse in* criticism. Such a shift neither privileges the community nor its activity, but creates instead a dynamic and creative intercourse between the two, a call and response—the "answer" for the Bakhtinian idea. Lionnet anticipates the potential for such discourse when she notes that it is the relationship between context, circumstance, and "cross-cultural linguistic mechanisms that allows a writer to generate polysemic meanings from . . . *seemingly* linear narrative techniques" (emphasis added).[30] The ideal result is that a community of critical theorists will turn their attention to the exercise of their power over the canons and the shifting metaphorical transformations of their critical glossaries in a humble acquiescence to their extensive and commual membership as they acknowledge the political processes of generation.

3

▲▲▲▲▲▲▲▲▲▲▲▲▲▲▲▲▲▲▲▲▲▲▲▲▲▲▲▲▲▲▲▲▲▲

Revision and (Re)membrance: Recursive Structures in Literature

> Had she paints, clay, or knew the discipline of the dance, or strings; had she anything to engage her tremendous curiosity and her gift for metaphor, she might have exchanged the restlessness and preoccupation with whim for an activity that provided her with all she yearned for. And like any artist with no form, she became dangerous.
>
> Toni Morrison, *Sula*

> There were no memories among those pieces. Certainly no memories to be cherished.
>
> Toni Morrison, *Song of Solomon*

Toni Morrison's *The Bluest Eye* opens and closes with a stream of linguistic madness that merges images of an internally fractured psyche and an externally flattened physical world. We learn that the injured spirit belongs to Pecola as, in the opening scene ("Here is the house. It is green and white. It is pretty. Here is the family. Mother, Father, Dick and Jane live in the green-and-white house." [7]), her metaphorically blued eyes see the one-dimensional remnant of the illusory world that has claimed her.

This fragmented and flattened stream is just one of the shapes of language in Morrison's shifting novel. There is also the ironically poetic and visually vivid language that describes Claudia's struggle to rise above the depression in her physical world: "She spent her days, her tendril, sapgreen days, walking up and down, her head yielding to the beat of a drummer so distant only she could hear. . . . She flailed her arms like a bird in an eternal, grotesquely futile effort . . . intent on the blue void it could not reach—could not even see—but which filled the valleys of the mind" (158).

Colors and textures thicken this novel as if they are the only dimensions left of language and vision that can frame the story of Pecola's madness. Even though the sisters who befriend her are saved by the "greens and blues in [their] mother's voice [that] took all the grief out of words" (24), Pecola is left with the biting shards of all the grief that surrounds her. "The damage done was total" her one-time friend Claudia reflects (158). The only language which remains for her is the internalized monologue of a narrative stream, whose shape, sound and sense contain the fractured psyche of the tragically injured Pecola. It alone can testify that her madness was framed by the recurrence of a shifting textural language. Each change in the narrative reminds the reader of another of its forms. Eventually it is the characteristic of a shifting language which frames the recursive structures of Morrison's first novel.[1]

Recursive structures accomplish a blend between figurative processes that are reflective (mirror-like) and symbolic processes whose depth and resonance make them reflexive.[2] The combined symbolic-figurative process results in texts that are at once emblematic of the culture they describe as well as interpretive of this culture. Literature that strikes this reflective/reflexive posture is characteristically polyphonic. Their textual characterizations and events, their settings and symbolic systems are multiple and layered rather than individual and one-dimensional. This literature displays the gathered effects of these literary structures to the extent that when we can identify and recognize them, we are also able to specify their relationship to thematic and stylistic emphases of the traditions illustrated in these writers' works. Because all of these structures share complexities—features of what I refer to as both the "multiplied" text and the "layered" text—I have chosen to use the term "plurisignance" as a means of illustrating the dimensions of vision and language in the contemporary literature of writers in this tradition.[3]

Plurisignant texts are notable by their translucence. A translucent moment in a text encourages the shimmering of its metaphorical layers. They strain against the literal narrative structure for an opportunity to dissemble the text through their diffusive character. Figurations that assert themselves over the literal level of text claim the reader's attention. Imagery and metaphor are the deconstructive mediations of translucence. A consequence of plurisignance is a certain posturing of the textual language. This posture places the narrative language upon a formative threshold rather than on an achieved and rigid structure. This is not to suggest that thesis and content are constantly in *potentia* in these texts. It means instead that these works are often characterized by the presence of a translucent flux and identified by a shifting, sometimes nebulous text. The narrative structures in these works force the words within the texts to represent (re)memories in/of events and ideas that revise and multiply meanings. A result of this revision is that what seems to be ambivalence is actually a sign of displacement. These translucent works have a textural dissonance.

Whether it is gender or culture or a complication of both that have directed the black woman's text towards its explorations of the state of being of its voices, the various linguistic postures within these texts are clearly intertextual. Gates suggests that: "shared modes of figuration result only when writers read each other's texts and seize upon topoi and tropes to revise in their own texts . . . a process of grounding [that] has served to create formal lines of continuity between the texts that together comprise the shared text of blackness."[4] Gender—the social, cultural, and linguistic frames that connect ideology to sexual identity—is a category critical to textual analysis. Any analytical perspective on the nature or the methodology of the text must bring to this construct whatever persistent, shared figures contribute to its identity. The black text, further specified as the black woman writer's text, involves the persistent figurations of gender, culture, and ethnicity—none of which independently inscribes the author's work. When gender enters into the sharing that Gates postulates at the crux of the continuity, it is necessary to explore commonalities in terms of what specific and formal understandings it brings to the texts. One would expect to find theoretical rationale within feminist criticism—especially that which has been directed towards understanding gender as an aspect of the writing process. The "loneliness" and "feelings of alienation" that Sandra Gilbert and Susan Gubar recognize as a cultural aspect of the "woman writer's struggle for artistic self-definition" are not unlike Addison Gayle's earlier attention to defining the cultural strangulation of black literature by white critics.[5] Gayle's point was that the definition of terms "in which the black artist . . . will deal with his own experience" was the central problematic of the conflicting literary aesthetics. Although feminist literary critics have consistently acknowledged a need to examine the intersections of race, gender, and culture, their texts too often assign marginal or limited space to work by and about women of Third World cultures.[6] However, at the intersections of Gayle's and Gilbert and Gubar's concerns, we can see a call for a critical attention to the gender-based sources of textuality. The "grammars" of such a textuality are rules that affect linguistic communities, the idea of discourse, as well as any recontextualizations of syntax by history, culture, and ideology.[7]

The "shared texts" that have had significance for black women writers certainly include those that specify the emphases of texts written within the black tradition. Those are texts which illustrate the plurisignance of their liminality, and I mean both the double-sided (ambivalent) quality of liminality as well as its complexity and multiplicity. Almost as a consequence, the carefully proportioned appearance of Third World women as either subject or object of feminist studies becomes an additional layer of the multiple qualities of plurisignance in the black woman writer's tradition. Wahneema Lubiano suggests that "textual production and textual interpretation are politicized in Afro-American literary discourse by virtue of that literature's relationship to Anglo-American literary discourse."[8] Lubiano underscores the inability to "cleanly separate" the interpretation of text from the production of text. She notes that this gray zone is related to whatever "traditions" (a term she suggests is as murky as "cultural") the literary critic identifies in the interpretive enterprise. I would further suggest that the politicization of text that Lubiano acknowledges is also an important issue in the characterization of text. A feminist text of the Anglo-American tradition grows more and more distinct, in contemporary criticism, from the woman-centered texts of the African-American tradition. It is, however, the discourse between the two traditions that forms their relationship, even if this discourse approaches a negative dialectic. In a sense, the African-American text's effective absence or marginalized presence in Anglo-American feminist discourse constitutes another "text" in African-American interpretive tradition.

The translucence I referred to earlier begins to have an interesting quality when viewed not only as method in literature, but as a subject within the literature. It is this kind of visual complexity that becomes a "formal line of continuity" and that identifies the discrete aspects in the texts of black women's writing. One might look, for example, at how black women visualize themselves in the literature of these authors. Instead of reflections that isolate and individuate, characters like Gwendolyn Brooks's Maud Martha and Shange's Sassafrass see themselves surrounded by a tradition of women like them. Sassafrass's ancestral women come "from out of a closet" and beg her to "make a song . . . so high all us spirits can hold it and be in your tune." The "Lady" that Sassafrass conjures calls to "multitudes of brown-skinned dancing girls" who become her spirit-informants about her past as well as her destiny.[9] Maud's vision of her place in this tradition is vision and revision as well—a call from her history and a response from her own psyche.

> A procession of pioneer women strode down her imagination; strong women, bold; praiseworthy, faithful, stout-minded; with a stout light beating in the eyes. Women who could stand low temperatures. Women who would toil eminently, to improve the lot of their men. Women who cooked. She thought of herself, dying for her man. It was a beautiful thought.[10]

Maud Martha learns to choose something "decently constant" to depend upon—like Morrison's Sethe from her novel *Beloved*, who discovers that she is her own "best thing"—and learns as well that "leaning was work."[11] Maud does not deny the procession of women a place in her imagination. Instead, she learns to revisualize the nature of their work.

In this novella, translucence is closely related to the shifting, diffusive presence of Maud and her dreams. Her husband tells her that the place he visualizes for her, their apartment, will be her "dream"; but the reader is confronted with textual structures that insist on their own dreaminess—the silences that fracture each scene and the stifling spaces of Maud's life (both the apartment and her marriage) that define her liminality. Maud's thoughts are translucent structures that replicate the kind of recursion discussed in the next chapter as syntactic revisioning of text. In an episode that describes Maud's sparing the life of a tiny mouse which "vanishes" after her act of liberation, Brooks writes, "Suddenly, she was conscious of a new cleanness in her. A wide air walked in her. . . . In the center of [her] simple restraint was—creation."[12] The moment that follows the embrace between Ciel and Mattie in Gloria Naylor's *The Women of Brewster Place* similarly illustrates the revision that occurs when modes of figuration are shared. I find in Maud's sudden and metaphorical translucence (the wide air that "walked" in her) a luminous quality similar to Ciel's moan, a sound so "agonizingly slow, [that] broke its way through [her] parched lips in a spaghetti-thin column of air that could be faintly heard in the frozen room."[13] Both moments mark occasions that initiate a cleansing of psychic despair. Maud realizes that she is good and Luciela realizes her grief.

Over and over again, black women's texts have characters that are poised between a spiritual place and a place that has been defined for them, assigned by some person, or because of some ritual of which they had no active memory. Amaka, Flora Nwapa's protagonist in *One Is Enough*, is clearly of the lineage of Maud Martha. However, where Maud's silences are telling, Amaka's voice is full-bodied and clear. She avoids another marriage because she understands that her own goodness does not reside in a definition of herself as a wife: "As a wife, I am never free. I am a shadow of myself. As a wife I am almost impotent. I am in prison, unable to advance in body and soul. Something gets hold of me as a wife and destroys me."[14] Her shadow is a metaphorical reminder of the liminal quality of the translucence and spiritual engagement that are topoi in these writer's works.

The quality of translucence that reveals the plurisignant text is also one that complicates the identities of the tellers of the stories. The boundaries between narrative voices and dialogue become obscure, merging one into the other. For example, Zora Neale Hurston's works illustrate an early interest of African-American literature in the merged textual voice. *Their Eyes Were Watching God* uses this device in the blending of a poetic narrative voice, the poetic dialect of Janie's storytelling, and her reflective conversations with her friend Phoebe. In the work of the contemporary West African playwright Efua Sutherland, the mystic and poetic monologues of characters like Abena (*Edufa*) have great resonance. Perhaps most indicative of the possibilities in such a resonant use of language is work by Ama Ata Aidoo, especially in the blending structures of prose and poetry in her novel, *Our Sister Killjoy*.[15]

The diffusive voice, an intertextual dimension of black women writers' works, directly contrasts with what is often a nihilistic obfuscation of speech that characterizes literature by male writers.[16] The traditionally privileged (and Western) restrictions of dialogue and narrative are shifted in black women's writings, allowing their polyphonic texts to claim the quality of translucence as part their methodology. For example, when Amaka in Nwapa's novel considers marriage with Izu, the narrative voice is clearly Izu's own conscience—but it is ironically a conscience of which he is not aware. He lacks the insight to understand what it knows, even though, as a minister sworn to celibacy, his conscience ought to be speaking out. Yet its frustrated speech is symbolically rendered by the narrative which asks for him, "What did he think he was doing? Cheating God and cheating his flock? He knew he was committing a mortal sin. . . . Sometimes he felt so guilty that he was afraid to associate with his colleagues *lest they know his thoughts*" (emphasis added).[17]

A (sometimes) tangential theme of frustrated speech is increasingly evident in contemporary black woman writers' texts. In works that indicate this kind of frustration, speech is manipulated—inverted from its usual dimensions and replaced into other spheres (layers) of the text. It becomes liminal, translucent and subject to disarray, dislocation (in the Freudian sense of *Verscheibung*) and dispersion in the text. Only the recovery of voice restores the balance to the text between its voices and the voices collected into its rearticulated universe. For example, Nwapa's purpose in *One Is Enough* seems to be to collect all life—

traditional village and contemporary—into a city like Lagos that metaphorically represents the corrupt center of this novel. However, Nwapa's protagonist Amaka is not salvaged from the victimization within these metaphorical structures. Neither the country nor the city offer her refuge. In consequence, both her psyche and her spirit are assaulted by the corrupt center.

Such empowerment at the metaphorical level: storms and hurricanes that have psychically disruptive potentials, trees that are serene and knowledgeable, rivers whose resident ladies (goddesses) hold the promise (or denial) of fertility, are examples of the poetic activation of the texts of black women writers.

Shift ▲

> Only the final section . . . raises the poetry to a sustained high level . . . recall[ing] English metaphysicals . . . fus[ing] African and European elements as in the best of Mr. Soyinka's early verse. . . .
>
> William Riggan, review of *Mandela's Earth and Other Poems*

> Indeed, basic differences between British and Igbo experiences and values . . . make it necessary . . . to have to *bend* the English language in order to express Igbo experience and value in it [emphasis added].
>
> Chinweizu, *Toward the Decolonization of African Literature*

I cite the Riggan review and the Chinweizu excerpt as a means of focusing on both the nature of textual revision and the substance of the interpretive discourse that often follows the work of writers whose cultural sources are non-Western. Central to my notion of the metaphorical revision in the texts of African and African-American women writers is an acknowledgment of the cultural sources of their (re)membered theses. What becomes increasingly important to my consideration of the intertextual nature of the literature produced by black women writers is the premise that the plurisignant text has a multiple generation as well as a multiple presence. Both source and substance are traceable through culturally specific figurations of language that are discrete figures in literature by black women authors. Shift happens when the textual language "bends" in an acknowledgment of "experience and value" that are not Western. A critical language that does not acknowledge the bend or is itself inflexible and monolithic artificially submerges the multiple voices within this literature. In consequence, critical strategies that address the issues within these texts must be mediative strategies between the traditional ideologies of the theoretical discourse and the ancestry of the text itself. Such mediation demands a shift in the scope (if not the tone) of critical terminology—a redirection that calls attention to different (and often contrary) ideologies. This is a task that demands a particular kind of assertiveness. This assertiveness directs the following discussion on the nature of shift and revision.

When the interpretive spaces of the Afrocentric text are culturally specified, and when theory attends to the dimensions of gender that are discrete in the figurations of texts by black women writers, the tangential accomplishment of such specification and articulation is a presentation of the plurisignant text as the ideal center of the critical discourse between the cultural etymologies of words within the critical and textual traditions. Texts by black women writers are those which are most likely to force apart the enclosed spaces of critical inquiry. These works represent perhaps the most liberated language of contemporary literature because their plurisignant nature models the cultural complexity of a revised critical community.

In exploring the nature and quality of "shift," it is important to acknowledge this as a generational term, one that has its genesis in the arguments of an earlier literary dialogue. This is a discussion that recalls my reflection (in chapter one) on the nature of the difference between subjectivity and objectivity. I believe that "shift" has probably always resided at the uncomfortable center between these two, occupying a cultural sphere of its own. It is important to identify this space as cultural because the distance between subjectivity and objectivity (being and form) is an occupied space—one that demands a degree of mediation as the literary critic bridges the area between

the text and its meaning. Mediation is a matter of claiming resi-
dence for critical meanings within an interpretive community, a
community that decides upon its membership not by any discrete or documented values, but by its tacit agreement on what
shall be the formal methodologies employed in critical inquiry.
This is the crux of the matter. By defining and enclosing the
terms of inquiry, the texts are selected a priori. By disabling the
definitions, i.e., deconstructing the terms of inquiry, the texts
have no prior claim to the method. Indeed, the methodology
itself is freed from lexical tyranny. However, such an abdication
cannot occur if the texts of the theoretical community do not
themselves reflect a plurisignant critical vocabulary. I would argue that it is precisely within the texts of black women writers
where an interpretive community is likely to find the most fertile ground for assuring a critical and pluralistic vitality.

In her consideration of the issues of critical theorizing, Barbara Christian's essay, "The Race for Theory," identifies black
women as having a historical claim to being the most appropriate "race" (and gender) for theory because

> people of color have always theorized . . . in forms quite
> different from the Western form of abstract logic . . . in the
> stories we create, in riddles and proverbs, in the play with
> language because dynamic rather than fixed ideas seem
> more to our liking. . . . And women . . . continuously spec-
> ulated about the nature of life through pithy language that
> unmasked the power relations of their world. It is this lan-
> guage, and the grace and pleasure with which they played
> with it, that I find celebrated, refined, critiqued in the
> works of [black women writers].[18]

Christian's familiar ("familiar" because it is a figure Zora Neale
Hurston used to describe "Negro" Speech) note that the form
of black women's textual language is a hieroglyph that is both
"sensual and abstract . . . beautiful and communicative" is an
appropriate metaphor as well for the activities of criticism and
interpretation of these texts.[19]

However, instead of grace and dynamism, pleasure and pithy
speculation, the literary assessments more commonly share the
cultural chauvinism of Riggan's assessment of Wole Soyinka's

1988 book of poetry. Riggan's perspective most values Soyinka's verse when it "reaches the level of the English metaphysicals" with poetry that reflects its European ancestry. This is a restrictive value that would yoke the African and African-American writers' literary domain. Such ethnocentrism is in fact responsible for disabling the relationship between these texts and their literary traditions rather than encouraging their (mediative) dialogue.

The plurisignant text calls attention to the syncretic relationship between individual novels and the novels within the cultural as well as gender-specified genre. This perspective suggests that the polyphonic nature of these texts is essential not only to their internal figurations, but is definitive of the tradition that collectively identifies them. Not only do the texts of African-American women writers articulate the dimensions of cultural pluralism in their world, but the perceptual "outsidedness" of these authors (a factor of both gender and culture) propels a revision in the critical discourse about their literature. In such a discursive space, "shift" becomes a necessary mediation between the reader and the text and encourages a dialogue among critical postures within the interpretive community. Shift positions the alternative interpretations represented by the assertions of gender and culture within the textures of this literature. The critical result is a theoretical acknowledgment of the multiplied text.

There are also dilemmas that accompany the mediative processes of shift. Which vision is clearest? Whose point-of-view is privileged? Which culture's traditions are most significant in the evolution of the text? Perhaps such questions should be anticipated because there is an implicit tension in any deconstructive mediation. Because of the potential dilemmas, however, it is even more important to clarify the origin of shift as extending from the text and shared with an interpretive community rather than shift being a construct of independent origins or of the community itself. In other words, the bend in lexicon comes not from the distinctions between, for example, phenomenology and structuralism, but it comes from the discourse that is possible, for example, between the works of Emecheta and Achebe, Morrison and James Baldwin, or Ngugi wa Thiong'o and

Gabriel Garcia Marquez. The conversations may emphasize distinctive narrative strategies in Morrison's *The Bluest Eye* and Baldwin's *Go Tell It on the Mountain* (both "coming of age" novels). Gender-based views of motherhood within the same (Igbo) society may be distinguished when looking at Buchi Emecheta's *The Joys of Motherhood* and Achebe's *Things Fall Apart*.[20]

Narrative shifts that happen when texts are translated from Spanish or Gikuyu to English might be a situation explored when discussing writers whose literature appears in more than one language. Writers like Marquez, Morrison, and Ngugi confront the political and cultural biases within language because of the wide translations their works receive. Within these considerations, shift cannot be explained through the preparation of the critical community to engage the questions raised by the texts, but through the community's understanding that these texts are layered with culture and ethnicity and gender. Once we are able to formulate a question relevant to the vision of an African writer in English, it is incumbent upon us to follow through that inquiry with an understanding of the version of vision that privileges the textual source. If, for example, orature is at the basis of that vision or if a prosopopoeic articulation is a discrete aspect of that visualization, then whatever lexicon we develop for the term expands as we shift our critical vocabulary so that it can speak of the generative text. The result is a dialogic intertextuality that recasts or shifts the meanings in critical terms.

In case a shifting text and a shiftiness in critical vocabulary seem too problematic for what is generally an urge towards stasis in literary theory, let me suggest a perspective of Paul Ricoeur's as a potentially stabilizing one. Ricoeur notes that "it is only when . . . interpretation is seen to be contained in the other that the antithetic is no longer simply the clash of opposites but the passage of each into the other." Ricoeur is certain of a *textual* point of intersection in symbols—the concrete moments of a dialectic, what he calls the "peak of mediation." He writes:

> In order to think in accord with symbols one must subject them to a dialectic; only then is it possible to set the dialectic within interpretation itself and come back to living

speech. This last stage of reappropriation constitutes the transition to concrete reflection. In returning to the attitude of listening to language, *reflection passes into the fullness of speech . . . the fullness of language . . . that has been instructed by the whole process of meaning.* (Emphasis added.)[21]

It takes only a slight shift of Ricoeur's comment regarding the "passage of each into the other" to understand it within the tradition of the Others who are the subjects and authors of African and African-American literature. The metaphorical figuration that results from this reformulated "other" (the symbols, the speech, the reflective language that Ricoeur includes in the processes that make meaning) is an instance of what I call the translucent nature of the plurisignant text. Such a refiguration brings me to a point where a reconsideration of gender and culture in what I have described as the translucent texts of black women writers is appropriate. Within this consideration, shift is now a necessary feature of the critical process.

(Re)membrance ▲

> The unconscious is the discourse of the Other. . . .
> The dimension of truth emerges only with the appearance of language.
>
> Lacan, "The Insistence of the Letter in the Unconscious"

Reflecting on the use of folk material as "imagery and motif" as well as "a basic element of the inner forms" of black literature, Keith Byerman's conclusion is that its use "implies a fundamentally conservative [i.e. preservationist], organic vision on the part of these writers" who recognize the "wholeness, creativity, endurance, and concreteness" in maintaining the perspectives of the past as "vital to their own sensibilities."[22] Byerman underscores an important relationship between folk material and the perspective of the past it recovers in his concluding chapter of *Fingering the Jagged Grain.* However, the wholeness and concreteness that he suggests are features of this (re)membrance of the past are in fact antithetical to the issue he attempts to resolve in that text. The search for wholeness characterizes the critical enterprise within Western cultures. An effort to revive the text through an internal critical network that restructures its symbolic systems (for example) reflects the cultural sensibilities of the West. This is a sensibility that privileges the recovery of an individual (and independent) text over its fragmented textural dimensions. Byerman's discussion illustrates the nature of the dialectic between the interpretive effort and the textual tradition he is exploring. He does acknowledge the ways in which these works thematically diminish the importance of "individual identity [which] does not exist separate from the community" (277). It is because the concrete history which engages the community and its members is a disabling (and therefore translucent) history that literature by black women writers dissembles the wholeness of this revived folkloric text.

This is, however, not an act of textual sabotage. Such activity in black women writers' texts is paradoxically an effect of (re)membrance—a phrase which cannot, in this canon where the shared tradition belies the scattering effects of the diaspora as well as its contradictory gathering, *simply* mean "wholeness." Such a dialectic in itself gives a critical edge to what, in *Beloved*, Morrison's Sethe calls "rememory." Sethe's vision of history has a translucence such as that described at the opening of this chapter. It is "a picture floating . . . a thought picture" that has as much a place in her vision of the past as it has in the actual past.[23] Consequently, it is a multiplied (and seemingly contradictory) form of memory because it has presence through its translucence, as well as being and form in its clarity. It is this kind of implicit dualism that calls attention to the cultural traditions within this literature and that questions the dimension of gender. Historically, women in Africa have dominated the use (and instruction) of literary forms that include proverbs and folktales. In consequence, it is important to determine the scope of the narrative traditions in black women's literature and to specify the nature of this relationship—to discuss folktales, for example, in conjunction with the voices of/in the tales. The tellers, the mode of telling, the complications and sometimes obfuscations of telling become critical not only to the folkloric traditions, but to the larger narrative traditions as well.

The specificity of voice as well as its assignation are factors relevant to the cultural and gendered (re)membrances in these writers' works. They are discrete features in the literature by women of the black diaspora. Claudia Tate makes this comment on the canon:

> Unlike the black aesthetics, black feminist criticism exam-
> ines not only its discursive territory but its own methodol-
> ogies as well, *realizing that they are not ideologically neutral*. . . .
> The criticism's placement in traditional, academic, human-
> istic discourse gives rise to this *reflexive posture* because crit-
> ics involved in this enterprise realize that the very terms for
> engaging in this discourse, that is, formulating hypotheses
> and evolving praxes, inherently valorize cultural produc-
> tion that is white, patriarchal, and bourgeois-capitalistic.
> (Emphasis added.)[24]

Tate recognizes, in this essay that reviews contemporary works in black feminist criticism, the "changing literal and figurative terms of the game."[25] Her analysis is a tacit recognition of the quality of shift and the nature of (re)membrance. The figura-tion that is accomplished in these texts is one that revises the familiar structures of memory and implicates a pre-text for black women's writing that would address the significance of their race, culture, and gender. The mythopoeic territory for these writers is therefore a territory defined through the refi-gurations of memory. (Re)membrance does not imply the wholeness Byerman (for example) figures as a result of the folk-loric traditions in black literature. Instead, (re)membrance is ac-tivation in the face of stasis, a restoration of fluidity, translucence, and movement to the traditions of memory that become the subjects of these works. The usefulness of literary traditions, whether European, African, American, or combina-tions thereof, is reconstituted in such a literary ethic.

Recognizing that the text of feminist literary studies is dis-crete, Lillian Robinson calls for the "next step in the theoretical process" which will be "for the female nontext to *become* the text."[26] Robinson identifies this nontext as the "creative incapac-ity" equated with silence, literate (as in the case of Tillie Olsen's *Silences*) as well as spoken (as in the example of Walker's Celie). Robinson sees the restoration of voice as a discrete aspect of a feminist critical tradition. Yet it is exactly that kind of definition which squeezes the black woman writer's literary tradition into a space too narrow to contain it. The (re)membered textual source of this gender-specified literary tradition includes a cultural source based in collective orature. Robinson, who seems to understand that there is empowerment through language, reaches for restoration of "a common literary heritage" within the restored voice of women's texts. However, such restoration may very well undermine the cultural specificity of women's language in the black text. The "common" heritage which Robinson concludes should be the focus of feminist criticism is one she artificially simplifies to a proclamation that "People have to live in a house, not in a metaphor" in a disagreement with Audre Lorde's dictum that the master's tools will never dismantle the master's house.[27] It is precisely because of this kind of goal that the black woman's text must clarify the distinctiveness and specificity of its tradition.

The epigraph from Lacan that opens this section suggests that truth, language, and alterity find their definition within the discourse of an interpretive community that values and affirms a multicultural and gendered ethic. A consideration of the text, specifically its language, is exactly what forces critical inquiry back into a textual tradition that unequivocally addresses the sources, the significance, and the histories *within* the textual language. Because black women's literature is generated from a special relationship to words, the concerns of orature and the emergence of a textual language that acknowledges its oral generation must affect the critical work that considers this tradition.

The revised and (re)membered word is both an anomaly in and a concretizing of the cultural memories and gendered ways of language that characterize the texts of black women writers. Rather than calling attention to weakness, this contradiction draws attention to the need to identify, call, and specify the plurisignance within the texts of this tradition. This is a task of definition as much as it is an act of interpretation. The critical enterprise participates in the layering that is intrinsic to the collective voices in the texts of black women writers.

Too often, feminist criticism has focused on the difficulties between the languages of their criticism inasmuch as they reflect a "male discourse." In my view, this concentration has confined

it to a dialogue of consciousness rather than unconsciousness—
familiarity rather than alterity. Even though the feminine Other
seems to be its subject, its objective effort, the decentering of
male androcentrism, has in effect fixed the critical inquiry to a
dialectic that does not include itself. I agree with Lacan that it is
our own unconscious that is the actual Other. The presence of
the differing self, the Other, is established through a reflexive
(recursive) project, one that repeats the text in order to produce
the text. Christopher Miller effectively argues this point:

> By defining the Other's difference, one is forced to take
> into account, or to ignore at one's peril, the shadow cast by
> the self. But without some attention to the African past,
> some effort to describe the Other, how can we accurately
> read the African present? There are in fact two ways to lose
> identity, be it one's own or someone else's . . . by segrega-
> tion in the particular or by dilution in the "universal." [28]

Miller's citation of Cesaire's comment on the loss of identity is a
maxim critical to the textual and accompanying critical need for
a reflective (re)membrance of the textual source. The position
of the ethnophilosopher, who values the metaphysical, the
mythic, and the *different* past in African cultures, is a position
that the literary theorist should adopt. Within such a dialectic,
the nature of a critical language is redefined and is subsequently
shifted away from a singular attention to a critical tradition and
toward the full-bodied voices of the shared cultural and gender-
based traditions reflected in the literature.

4

▲▲▲▲▲▲▲▲▲▲▲▲▲▲▲▲▲▲▲▲▲▲▲▲▲▲▲▲▲▲▲▲

Revision and (Re)membrance: Recursive Structures in Language

> When each member of a collective of speakers takes possession of a word it is not a neutral word . . . the word is filled . . . with . . . . voice [and] arrives . . . already inhabited.
>
> Mikhail Bakhtin, *Problems of Dostoevsky's Poetics*

The dimensions of recursion become apparent when literary (re)membrance and revision are interpreted with a focus on syntactic (grammatical) as well as cultural (metaphorical) categories. In this discussion I want to emphasize the grammatical features within language that specify concepts of time. However, instead of the traditional grammatical reference to these features as notations that identify tense, I prefer to identify them as being concerned with aspect.

Morgan Dalphinis makes an important distinction between aspect and tense. His discussion explains how aspect claims a broader conceptual category than tense because aspect, unlike a "time-based yardstick of concepts such as past, present and future," includes consideration and measurement of "parameters such as completed action versus uncompleted action, progressive versus non-progressive action and futuritive versus non-futuritive action." Dalphinis argues that because of this extension aspect is "consequently a different yardstick to that of time."[1] Dalphinis discusses parallels between grammatical features in languages of West Africa and grammatical features found in languages and dialects of the Caribbean. This syntactic confluence is a significant point of cultural intersection between languages across the Atlantic and calls attention to the West African origins of the Caribbean languages and dialects. These parallels, found in the most linguistically basic levels of structure, carry important cultural implications for the study of linguistic patterns in oral literatures. Patterns of cultural sharing, what Dalphinis calls the "tenacious survival of African culture," between African and Caribbean languages become increasingly significant as we explore the ways that oral literatures are rendered literate.

Related to a consideration of the nature of aspect is a recognition of the linguistic principle involved in this kind of deliberation. This principle concerns the traditional linguistic distinction between the notions of synchrony and diachrony. It is my argument that the methodology of the black text, specifically the black woman writer's text, often dissolves the distinction between these linguistic principles. In these works, simultaneity (synchrony) is often compatible with, rather than distinctive from, the long expanse of historic time and the changes that occur within this expanse (diachrony). Bonnie Barthold's sustained discussion of synchronicity in the African world suggests a point compatible with Dalphinis's distinction between tense and aspect in the synchronic equivalency she draws between being and duration: "each [durative] moment embodied a recurrence of a past moment, and implied was a potential future recurrence."[2] The persistent paradox in black women's literature is not simply that historic events often exist in the same space as the events of the present. In addition to literary synchronicity, a figurative sharing of metaphysical space between historically recoverable events and events metaphorically retrieved through the instantiation of memory and myth occurs. This blurring of what in Western literatures are traditionally discrete constructs marks an important shift in this linguistic principle as it is applied to the black text.

There is an interesting corollary here to what Jonathan Culler identifies as deconstructive potential in what I describe as the reflexive/reflective nature of recursion. Recall, for example, Culler's argument that deconstruction has the potential to emphasize the historicity in "discourse, meaning, and reading" which he subsequently identifies as the end products of "processes of contextualization, decontextualization, and recontextualization."[3] The recursive structures within black women's literature simultaneously construct (historic) contexts (for discourse, meaning, and reading) and revise those same contexts *in an intentional effort to destabilize them*. The end product of this activity is that the past, present, and future are synchronized into what is essentially a deconstructive configuration.

In one sense, this rather paradoxical posture implicates the historicity in discourse, meaning, and reading and in another sense it reconstructs our notion of historicity. Because of recursion's tendency towards revision, the dissolved distinction between synchrony and diachrony has a critical effect on these texts. A subjectivity (and I will argue it is the subjectivity of culture and gender) becomes a significant presence within the discourse created by the recursive text and its reflexive meanings. Alton Becker (somewhat radically) suggests a similar project for the linguistic enterprise when he proposes that linguists "look at something which I think is important to do but which can't be handled within scientific linguistics. . . . I think the job to do is simply to put the observer back into our [linguistic] work. Put the observer back into our knowledge. Put the knower back into the know."[4] Becker's return of the observer to linguistic work has the significant consequence of placing the considerations of culture and gender into a critical relationship with the discourse of the text.

Several features in the literature of black women writers in English illustrate the textural and textual effects of the synchronic/diachronic confluence, but their parallelism is especially clear when we consider the concept of aspect. Sometimes aspect functions as an implicit concept and at other times it is an explicit structural feature within a text. For example, in Ama Ata Aidoo's story, "A Gift from Somewhere," recursive textual structures are of interpretive significance because the dimensions of aspect that are woven into these features are intentionally oblique. The story's opening lines are: "The Mallam *had been* to the village once a long time ago. A long time ago, he *had come* to do these parts" (emphases added).[5] It is fairly easy to recognize the most superficial feature of recursion—simple redundancy. This is illustrated in the repetition of "a long time ago;" but we learn in this story that Mami Fanti is not quite certain of what happened in that distant past or whom to thank for the life of her child. "Do I thank you, O Mallam . . . or you,

Nana Mbemu, since I think you came in the person of the Mallam ... or Mighty Jehova-after-whom-there-is-none-other?"[6] Her ambivalence is initially expressed through grammatical structures, the ambiguity of the verb phrases "had been" and "had come."

The thesis of this story revolves around the being, the nature of whomever it is who comes. The syntactic consequence of this ambiguity is that the verbs "be" and "come" are conceptually marked for recursion. Because of its thematic significance, this recursive instance is reflexive. Only at the end of the story does the reader come to understand the interpretive significance of the verbs even though the text has already signaled this intent through its repetition of "a long time ago." The Mallam's being ("he had been to the village") and his coming ("he had come to do") are linked through the repeated adverbial phrase ("a long time ago"). In this kind of recursive repetition, the expressive nature of the intertextual relationship between the parallel verb phrases "had come" and "had been" is emphasized.

The distinction between the concept of aspect and the notion of time (especially a Western notion of time past, present, or future) expands the reflective/reflexive potential within the literary event. A consideration of aspect prompts a consciousness of being and existence more complex than a simple identification of the relationship between the moment of event and the nature of the character involved. Benjamin Whorf's classic explication of time in the Hopi language suggests that there is a need for another kind of lexicon to clarify the sense of aspect within non-Western cultures. Whorf chose the categories of "manifested" and "manifesting" to explain the presence of being and existence in the conceptual reality of the Hopi's worldview.[7] There is a parallel need to create, or to appropriate and relexify (an accurate description of the theoretical process of *Moorings and Metaphors*), a specific vocabulary for the interpretation of syntactic categories in English used by culturally distinct speakers.

Although linguistically this matter is clearly relevant to verb phrase structures and is a matter of syntax, it is not an issue discussed in linguistic theories of grammatical transformations relevant to recursion or reflexivization. For it to be so, recursion must be identified as a syntactic process as well as a lexically relevant process. However, recursion as figurative reflection, a sort of mimetic inversion of given syntactic or semantic information, is quite clearly related to the behavioral given of habit. Because this sense of recursion is related to repetition, a theory of black literature that privileges the interpretive significance of repetition can be applied not only at the semantic (traditionally literary) level of signification, but at the syntactic (grammatical) level of recursion. My argument is that the intertextuality of repetition at both syntactic and semantic levels is central to an understanding of the speakerly text because it behaves as both subject and object and its collective structures of repetition, signification, and figuration represent the intertextual nature of its being.[8]

I believe these features are of interpretive significance to black women writers' texts not because that is the only place they can be found, but because women's stories persistently use them as method. The author's gender is implicated in the emphasis of features that appear in both the literary and linguistic dimensions of the text.

Recursive structures that appear in linguistic and metaphoric patterns and that multiply narrative structures through an interplay of orature and literature are further complicated in these writers' works by the metaphorical presence of ancestors and feminine deities. When these features are joined to the culturally extended metaphor of the ancestor/goddess, they construct a gender-specific frame that specifies the context and structure of literature by women of the African diaspora. Their choral nature further specifies patterns in the textual/textural weave that liberates them from the strictures of Western individuation and clarifies their source as external to the West.[9] A Eurocentric critical theory applied to these texts would mask their membership in this tradition. The interaction of elements within the group gives entree to texts written from a tradition where the practice of recursion was, through the traditions of the griots, praise-singers, and oral archivists, a cultural reality.

Attention to the primary and oral sources of this literature testifies to the importance of conceptual collectivity in West African cultures. Gates explains that "the nature of black poetic expression [means that] the black poet is far more than a mere point of consciousness of the community. He or she is a point of

consciousness of the language." [10] Such proverbial expression as
the extended family, the coming of a first people (rather than
the first man or first woman), the rejection of isolation both in
social behavior and ways of feeling about belonging are concepts and patterns that follow the culture into its spoken and
written language. [11] If structures of recursion are identifiable
and discrete aspects of black women's literature, how shall we
look for them and what shall we understand them to be telling
us? I will answer the second part of this question before I return
to the first.

Initially, it is black women writers' concern with the behaviors
of telling that is especially significant here. Language structures
that tell serve as another layer in a text multiplied through the
condensation of figures of language and figurations of language that speak. However, they are text-specific. It is certainly
not my intent to claim that black women's literature is all about
the same thing. The complexity of the community rather than
its sameness is distinctive. I do maintain that the syntactically
supported intention of this literature to reveal, call, tell, an-
nounce, and (re)member is the achievement of linguistic structures that are recursive. Susan Willis understands the
significance of this event when she writes of the fear Zora Neale
Hurston felt. Hurston was worried she would be a teller of tales
that would "be in some lone, arctic wasteland with no one under
the sound of [her] voice . . . [within] the cold, the desolate soli-
tude, the earless silences." In an explication of her thesis of
Hurston's "motif of wandering," Willis underscores Hurston's
description of her fears of an "earless silence" and of "casting
her words into a void"; Hurston's "earless silence" is quite no-
ticeably a dissembling metonymn indicative of the recursive
text. [12] I have noted that a telling language is a hallmark of black
women writers' texts. "Earless silences," encloses voice rather
than liberates it, and serves as a lucid example of the kind of
interpretive significance we can attach to recursive structures in
language because of its redundancy. A classic Hurston double-
descriptive, it implicates auracy as well as oracy. [13] What recursive structures like these tell us is how to attend to the interpretive significance of aspect.

My first question—How shall we recognize these structures?—calls for consideration of both structure and context.

Textual attention to certain kinds of contexts may indicate the presence of recursive structures and point to a layered text.

Repetition is an important structural signal in these works. A repeated phrase signals a linguistic (language-based) recursion. The message is to go back, say it again, repeat it for emphasis.[14] There is certainly a strong tradition of repetition in oral literature. Repetition gets some of its earliest use as a signifying device from folksongs of the African-American culture and praisesongs of African cultures. A contemporary example of the persistence of this tradition may be found in the interview NBC television ran with Olympic gold-medalist-to-be Florence Griffith-Joyner in a pre–1988 Olympic promo for the network's coverage of the summer Olympic games. Joyner introduced her three nieces to the television audience. These young girls had composed a rap and proceeded to perform it for their aunt (and the television cameras). The image of ancient village singers, composing a song in praise of a relative, an event, and directing the development of an oral text that would serve as a record for that moment was recalled by the three girls who rhythmically repeated their aunt's achievement and her name. Their oral artistry, offered to their aunt as a gift of telling, underscored their prepubescent understanding of their role in a black and female culture.[15] Whether as a celebrated or a domestic art, women's songs have defined and shaped the culture's value systems.

The history of repetition is telling and rich. In literature, repetition is a restorative act because it recalls the orate voice to the literate structure. Literature that repeats also interrupts the linear progression of the text—a conceptual (but not always a literal) movement from subject to object. The repeated text is evocative and conjures its voice back (again) to the reader's attention. This is a process similar to, but still different from, a discussion that engages Gates. His discussion of repetition is as revision, a signification accomplished by indirection. My discussion of repetition as recursion and Gates's discussion of repetition as revision both underscore the figurative indirection found in the black text. However, the figuration achieved for the black woman writer is dependent upon her acknowledgment that her ownership of a creative word is an opportunity to revive the spoken text she has been denied. For a contemporary writer, repetition evokes the power within an artistic word, reminiscent of an historic Africa where the artists' place in the community was central to preserving its traditions. These were logocentric cultures and what the recursive word accomplishes in texts by black women writers is to return to voice as the center in an intentional displacement of the scriptocentric West.[16]

A repeated structure (as opposed to phrase) signifies a deepening of the syntactic level of text, and this implicates recursion as a feature of the deep structure. Often a verbal element in the syntactic structure is repeated and signals recursion. For example, there is room to argue that Walker's constant use of "say" in the first half of *The Color Purple* is simply the way that Celie communicates her own speech and that of others.[17] Yet because of the text's concentration on the subverted voice, it is clear that to "say" at all for Celie, who has been threatened with her life if she dares to tell, is a signifying event. It is especially important because she can lose her spiritual life if she does not talk. A syntactic repetition at the verb phrase level, then, is important to aspect—"being" in/of the text. Both place and time are implicated in syntactic recursion and repetition because *displacement is the thematic result of repetition.* It moves the text away from itself and the reader away from a subjective/objective process of understanding it. Instead, the text becomes circular, its referentiality no longer given through the perceived, linear arrangement of words. Meaning is never achieved by a process of adding together words in a sentence string. To discover meaning there must be some acknowledgment of figurative abstraction. Layers of rhetorical meanings extend from the textual organization.

The appearance of dialect is generally significant in texts that shift between dialect and standard structures either as a narrative feature or as speech. The simplest explanation, one that I would use, for example, in a discussion of William Faulkner's shift between dialect and standard structures, would be that dialect signals a regional or cultural speech pattern that the author sought to emphasize as a way of identifying character. However, identification is merely a superficial factor in the black text that uses these structures. Dialects that are not standard indicate a signifying text. They reveal a complicity within language structures within the text to invert the potential of the word away from what it "seems" to mean. Narrative and characters' voices shift back and forth between dialect and standard usage in Hurston, especially in *Their Eyes Were Watching God.*[18] In Gloria Naylor's *The Women of Brewster Place,* dialect becomes a class issue—marking the women's speech for the kind of history they bring to the community of Brewster Place and complicating it with their rural or urban, privileged or impoverished circumstances. The narrative voice indicates its understanding of each of these voices by dislocating itself and allowing their dialogue to dominate or poetically intrude as a compensation for the silence in the text.

V. N. Volosinov, explaining a theory sometimes attributed to his theoretical colleague Mikhail Bakhtin, noted:

> Existence reflected in sign is not merely reflected but *refracted.* How is this refraction of existence in the ideological sign determined? By an intersecting of differently oriented social interests within one and the same community. . . . Thus various different classes will use one and the same language. As a result, differently oriented accents intersect in every ideological sign. Sign becomes an arena of class struggle.[19]

Susan Stewart cites this passage (and attributes it to Bakhtin rather than Volosinov) and notes that "once he moves the materiality of language away from essence into the domain of practice, Bakhtin can present the cacophony of voices present in any utterance." His purpose to then "place the subject within a social structure, a place where subject and structure are mutually articulated," is served through such a shift in place, resulting in ideology as an "ongoing product and producer of social practices."[20]

"Cacophony" is the operative word here. Syntax is a contextual issue for Bakhtin that affirms the operative processes of sociohistorical reality. Cacophony within a speech community at once rejects a Western notion of community and supports a community that is identified by its linguistic diversity and its (paradoxically harmonic) thematic complexity. This articulation belongs to the novelist who preserves dialect. Speech differences do not merely distinguish character from character, but collect characters under a rubric of their linguistic refraction. Then what becomes important to the choice to preserve dialect is the significance of its appearance and the ways it allows culture and history to emerge from the linguistic parameters of the text. Therefore, the appearance of a dialect structure is a message to attend to the construction of the story, to watch for the narrative or spoken indirection that dialect signals, and to work toward an interpretation that includes a consideration of what the language has done, at that moment, to the story.

English language texts by African women writers do not, as a matter of course, include the use of American dialects. Instead, dialects in these texts reflect the pidginized and creolized languages that are the result of their colonial pasts. The appearance of such dialects has more historical textual significance than can be claimed for dialects of American English. However, dialect used as a creative practice is a rich strategy in both the African and the African-American writer's texts. As an example, consider a short story by Ama Aidoo, "For Whom Things Did Not Change." As a figurative mask, the use of dialect in this story is a trope. The speaker assumes dialect as intentionally as he assumes his servile persona for his "master." The inverted tropes of this story are multiple. The master is not a white colonialist; he is a black African. The textual confusion of voices is dense (the narrator speaks in at least three forms, the self-reflective narrative, the dialectal dialogue, and a standard English monologue). The thematic inversions possible with the assumption of dialect multiply the syntactic and symbolic potential within the words of the text. In both literatures, African and African American, expression is creatively empowered through the artistic use of dialect.

What I shall label the "persistence of speech" in African women writers is comparable to the manipulations of language in African-American women writers. Lloyd Brown has commented on the "sheer volume of talk" in Flora Nwapa's novels, a description that could apply as well to Emecheta and Aidoo.[21] Written talk seems to be the technical achievement of both the African and African-American writer. However, for the African writer, written talk is a complicated verbal signal system that literalizes the poetry of the myth in the (re)membered roles of women's speech. Attention to the representations of speech and awareness that the activity of speech is a spiritual engagement for both cultures are considerations that must enter into an interpretive analysis of this literature.

Shift and aspect may appear as an inconsistency in tense, a shifting narrative voice, and/or a disappearance of the syntactic form within a sentence. These are additional signals of the linguistic recursion of the text. The latter sign, the dissolving syntax, is a feature traditionally spoken of as stream of consciousness. It needs no further distinction in a consideration of these texts except to note again that its appearance is a signal about both the text and the character. This is very different from Virginia Woolf's (for example) use of this technique as a narrative mode in *To the Lighthouse*, and different as well from the interior monologue. In the texts we are concerned with here, the dissolved narrative signals a cooperative dissolution of the narrative voice, the character's voice, and the textual structure. Among contemporary writers, Toni Morrison's various forms of a streaming narrative, evident in the opening pages of *The Bluest Eye* and the closing chapters of *Beloved,* are perhaps the most luminous. However, the intertextual significance of the technique is a feature in black women's writing which, in conjunction with these other aspects of language, identifies the traditions in their texts.

It is important not to misinterpret the expanded and complicated vision of the narrative voice in African and African-American women writers' texts. No longer a simple, careful moderator between text and character (and author and reader) the involved narrator enters into the event of the text. Often, the narrative awareness shifts according to the degree of involvement. Although this is a participant structure that may be interpreted in reference to the literary structures of the text, it is of linguistic importance as well. Shift may be most obvious in the subjective element of a sentence. Voice, for example, may shift from "I" to "we." A choral structure may replace an individual commentator. The narrative voice may suddenly seem to leave the text and speak directly to the reading audience. Black women writers seem to understand, predict, and speak to the presence of an audience, returning their audience to the community of tellers for whom the oral text was originally prepared. In other words, in noting narrative shift, we must also be prepared to give interpretive significance to this linguistic diversion of the text. A shift in narrative perspective (combined with a recurrent textual structure) in *Second-Class Citizen* illustrates the textual importance of this kind of diversion. Buchi Emecheta writes of her character, Adah: "The slamming of the door, the finality of it all, reminded her of something she had seen before. She had seen it all before, this cruel finality. The other person who was shut away from her like that never came back. Where did it happen before? She searched her memory as she stood in that scorching Nigerian sun."[22] Several linguistic signals in that passage point to its recursive structure. The most obvious may be the narrative repetition. The final element of the first sentence becomes the initial element of the second sentence (a structure Aidoo also uses). The rhetorical question is asked in Adah's voice. Rather than "Where had she seen it before?"—the appropriate subjective form for that query—the narrative shifts to her own voice ("Where did it happen?") and replaces not only the subject but also the aspect (from past perfect to simple past). Emecheta's text continues: "It all came back to her now. It was Pa who was nailed down . . . it had the same aura of finality."[23]

Second-Class Citizen opens with the event of her father's death and her becoming a "girl-orphan" (although she has a mother). Her husband's temporary leave-taking brings back the memory of her father's funeral. His trip to London effectively makes her an "orphan" again. The social structures of her culture will force her to acknowledge the authority of his family. The recursive structure within that repetition and syntactically shifted narration is of interpretive significance to the text. The careful placement of "it all" grows in its capacity to include the present event of her husband's leaving. The "aura of finality" is of critical proportion to other like events in Adah's life, as well as to the scene from her childhood, which Emecheta renders in great and poignant detail in *The Bride Price*. In *Second-Class Citizen* we know from the repetition and recursion that "it all" is a large and overwhelming category of the emotional upheavals in Adah's life. We suspect, with this repetition and recursion, that this category will grow. Such narrative features are among those that are important to the structures represented in the traditions of black women's literature.

In *The Newly Born Woman*, Hélène Cixous writes of ideology as a kind of "vast membrance enveloping everything." Obviously, syntactic structures that are morphologic cannot be considered as insular in a critical theory of literature. They envelop the ideology of the text itself. The "membrance" that Cixous refers to is an appropriate metaphor for their textu[r]al effect.[24] The canonical argument is therefore quite seriously an argument of the politics of ideology. Gayatri Spivak underscores this argument when she writes: "We will not be able to speak to the women out there if we depend completely on conferences and anthologies by Western-trained informants. . . . In inextricably mingling historico-political specificity with the sexual differential in a literary discourse . . . [we] begin effacing that image."[25] Spivak's argument for Third World women, that "when we speak for ourselves, we urge with conviction: the personal is also political," frames the cultural argument within black women writers' texts. When criticism of these texts acknowledges the activity of speech as its challenge, both in its direct engagement of a victimizing silence and in the specific (re)membrance of a tradition that has been socially and politically devalued in a modern world, then speech itself—the discrete (albeit fragmented) units, its patterns, structures and ways of making and (re)membering sense—becomes a critical part of a theory that speaks, not only to "the women out there," but to a tradition in literature that has waited for its own voice to emerge from the text.

Patterns of recursion concretize the formal, linguistic structures found in black women's texts. However (and perhaps surprisingly), the result is not a stylistic unity; it is instead the kind of multiplicity that Bakhtin identifies as a characteristic of seriocomic literature. Writing in *Problems of Dostoyevsky's Poetics*, Bakhtin notes of this genre, which he identifies as having the power to transform an "unfinalized" present, that,

> multiplicity of tone [is] typical; they make wide use of introductory genres—letters, manuscripts which have been found, parodically reconstructed quotations, and the like. In some of these genres the mixture of prose and poetic speech is observed, living dialects and slang are introduced . . . and various authorial masks appear. The *represented*

word appears alongside the *representational* word, and in certain genres double-voiced words play a leading role. *Thus there appears here a radically new attitude to the word as the material of literature.* (Emphasis added.)[26]

Here, in Bakhtin's notes, are mirrors of the black woman's text: "mixtures" of speech; the necessity of authorial masks (a tradition that has marked black letters in America since its earliest days), and the polyvocalic word that nullifies the chasm between objectivity and subjectivity. All characterize the narrative dimensions of these texts. They are shifting, shape-changing texts in the ways they acknowledge a tradition based both in a culture for which the orate word is privileged and in a gender where the preservation of that word explicates this tradition.

5

▲▲▲▲▲▲▲▲▲▲▲▲▲▲▲▲▲▲▲▲▲▲▲▲▲▲▲▲▲▲▲▲▲▲

Mythologies

> I wanted to write out of the matrix of memory, of recollection, and to approximate the sensual and visceral responses I had to the world I lived in.
>
> Toni Morrison, "On the Spoken Library"
>
> But isn't the truth of the voice to be hallucinated?
>
> Wole Soyinka, "On Barthes and Other Mythologies"

Buchi Emecheta's *The Bride Price* opens with the striking image of Ma Blackie, "a giant of a woman . . . a 'palm tree woman.'" Ma Blackie was not only a large woman, but she had a glossy black skin that had distinguished her presence in her village since the time of her childhood. Therefore, when we learn that she is absent from her home at the story's opening, the symbolic contrast between her physical presence and literal absence at what is the opening event of the novel, her husband's death, is an especially poignant image. Because Ma Blackie had gone to her childhood home in Ibuza to "placate their Oboshi river goddess into giving her some babies," her son Nna-nndo and daughter Aku-nna are left alone to experience the emotional trauma of their father's loss. Emecheta's is a story marked by dissolved contrasts between presence and absence, light and dark, and myth and actuality. At the end of this novel Aku-nna's physical life is cut off at childbirth. But her death is not at all a spiritual closure. The story of her tragedy (she had betrayed a village superstition by choosing to marry without a bride price having been paid) makes the events which culminated in her death a "present absence" as well. Her spiritual destiny was to become the embodiment of a myth that exacted "a psychological hold over every young girl" in Ibuza.[1] Aku-nna's susceptibility to this myth was foreshadowed in the earliest pages of Emecheta's novel.

The legend of Sapphira Wade, "a true conjure woman" forms the opening event of Gloria Naylor's *Mama Day*.[2] In a story fraught with overwhelming psychic and physical intensity, Sapphira's (absent) presence is the single most powerful image in the book. The ramifications of her necromancy in 1823 are still being played out in the contemporary lives of her children's children's children on the island of Willow Springs. They are left to inherit the shimmering spirit of her memory and the unavoidable stature commanded by her mythic presence.

Both the girls in Aku-nna's village and Sapphira Wade's grandchildren are left to a legacy that promises them that they have no choice but to re-collect the significance of their ancestor's living into their own. Vulnerable as they are to the mythologies that have preceded them, their own living will be enacted in the shadows of stories that represent the most primary beliefs and the earliest of rituals within their cultural histories. Sapphira Wade's mysticism and magic continue to reflect into the present-day terror of her great-granddaughter, Cocoa. Aku-nna, who flirted with the tragedy implicit in failing to acknowledge myth predictably became the embodiment of that myth. Now her life's story is attached to the warning village girls in Ibuza have been instructed to acknowledge.

Although Lévi-Strauss would emphasize mythology as a facet in the articulation of religious anthropology, it would seem that the mythology (re)membered in these writers' works has a far more intimate relation to a perceptual universe and a felt-life than a religious anthropology would experience.[3] In these works, the literary concept of archetype extends itself beyond the particular and specific meanings or patterns of literary arrangement that a religious anthropology would support. Instead, it embraces a communal and culturally determined archetype. The mythologies in literature by black women writers seem closer to a metaphorical revisioning of experiential knowledge—the antithesis of Lévi-Strauss's claim that myth "should be placed in the gamut of linguistic expressions at the end opposite to that of poetry."[4]

Lévi-Strauss's theory of mythology illustrates the effort in the Western tradition to distinguish myth from other acts of language. This effort forms the basic difference between Euro-American thought and mythology in non-Western cultures. In some myths of West Africa, for example, one can identify the effort to preserve both original meanings and primary models of symbolism. The constant presence of mythic systems of meaning in processes of orature and literature makes them a familiar matter of everyday use. Consider, as an example of this constancy, the quilt in Alice Walker's short story, "Everyday Use."[5] In Walker's story, the quilt is a metaphor that represents the everyday necessity of such ancient objects. Either the quilt, whose ownership causes the dispute between two sisters, is an object to revere at a hanging-on-the-wall distance (the Lévi-Straussian theory of myth that separates it from ordinary language), or it is an object for everyday use because memory is one of those features of aspect in these texts that dissolves the boundary between the past and the present.

Archetypes that render mythic structures into systems of meaning are generally archetypes of behavior and cognition. In black women's literature, temporicity (an emphasis on specific times and certain places for metaphorical meanings) acts not as the generative spark for what Northrup Frye would label "associative clusters" of archetypes, but rather generates clusters of community from the gathered (re)membrances of language, voice, and psyche. Frye's term "cluster" is a helpful descriptor of such a framework, but it is also slightly misleading. Again, the element I have described in chapter three as shift is instrumental in illustrating how recurrence, which Frye associates with a dialectic ritual, is in black literature a linguistic ritual.[6] What shifts here is the traditional distinction between behavior and language. Linguistic rituals of black literature associate speech and act rather than dissociate or displace the two. The moment of genesis for this relationship occurs when voice is linked to creative activity. Recurrence (recursion) is the cyclic repetition of frames of thinking about the patterns in our physical and spiritual lives that have come to be associated with a specific culture. This cyclicity follows cultural patterns of orature and literature. Linear progression is but a delusion, a momentary displacement of perception in the actual recursive universe represented in this imaginative literature.

Literature by black women writers acknowledges that displacement has occurred and compensates by placing a massive energy into structures of orature within their texts. The specificity that generally accompanies archetype is diffused and often even obliterated in this literature. As a result, we find sequences specifically written to supersede the expected and traditional narrative use of the agencies of time and space/place.

Note, for example, Avey's vision in Paule Marshall's *Praisesong for the Widow*. Avey, who is on a cruise, has decided that she is unable to complete her planned journey, so she has shifted her itinerary to return home. Ironically this is exactly what happens although the home she returns to is as much a spiritual as physical place. The ancestral presence of her great aunt figures strongly in the text's evolving outside of the anticipated structures and flowing into a timelessness where Avey becomes vulnerable to what I call "mythologies." She is seasick and her illness forces a (re)membrance of a childhood illness. More than youth and age are dissolved in this psychic revisioning. Avey's immediate past is juxtaposed against the stronger mythology of her historical and ancestral past. Rather than a descent for Avey into some form of memory even more shadowy than her childhood, Marshall uses this moment for the time "when the pall . . . lifted momentarily and she became dimly conscious."[7] Marshall quite intentionally makes use of this quasi-oxymoron (dim consciousness) to indicate that mythology, as an instant of memory, is not an occasion to doubt the veracity or accuracy of the myth, or its figuration into memory, or its agency in the present.[8] Instead, it is a moment when a metaphysical disturbance substantiates the physical. The history in this event is compelling. The passage that connects Avey to her slave past recalls a slave ship. Marshall writes:

She was alone in the deckhouse. That much she was certain of. Yet she had the impression as her mind flickered on briefly of other bodies lying crowded in with her in the hot, airless dark. A multitude it felt like lay packed around her in the filth and stench of themselves, just as she was. Their moans . . . enlarged upon the one filling her own head. Their suffering—the *depth* of it, the weight of it, in the cramped space—made hers of no consequence. (Emphasis added.)[9]

The "depth of it" is the depth of her own history being forced into the "cramped space" of a culture and tradition that would deny its significance and even its occurrence. Susan Willis cites this passage in order to emphasize that the images that are a part of the descriptive elements in Marshall's book (the iron, the manacles, the physical memories of slavery that Avey both psychically and physically endures—again) are metaphors "articulating the individual's access to racial consciousness and liberation."[10] However, these metaphors also specify what I term "mythologies"—the diffusive agencies of language by black women writers that substantiate a metaphorical presence in the language of the text. In this particular novel, evidence for this agency, an activation of metaphor, is found in the memory of Cuney's grandmother. Her story serves as the living embodiment of the myth of the Africans who came to Tatem Island and who, in rejecting its isolation and system of slavery, turned back toward the sea and walked across it back home. (The incident is both mythic and historical because of the Africans' power over the water and because this is an event that she had witnessed; the ship and the [re]turn happened.) Cuney's grandmother, whose "mind was with the [returned] Ibos," was the spiritual presence that maintained the past in the present and that obliterated the distinction between them.

The presence of mythologies in black women writers' texts points toward the elements of myth—metaphor, spirituality, and memory—as they appear in the systems of literature, rather than toward individual myths of West Africa. The cultural presence within literature acknowledges spoken language as its source. The potential to reformulate story, not into constituent patterns but into frames that reconstruct more ancient patterns of memory and telling—mythologies—is of interpretive significance. Texts by black women writers privilege an older understanding of literature. Because their structures acknowledge the mythic traditions that have generated them, these works are not distinguished from their ancestry. Used in this way, myth is a linguistic mediator between spirit (the objective/perceived world) and self (the subjective/experiential world).

The Matrix of Memory ▲

I recognize appearances of myth as explanations of natural orders, as personifications of natural phenomena, and as rationale for the seemingly irrational. However, the interpretive distinction between Western and non-Western mythologies is the extent to which myth has been, in West Africa, assimilated into the ordinary dimensions of human life. Rather than the extraordinary and distant environment of, for example, the Graeco-Roman mythologies, the nearness of myth to reality in West African cultures is enabled by the realm of the ancestor. Ancestors continue to make their spiritual presence felt after their deaths; they are unseen but neither uninterested in nor dismissed from the lives of their families. Their constantly mediative presence between the spiritual and physical worlds maintains a relationship between subjectivity and objectivity so critical and so intense that it demands a vocabulary distinct from that of the Western world. Indeed, the very concept of religion in some indigenous African societies reflects an ideology that is far more inclusive (communal), than the Western intepretation of this term would allow. Religion as a way of living and a system of belief extends throughout African cultures and is often dissimilar from the more discrete ideologies that Christianity, for example, would acknowledge. All artistry, the natural world, the spiritual universe, and the mundane are integrated into a vision of religious sensibility in indigenous African religions to the point that it is almost inappropriate to call this pervasive belief system "religion" in the Western sense of this term. Some African theologians go so far as to claim that the word "religion" has no exact translation in African languages.[11]

Lévi-Strauss writes of the originality of myth "in relation to other linguistic phenomena."[12] In contrast, I suggest that the *resemblance* of myth to literatures and oratures marks the West African tradition in black women writers' literary and cultural traditions. This interpretive difference has a significant critical

dimension. For instance, Northrup Frye relates an Egyptian tale
of "Two Brothers" whose argument leads to the attempted escape of the younger from the older. The story reaches a climactic moment when the god Ra intervenes and places a crocodile-
filled lake between the two. Frye's interpretation is that at this
point the story gives "the external analogy" to "life" and obtains
an "abstractly literary quality."[13] However, its story status positions it as different from "life" and its intention to be something
other than (and I would argue, larger than) life. It is as *dimension*
rather than *distinction* that myth has its presence in the non-
Western world.

In a Yoruban myth of two brothers, the rivers that would satisfy the younger brother's thirst (and, it is implied, help to rid
Apasha of the jealousy he feels for his elder brother's hunting
prowess) are continually muddied by the orisha and trickster
Eshu. Apasha kills his elder brother, thinking that he was the
one who had been deliberately preventing him from quenching
his thirst. When Apasha realizes that Eshu was the culprit who
dirtied the rivers and spoiled the drinking water, he mournfully
sits by his brother's dead body until he becomes a mound of
earth and his dead brother becomes a sparkling stream—assuring that Apasha's spirit would never know thirst. This interven-
tion of a god, or orisha, is similar to the story that Frye relates.
According to Frye, it would be toward the conclusion where the
story assumes an "abstractly literary quality" because at that
point the brothers become the mound of earth and the stream.
I would argue that the story is mythic throughout—just as Eshu
hides behind the bushes, following the brothers' hunt throughout their day. There is no particular moment when mythic proportion is achieved—no shift from the world that Frye sees as
analogous to life to the "abstraction" of mythology. Instead, the
mythic dimension of this story is synchronous to the story itself.
It is not distinct from but intimately an active presence in the
unitary lives represented in the story that are shared equally
between spiritual (Eshu), ancestral (the protective presence of
the dead elder brother), and human presences (the living
brothers).

Although I speak of a structure of mythology, my label is different from the structures that occupy Lévi-Strauss's structural
criticism or the archetypal theory represented in Frye's work.

When structure refers to memory rather than device it shifts from the sort of binary explications that Lévi-Strauss brings to the Oedipus myth or the cycles of mythology in Frye's analyses. Indeed, even this cyclic concept of Frye's is undercut by his emphasis on a dialectical movement between order and chaos within narrative structures.

An example of the privilege that memory asserts in myth can be found in Zora Neale Hurston's identification of the features of dialect that call attention to what she labels as a "Negro way of saying." Her specific reference is to such syntactic and semantic elements as double-descriptives and verbal-nouns. Including metaphor and simile in these categories, she anticipates a critical perspective that privileges the mythologies that I identify as features of black women's imaginative literature. Hurston's observations come very close to specifying what is a way of (re)memory in the literature of black women writers. This reconstruction of memory elevates that event and its surrounding structures, whether syntactic or semantic, to mythic proportions. This is what happens when Denver asks Sethe in Morrison's *Beloved* if this means that "rememories" never die. "Nothing ever does" is Sethe's reply to her (36).

Within such an omnipresent universe, the events of ordinary life may loom larger than the living we would anticipate, or the dimensions of time and place may exceed themselves, or the uses of language itself may shift away from the boundaries of literature and extend into the realm of orature. In a section of *The Women of Brewster Place,* Gloria Naylor's description of a preacher's sermon defies the definitions of either poetry or prose. The rhythms of speech dominate the passage, but its sensual level is poetry and its visceral level is painfully (and erotically) prosaic.

> He needed their attention for [a] split second because once he got it, he was going to wrap his voice around their souls and squeeze until they screamed to be relieved. . . . First he played with them and threw out fine silken threads that stroked their heart muscles ever so gently. They trembled ecstatically at the touch and invited more. The threads multiplied and entwined themselves solidly around the one pulsating organ they had become and tightened slightly, testing them for a reaction. (65)

This text gathers together a fractured community—and whether the preacher's purpose is nefarious or fine, he knows, the text knows, and the reader should feel the powerful potential in the way he renders his sermon. Naylor, in recognizing what such linguistic structures accomplish, uses the mythologies of telling as a way of signalling her reader that here is a man who has "permission to take that short hop from the heart to the soul" and who can even obliterate reality until "there's no room, no room for nothing else, not even that great big world out there that exacts such a strange penalty for my being born black." She begins to wind this emotive section down with a cryptic assessment: "It was hard work" (65).

Within such a literature, myth does of course survive as the stories of orishas and tales of genesis, but it also takes on the patterns of "ways of saying"—the aspective literatures that represent not only ways of thinking about the world but ways of behaving (saying) in the world, ways of culture, and mythologies in communities. Such signification, such signs of the world, the culture, and the systematicity within communities are not quite as fragile as the kinds of stories and legends we have come to identify with the term "myth." These are actually very small in number when one compares the extant literary texts of myths (always, of course, in the Western world "in translation"). Although this body of literature is certainly telling about the African world and its peoples, it is a fragile record as well. Its literate preservation, even downplaying the bastardizations in the process of translation, is an extremely selective process. Western literatures have generally salvaged those stories and tales that match their own anticipated frameworks about myth. The genesis of the world is an accepted topic, as are sibling rivalry, human deceit and conceit, war, and celestial events. For all of these myths there are parallels in the myths of the West. Perhaps it is as a consequence of these parallels that we have developed such specific critical schema, a very particular way of talking about such myths. Northrup Frye can, after all, discuss mythologies of rivalry in an American Indian culture with as much ease as the European myths he recounts in *Fables of Identity*.[14] Yet Frye's perspective suggests a priori interpretation: perhaps it was the European myth that paved the way for his interpretative posture in reference to the non-Western mythology. Certainly, there is no evidence that he followed a reverse interpretive process. Therefore, when we proceed to depart from the example of the West, along with a host of other interpretive questions we must ask, we should also concern ourselves with the process of selection—a concern that begs the (rhetorical) query, What culturally specific interpretive frames have been excluded? My thesis in this chapter embeds the sense of cultural mythologies into ways of saying.

Mythologies in language are structures that I place in the same arena as mythic archetypes, constituent units of myth (Lévi-Strauss) and formulaic constructions of myth (Barthes).[15] However, mythologies are not discrete units of structure as much as they are features of a surviving sense of how language enables the survival and transference of memory. This is its critical distinction from a definition that uses as its standard the formulas that parallel received structures from Europe. Because memory is critical to mythologies, then the privilege that memory traditionally represents over myth—that of representation (accuracy) over figuration (metaphor)—is dissolved within the disappearance of the chasm between memory (history) and myth (figuration). What remains are the historical figurations of mythologies.

The Truth of the Voice ▲

If we were to place Hurston accurately in the history that is expressed in her texts we must first replace the linear vision of history, essentially a Eurocentric perspective, with a cyclic vision. Hurston is an African storyteller. Her literary perspective of the world is dominated by a circular view of time. Its historical events and people and her linguistic revisioning of the oral text are recirculations of story, an appeal to the ritual of an oracular word that centers and grounds the literate text.

Moses, Man of the Mountain uses the power of oracy to serve as documentary evidence of the literate text.[16] I have written in *Character of the Word* that in this book she acknowledges the word's creative potential. The embracing (note that I have not said the "extending") of literacy pushes words and language outwards towards its community.

West African myth presents the genesis of humankind in a community (the group or company that Gabriel Setiloane references). This vision of community is critical in literature by Africans and African-Americans.[17] The sense of individual generation is not corroborated by myths of genesis. Communal generation is historically a part of black culture. As an example, note the figures sculpted in this Yoruban creation myth:

> Obatala, the Sky God Olorun's son and representative on earth, was authorized by Olorun to create land over the water beneath the sky. After he had created the earth, and illuminated it he thought, "Surely it would be better if many people were living here." He dug clay from the ground, and out of the clay he shaped human figures which he then laid out to dry in the sun. And when he had made enough figures to begin the populating of Ife, he called out to Olorun. . . . They arose and began to do the things that humans do and in this way the place Obatala named Ife became the city of Ife.[18]

The language of *Moses* acknowledges the power inherent in a collective telling in a manner that asserts the potential of words to themselves represent this creative potential. An early recursive passage in the text is a litany—a chant that calls together the respondents in the manner of the folkloric tradition: "He had crossed over. . . . He was not in Egypt. . . . He had crossed over. . . . He was not an Egyptian. . . . He had crossed over so he sat down on a rock. . . . He did not own. . . . He did not have. . . . He had crossed over. . . . He felt empty. . . . He had crossed over."[19] The divestment of Moses's community and his place is a telling feature of this event. The repeated words gather together the remnants of this psychically and spiritually fractured man who eventually finds that he is literally and figuratively a "man of the mountain"—the rock. Whatever these figures metaphorically represent in the novel, Moses will come to embody as well. It is important to note, however, that Moses has no power (neither an external magical power nor an internal power of recognition) until he meets Jethro and joins Jethro's community. Only then is he energized and ready for the power in the words of the text. Hurston winds the energy of its eventually explosive power with the early incantation and readies both her novel and the reader for the realignment of word and speaker/writer.

If we sense that Hurston speaks in this story because of the power and strength in the narration, then we have recognized the glimmers of this reassociation. The new text, revisioned in Hurston's crafting, is one that acknowledges a West African sense of the generation of the world as a community—the proverbial expression of a black culture. In the restructured folktale, the characters and event are known qualitites. The revisioned story simply repositions them. In *Mules and Men* Hurston noted that "belief in magic is older than writing."[20] This belief restructures the community in *Moses* and places this allegorical tale in a direct relationship with its spoken language. The characters and events of *Moses* simply fit into the schema of rocks and crossing over. Centered by the activity of an incantatory word, they move, tighten, and collapse into the linguistic center of this ancient and revisioned story.

The activity is accomplished in three ways. First, the story itself is taken away from event and behavior and returned to language. Second, language restructures the community—places men in correct relationship to their rocky places, reconvenes peoples separated by sociolinguistic trickery and reestablishes original communities and their relationships to the natural world. Finally, the text links oracy and literacy and reiterates the relationship of the word to God (creation).

This gathering of voice, words, text, and story is present as well in the stories of *Mules and Men*. In this collection the stories are returned to language because their focus is not event and interaction. Certainly these features of plot are important to both the novel and the collection; but in both the story collection and the novel, the activity of language—the movement in and of words—is ultimately responsible for the texts. It is, however, in *Moses* that Hurston assigns final authority to the word and accomplishes the cultural revisioning of storytelling in full textual form.

My first point, that the folktale's energy extends from its linguistic arrangement, is illustrated in the opening lines of *Moses*. We are confronted with a prayer: "Have mercy! Lord, have mercy on my poor soul"(11). This invocation signals the beginning of a ritual storytelling posture and pulls a creative energy into the story. Hurston's authorial voice is certainly the primary structuralist of this story; but it is not an individuated voice, it is a shared voice as the prayer/plea indicates. The next paragraph begins with a transitional phrase—"so"—which acknowledges the link between the preceding text and what is yet to be crafted. As much in response to the laws of Pharaoh as to the opening prayer, we are told that "So the women in the pains of labor hid in caves and rocks. They must cry, [a recursive reminder of the opening plea] but they could not cry out loud" (11). We learn, this early, that the now familiar thesis of "silence" is the event of this story. The opening incantation to the creator is all that they have left. If we acknowledge the artist/author as creator we can certainly see how this novel fits into the patterns of the canon. There is a critical internalization of language and it is through this internalization that the text itself gains power. Moses learns to talk to rocks, trees, and the caves that echo with the thwarted cries of women in labor and hold the memory of their terror. This initial chapter ends with the ancient Hebrew's learning to "crush the agony inside"—a functional interiority because only within their spirits will they find the linguistic honesty of the natural world. They sank "lower and lower" the narrative voice tells us (12). It is implicit that they are gradually grounded, recovering their relationship to the earth, and rediscovering their creative places.

My second point, that language restructures the community, is evidenced in numerous ways throughout the text. As a child and as a young man, Moses revels in the Egyptians' adulation of his wonderful military talent; but it is his hearing of the old story of the Book of Thoth that will bring him to the gods. At that point, his life is redirected. His goal shifts from military acrobat to a sort of mental acrobat—he immerses himself in print, searches for, reads, and follows the instructions of the old story in order to find God. Here Hurston's emphasis is on positioning words into places where they have the potential to direct and redirect action. The enslaved Jews (of whom Moses is one) already know what Moses will learn in this text—that they can change events through language. "Did I tell that Prince something? I told his head a mess!" (96). This phrase signals a linguistic disruption, forcing Moses not to "follow his usual pattern" the evening he learned of the book's existence. The power of the word interrupts and dislocates place and pattern. Instead of the usual court functions, Moses readies himself for his journey out of Egypt and the meeting with the rock that Jethro says is a "call waiting for him" (137).

Once Moses meets his teacher and becomes a part of Jethro's

community he has a particularly thoughtful response to the experience, feeling that "he had achieved a certain calm by forcing
an internal silence on his soul" (139). His experience of interiority is a ritual Hurston signal. All of her characters in search of
self are readied for what is essentially a spiritual quest by an
external silencing. Janie experiences this in *Their Eyes Were
Watching God;* so do John Pearson of *Jonah's Gourd Vine* and Ar-
vay Henson Meserve of *Seraph on the Suwanee.*[21] That this silence
anticipates search and spiritual recovery is the ultimate folkstory of *Moses* and indicates its ancient status. The profound
calm the narrator says "took up" in the face of Moses and that
"grew rugged like the mountain and held its power inside," metaphorically and visually restructures this calming silence (144).
His role in Jethro's community is shifted after this experience
with silence. Although Jethro is master wizard, Moses becomes
a master student who eventually "leaps past [Jethro's] stumbling
mind to the *inside* meaning of things" (149; emphasis added).
Again, the forced interiority dictates a shift in the organization
of the community. Moses finds that "them secret words" are the
"keys to god"—a power that eventually enables him to battle the
legendary snake guardian of the Book and to sit atop the mountain, passing "nations through his mind" (151, 160). Once he
learns that life could never be again what it once was, the redefined community has a leader, a slave, a dispossessed man, a
deified man, and a magician all layered into the body and spirit
of Moses. At the base of all these incarnations, each of which is
followed by a shift in social structures, is voice, word, or text.
Somebody *tells* that he was Hebrew; he *speaks* the language of
the natural and magical worlds, he *reads* the Book of Thoth.

That voice and text are linked and reestablish a relationship
to God (and metaphorically to creation) is the issue of the final
chapters of *Moses.* We know the myth well. Its events are familiar to Western cultures. However, Hurston's point is not to retell
this known story. Instead, she uses the events of what she reestablishes as a collective myth to gather us into it. "When are we
crossing over?" is the elliptical query of the freed Hebrews at
the novel's end. But like the recursive text this is, they contradict
themselves: "When are we crossing over? We are here!" (338).
Moses however, does not want them to forget that "it ain't everybody who can go right up and talk with God . . . and then bring

back the right word from the talk" (340). Moses learns, as does
the reader, that the trick of this story is not in winning battles.
The trope of this story is in the revision in its words, that the
narrator says "would be according to their own dreams" (346).

Hurston's epilogue to this tale is the prologue "Lord have
mercy" revisioned, a technique indicating the nature of a reflexive recursion. The revelation at the story's end, that "now God
had a voice and a glory," is a recursive acknowledgment of the
thesis of silence and voice that opens the story. In a translucent
oxymoron that underscores this recursion, Hurston explains
that a "dimming sunlight" gives Moses an "inside vision" (347).
Then, just in case we miss this point, the lizard tells Moses that
memories are not of a body, but that there is a keeper of memories that would give voice and body, through a collective language, both history and truth, and further, it would explain to
Moses how the world was made. With this assurance that he
would know creative power and with the elliptical message that
he could not hold this knowledge within his own, individual
body, Hurston returns the power of creation to a word Moses
must learn to share. The community refigured through this
spell includes the ancient Hebrews, the Egyptians, the lizards,
and the rocks. This group is destined to rediscover their relationship to each other because Moses had bothered to learn the
power in the word.

Literacy is a visualization of the mythologies of language. It is
a magical act itself, pushing experience and knowledge into a
specialized sphere. This textual vitalization is accomplished by a
sharing of power between the literate and spoken word, a divesting of the oppositional space between them and a creative
regathering that, in *Moses,* includes the moon, the sky, the seven
suns of the Universe, the lightning, thunder, and flame as an
accompaniment for Moses's final word—"farewell." This word
is an instructional directive to that regathered community who
had yet to recognize that the crossing over point is "here."

Historical Displacement ▲

In "The Limitless Freedom of Myth," Houston Baker argues for
an interpretation of myth that supports its inversive nature—
that which Victor Turner has defined in "Myth and Symbol" as

a state of "liminality" that is "pure potency, where anything can happen, where immoderacy is normal, even normative, and where the elements of culture and society are released from their customary configurations and recombined." Baker supports Turner's understanding of this inversion in myth as a "countermanding of social norms by symbolic means" that "governs the mythic universe of discourse."[22] This is a particularly interesting formulation of myth because it accepts an inversion of the norm as rendering a presentation of a symbolic, and therefore abnormal, mythic discourse. Rather than begin with the thesis that myth is representative of a subliminal historicity, Baker asserts the nonrepresentation of myth (it is inversive of history). Within such symbolism lies a limitless, liminal freedom wherein the critic of African-American literature can move betwixt and between Western critical methodologies. This is a particularly useful perspective for me, because it engages a view of history basically opposed to the frame I suggest informs the texts of black women writers. The critical distinction is whether or not one accepts the history external to the black text as relevant to the history within the black text.

Baker persuasively argues that the "logic of [a] traditional historico-critical approach to Afro-American literature sharply curtails the attention that is granted to writers [of early African-American literatures] such as Wheatley and Dunbar." Further, he claims that "the logic of socio-historical criticism also includes the proposition that Afro-American literary texts (in their supposed historical reflexivity) directly mirror social, political and psychological conditions prevailing on Afro-American culture at any given time"; and this certainly is true.[23] However, such interpretation represents a logic that only works if we accept the proposition that the history in the African-American text is merely a reflective one that mirrors the Westernized version of history appearing in the texts and journals of the eras.

My argument is that the mythologies in black women writers' texts are self-*reflexive* and their history is the history of orature—the primal mythic source. For example, the history of slavery that is documented in the sociohistory written by Western historians shifts when black women writers such as Paule

Marshall make it a psychohistorical (re)membrance for characters like Avey. We cannot trust, within the dense characterization that Marshall offers, the simplistic and self-serving
textbook histories of slavery. Joan Kelly, writing of the moment
when feminist scholarship in history placed women into the humanity that history includes in its discussions of events, activities, politics and culture, notes that then will "the period or set
of events with which we deal take on a wholly different character or meaning from the normally accepted one."[24] She writes
that feminist historiography has unsettled accepted evaluations
of historical periods. However, historians eventually address in
some form the populations that have been marginalized by the
dominating male and Eurocentric perspectives. Yet, these observations immediately bring to the fore the kinds of questions
that should accompany the historical and social perspectives
that Baker is willing to say are inverted from a range of normalcy into a range of abnormalcy in the black text.

What is normal? Whose ethic is operative here? Whose values
are embraced? When Baker argues for an African-American
critical orientation that "looks, not to *real* history, but to the limitless freedom of myth . . . [that] offers the unreal prospect that
[he] has in mind" (emphasis added), he unnecessarily acts as a
literary contortionist in order to value the vision of the black
text.[25] His vision of history is strange indeed. "Real history" is
the history in the Western textual tradition. Just as it has marginalized women, it has marginalized and even eliminated the
Third World from its vision. Unlike Baker, I am not willing to
call such misrepresentation a "real" history. Instead, I suggest
that we view literary mythologies through a historic filter, but
that that history be the history within the text, that it be an internally derived perspective and that all mythologies—historical and metaphorical—share equally in the literary figurations
within the composition of the text. (The kind of cycle I visualize
is represented in figure 1.) The representative schematic I
sketch in figure 1 stresses the constantly interactive nature of
the movements between each of the aspects that become mythologies in black women writers' texts. Ancestral events and
the appearances of goddesses fall into this schematic because
the spiritual realm of the goddess is a dimension of ancestry.

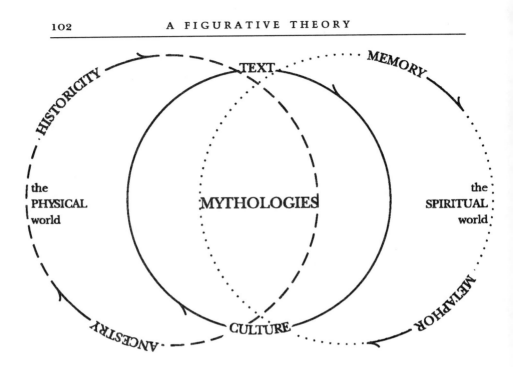

The idea of ancestry obviously implicates a spiritual history, one that is enabled through memory and that reflects, in the energies vested in orate structures of their texts, the density of the mythologies.

The element of shift (defined in chapter three) works within the structures of mythologies as well and links memory with metaphor through the kinds of events that are beyond what one would consider ordinary. Historicity and ancestry are linked by considerations of time that exceed its anticipated boundaries. The qualitative rather than quantitative conceptualization of time is a distinction between West Africa and the West. Although specific time (precise time) is of value, as Joseph Adjaye notes, "African history and oral traditions are based on *relative* time until events enter the most recent past" (emphasis added). Adjaye illustrates this point with a reference to the Akan of Ghana, for whom,

> as with other African groups, time exists and is seen to exist only in reference to specific events. Time . . . does not

exist in a vacuum. In contrast to the West, specific time is less important. . . . In Akan (and African societies) however, time does not exist for its own sake [as in the West where] time has to be *produced*. (Emphasis added.)[26]

In literature when time is not "produced" in the Western sense, what we find is not as much a suspension of real time as it is a freedom from the production of it. The Western sense of time would disable the activating of the mythologies that have been contextually shifted and internalized to the universe the text represents. Events that experience this shift are not treated as extraordinary by the narrative within the text. Their relationship to the story is intimate, even quite ordinary. Questions about chronological time (for example, my students always ask if Circe in Morrison's *Song of Solomon* is really "that old") beg not the questions of the textual traditions but focus instead on an unnecessary, and even misleading, assumption of an interpretive schism between myth and literature. Such a division is assumed in Frye's explanation that mythology supports a movement from a "level" of myth to a "level" of the low mimetic or "representative likeness to life."[27] Houston Baker's analysis also articulates a position for mythology that is quite compatible with the traditional Western perspective:

Mythic and literary acts of language are not intended or designed for communicative ends. Rather than informational or communicative utterances that assure harmonious normalcy in human cultures, such linguistic acts are radically contingent events whose various readings or performances occasion inversive symbolic modes of cognition and other extraordinary human responses.[28]

Baker distinguishes between acts of language that are communicative and those that are not—an approach similar to what Frye terms "levels" of likeness to real life. Such a distinction may be appropriate for the critical theory that Baker articulates, especially as it concerns such male writers' work as Dunbar's *Sport of the Gods*. Nonetheless, Baker's analysis of an axiological division between the kinds of speech acts that are performative and those that are mythic is antithetical to my view of black women's literature as representing an axiological *unity* within the narrative structures of the text, its patterns of discourse, and its assumption of an intimacy between history and memory. Because "historically conditioned modes of discourse" are determined by the nature of history within the text, the internalized tension that would fracture a relationship between the mythic and the literate (and demand some sort of critical and/or analytical reconstitution) does not exist.[29] In other words, the literate owes its ideology to the mythic and the mythic owes its being to the orate. Either these systems of ownership are acknowledged in the textual structures or they are not. For Baker's criticism, the schism is a juncture that critical interpretation bridges. The theoretical posture of my argument acknowledges no such schism.

The events of the text are evidence of the internal mythologies; they exceed the normative (in the reader's view) but they are clearly a part of the norms within the text. Consider situations like those found in Morrison's *Sula*. In this novel, Eva, the community matriarch, disappears early in her life and returns to the Bottom with only one leg. The talk surrounding this event becomes a part of the community gossip and the various explanations for her loss—she stuck it under a train to get the insurance money—seem at once both ridiculous and probable. So we are prepared in this text to accept that Sula may well be responsible for any unexplained death in the community, that the plague of robins is due to her return to town, that the scar(?) on her face does indeed change its shape from a rose to a tadpole to a snake, and that she probably did stay conscious long enough *after* she died to reflect that "it didn't even hurt" (149). The ridiculous, the sublime and the probable are all a part of each other in Morrison's universe. Mythologies are acts of both the spoken and the literate texts *within* her texts; but Morrison is not alone in this coalesence of mythologies in events. Meridian, in Alice Walker's 1977 novel, *Meridian,* is elevated through and beyond the time of her childhood memories. The ancient Indian burial ground on her father's farm serves as the locus of her transcendence over the time represented by her present and her ancestral past. It is an event similar to Avey's experience (*Praisesong*) in its relevance to the character. Meridian retains the knowledge of transcendency and is able to will its ecstasy. Like Morrison's Eva, the mythology becomes a part of Meridian's very nature.

In Bambara's *The Salt Eaters,* the plight of "the daughters of the yam"—the set-adrift, groundless black American women whose primal ground is Africa's—is bemoaned by the ancestor who hovers over the events. The narrative language supports the temporal disarray in the text and we learn quite early the significance of the various mythologies—the threads of event, time, memory, ancestry, and history that run consistently throughout the story and that are devices of its weave and formulations of its texture. Velma Henry, the psychically disengaged revolutionary of this story, tries to hold on to herself because "there was nothing but herself and some dim belief in the reliability of stools to hold on to"; but a voice that represents Velma's internal monologue, the narrative voice, and the omnipresent ancestors says:

The reliability of stools? Solids, liquids, gases, the dance of atoms, the bounce and race of molecules, ethers, electrical charges. The eyes and habits of illusion. Retinal images, bogus images, traveling to the brain. The pupils trying to tell the truth to the inner eye. The eye of the heart. The eye of the head. The eye of the mind. *All seeing differently.* (Emphasis added.)[30]

Events that link memories and that are metaphorically rendered in the text as "time" also connect history to the idea of ancestry. These are simultaneous considerations within the contemporary texts by black women. (See chapters six and seven for further discussions.) The vitality inserted into language by the mythologies in black women's writing becomes their especially distinct means of allowing the presence of historical, mythic, and contemporary figures to exist simultaneously in the text. Their insistence on making the worlds of the past and present collide creates a literary history that indicates a different world view operating—one that both denies the primacy of Western historiography and that challenges standards external to the text as a means, a frame of understanding. In Gayl Jones's novel, *Corregidora,* Ursa Corregidora's grandmother reminds her that the truth of the family's slave past cannot be found by searching for traditional historical evidence. The written records—papers, logs and journals—were not the kind of evidence of truth that she could rely upon "because they didn't want to leave no evidence of what they done. . . . That's why they burned the papers, so there wouldn't be no evidence to hold up against them." It is the evidence of "generations" that her grandmother and mother remind her to "make . . . [and] go on making."[31] Ursa, who has lost her generations and her evidence, is fragmented by this denial. Motherhood for her would have meant her membership in a line of women who had survived; it would have made certain that her body would "tell." The mythologies of this text are cultural memories. The fracturing of families, the enslavement of a people, and the interference in history are (re)membered by her grandmother's decision to make her generations a testimony and a validation of her own living and her own history. It is a reunification of what another history would insist upon as fractured. Yet, the regathered community insists on its own linguistic traditions (what I am telling you, not the records) to give evidence to the quality of their survival. Ursa's tragedy is that she is separated from the mythologies in her mother's and grandmother's lives because she is "different now . . . I have everything they had, except the generations. I can't make generations" (60). Gayl Jones's women, the grandmother, mother, and Ursa, model a matriarchy; through them the evidence of their slave past is salvaged and defined. However, when Ursa's pregnancy is terminated by Mutt's violence, her loss is a loss of self, matriarchy, community, and story—the tragedy of Jones's novel.

The telling that is generally an activity complicated by our (the readers') awareness of a history outside of the text and dominated by an ethic (male) that would privilege either behavior (performance) or a written word seems to be the constant element of both tension and creation in the text. It is an element of tension because telling is consistently challenged and denied. The works of Hurston, Walker, Jones, Naylor, and Morrison testify to the dangerous position black women assume when they dare "tell." The contradiction that removes their novels from a simplistic linear narrative that explores the tragedies of a singular theme is that "telling" is also a creative activity. In Emecheta's *Second-Class Citizen,* Adah's husband burns her novel in a jealous and fearful acknowledgment of his wife's variety of expressions. She is a mother, a writer, and a librarian—a keeper of words. She calls the novel her "brainchild." Emecheta describes its writing as a process that occurred "throughout all those months when she was nursing Dada" a reminder of the "white ink" imagery that French theorist Hélène Cixous uses to illustrate the spirit of women's writing "the body."[32]

It is possible to understand within this context Mary Poovey's sense of the "inadequacy of binary logic" in the face of the multiple presences within a feminist historiography.[33] Even in the face of "real" historical women, the characterization within the black text supports a theory of multiplicity (mythologies) as a vision of reconstructed lives, either historical or textual. In a wonderful and important recovery of the events surrounding Gwendolyn Brooks's receipt of the Pulitzer Prize, Mary Helen Washington notes that a *Negro Digest* article "begins with a list of people who didn't believe Brooks had won the prize—her son, her mother, her husband, friends" and ends with "the son's rejection of his mother's fame because it has upset his life."[34] If we remember the similar skepticism that greeted Phillis Wheatley's book of poems nearly two centuries prior to this, an experience Gates calls one of the "oddest oral examinations on record" in American letters, the patterns of disbelief seem uncomfortably repetitive.[35] However, the parallel thesis of recovery and creation that accompanies the activity of voice makes clear Bambara's sense of words as "spirit-force." Mythologies are the reconstructions of memory—the meta-matrix for all uses of language and the primary source of a literature that would recover a historical voice that is at once sensual, visceral, and real.

I can now return to the opening argument of this chapter: that there is an important difference between an African thesis of mythologies as literature and a Western thesis of mythology as a facet of literature. Critical theory can use this distinction as a point of genesis in understanding the literary trajectories of black women writers' texts. Mythologies become significant elements within the text not because of their relationship to a textual prehistory, but because of their proximity to the sense Morrison understands, in *Beloved,* as "rememory."

I don't pray anymore. I just talk. . . . I was talking about time. It's so hard for me to believe in it. Some things go. Pass on. Some things just stay. I used to think it was my rememory . . . a thought picture. . . . It's never going away. . . . The picture is still there and what's more, if you go there—you who never was there—if you go there and stand in the place where it was, it will happen again; it will be there for you, waiting (35, 36).

Prehistory moves the conceptualization of myth as a religious anthropology (a frame of culture that supports prayer as well as a binary logic) away from what happens in these women writers' texts. It is hard to believe in time because the records of time are not reliable for what has happened to them, and prayer is not a responsible reaction. (Remember the painful inarticulate-ness, in Morrison's *The Bluest Eye*, of Mrs. Breedlove's prayers to Jesus and their inability to relieve her suffering and the suffer-ing of her family. Remember that Flora Nwapa's Efuru prays for fertility to ancient gods and goddesses but she is destined not to know the joys of motherhood and her prayers are not the vehicle by which she or the text is empowered.) Instead, just talking (telling) seems to be the way for memory and time to work out some sort of textu[r]al truce. History is reconstructed within such a frame and the writer is able to write out of a matrix of memory that is both sensual and visceral, as well as to reconstruct a logic of repetitive, circular complexity rather than a binary and linear polarity. The community of writer, text, and reader engages in this spiritual reconstruction—a project that both redefines the nature of the text and insists upon a theoret-ical articulation that recognizes the energy of that community. So, although theoretical contention seems to be the issue here, it should not be.

Stanley Fish comments on the nature of change and/in theory by calling to our attention that "a theoretical pronouncement is always an articulation of a *shift* that has in large part already occurred; it announces a rationale for practices already in force; it provides a banner under which those who are already doing what it names can march" (emphasis added).[36] Viewed as such, shift does not produce a contending theory, it announces an existence that has not yet been named, or one that has been subsumed, erroneously, under the rubric of an inappropriate title. One is not, in articulating a theory of black women's literature, either announcing something or making anything "new." It has an established presence, one that has heretofore occupied the marginalized spaces of a theoretical dialogue that represents the assignation of a "single identity and marginal place" to all women and their work.[37] A theory of mythologies is one way of articulating a frame that privileges the concurrent activities of spirit and mind unencumbered by paths toward memories—trajectories that are both tactile and insistent on their generation within the community.

Part 2

An Intertextual Study

6

▲▲▲▲▲▲▲▲▲▲▲▲▲▲▲▲▲▲▲▲▲▲▲▲▲▲▲▲▲▲▲▲

The Idea of Ancestry:
African-American Writers

> These people were my relatives, my ancestors. And
> this place could be my refuge.
>
> Octavia Butler, *Kindred*

Octavia Butler's *Kindred* provides an especially clear illustration
of the idea of ancestry—a metaphor that emphasizes the cultural frames in texts by African-American women writers. The
first person voice of the narrative intensifies the visceral nature
of the (re)memory that the protagonist Dana experiences. Consequently, voice assumes a paradoxical posture in this narrative.
It is simultaneously a voice from the past as well as a voice in the
present. Butler's narrative complication underscores the fracturing quality of Dana's experience. Her physical loss (her arm
is severed) offers figurative support to the imagery of this fragmented voice. Because Dana's psychic fracturing takes both a
physical and a spiritual form, it is doubly disabling. The searing
tragedy of the story's conclusion ("And suddenly, there was an
avalanche of pain, red impossible agony! And I screamed and
screamed.") which is this recursive story's opening ("I lost an
arm on my last trip home. My left arm.") enfolds the entire narrative into the fractured dimensions that are the remnants of
her physical and spiritual disembodiment.[1]

In this novel, Butler's strategy complicates the perceived distinction between the past and the present until their intersection becomes more real than their separation. When Dana is

being pulled from the past into her present, she says that "I felt myself losing consciousness, falling back. I caught hold of a tree and willed myself to stay conscious" (43). There is ambivalence here—between consciousness and unconsciousness, between what Dana considers to be falling back (actually, she falls forward, not backwards, to her own future) and being stable (which would mean staying in a dangerous past). The complications between safety and stability, and the historic past and her quirky present, become increasingly more threatening as the story develops. For Dana, the collision of the past and present is a shuttling between what is the objectivity of her essentially unrecovered past and the subjectivity of her contemporary life.[2] The novel retrieves the past through a collision between the two dimensions. What Dana had read in family histories or had been told about her ancestry becomes mostly unusable when, in 1976, she is pulled back into her past, an 1813 plantation where her grandmother had been born. At this point she is faced with an immediate need to subjectify the experiences she had known only academically.

Dana is clearly aware that dissonance is at the crux of her dilemma. She explains to her husband (who is white) why her perception of this experience is qualitatively different from his. He can protect himself, she says, because he is "able to go through this whole experience as an observer" (101). Her inability to maintain the distance between subjectivity and objectivity is the source of much of the novel's psychic tension. In a recursive twist, Dana's husband represents the culturally and socially constructed Other, a role generally not associated with white males. Anthropologist Clifford Geertz notes that this Other must develop an "ability to construe [culturally different] modes of expression" in order to dissolve the kind of subjective/objective dilemma Dana perceives.[3] As an African-American woman, Dana has this ability and uses it to move between worlds—white and black, past and present. Because there are white slaveowners who complicate her generational history, she has some degree of familiarity with the disruption that her husband barely understands. Because her history is fractured, recognizing and managing dissonance are not unknown to her. In similar ways, African-American women writers, in general, position their narratives in the figurative dimensions achieved through narrative disjuncture. The dissolution between objective and subjective dimensions becomes a strategic textual event in their texts.

Each of the novels that focuses my discussion in this chapter (Gloria Naylor's *Mama Day,* Paule Marshall's *Praisesong for the Widow,* Ntozake Shange's *Sassafrass, Cypress and Indigo,* Gayl Jones's *Corregidora,* and Toni Cade Bambara's *The Salt Eaters*) features the presence of a mediating ancestor. As a metaphorical construction intersecting these texts, the ancestor characterizes the shared textual/cultural histories that collect the writing of African-American women. Still, the authors' use of the ancestral metaphor is stylistically different in each of these stories. Sometimes the presence is mediative and instructive, sometimes it is mediative and condemnatory, sometimes it is mediative and silent. However, because she serves as a recursive touchstone for the simultaneous existence of and revision in the idea of mediation, the ancestral presence constitutes the posture of (re)membrance. She is the linking of gender and culture that pulls these writers' works together. She accomplishes mediation in the connection of her figurative and metaphorical presence to the textual strategies of (re)membrance, revision, and recursion.

The ancestral voice can echo the structures found in women's autobiographies. Françoise Lionnet describes Maya Angelou's narrative strategy with a perspective akin to the idea of ancestry in imaginative writers' works. Lionnet notes that Angelou's narrator represents an "alienated form of consciousness" and "alternates between a constative and a performative use of language . . . using allegory to talk about history and myths to refer to reality." She notes that the voice in Angelou's works "is a *parole feinte* that mourns the loss of the illusory possibility of pure *parole-recit,* of direct and unmediated communication with interlocutors who share the same referential and mythic world she does."[4] When this autobiographical loss is recast in an imaginative work, the ancestor's voice mediates the restructuring of the community. Its textual presence is figuratively expressed as either a being in the work or as an essence of its mythic world.

Mediated Wholeness ▲

In these writers' works, mediation does not honor its traditional meaning. These writers seem to feel no pressure to force a positive reconciliation out of the overwhelming emotional and physical confrontation between the past and the present. Instead, their effort inserts a translucent (diffusive) presence into these texts that specifies the cultural traditions in the story and explores the nature of the dissolved space that lies between objectivity and subjectivity. This ancestral presence eventually exerts enough textual control to moor the thesis in the places of the spirit. Positivism is essentially irrelevant to this variety of mediation.

Melvin Dixon suggests that alternative spaces in the black text (like those I am suggesting are spiritually recovered by the ancestor) "lead to control over self and environment." His is a utopic vision characteristic of a folkloric perspective. Consider the parallels between Dixon's idea of control over self and environment and Keith Byerman's understanding of wholeness. Byerman's thesis suggests that the vision offered from folk material is compelling because of its tendency to imply the authors' "organic vision." However, Byerman also acknowledges that the desire for this vision of wholeness is met with a text of the African-American canon that represents a "three-dimensional reality, full of contradiction, paradox and masking."[5]

Byerman's assessment of the text argues against both his thesis of organicism and Dixon's view of control. I suggest that a gendered and cultural reading of these texts indicates their emphasis on something other than an organic re-creation of psychic wholeness. Instead, works by these writers unambiguously explore the consequences of psychic fracturing without any necessary trajectory towards conciliatory wholeness. Works that focus on fracture indicate that disjuncture is the legacy of women who struggle toward a contemporary reality without having confronted or acknowledged the persistent spiritual histories of their pasts. Regardless of the effort of theorists like Byerman and Dixon, whose critical vision leads them to imagine a kinder and gentler conclusion for these stories, wholeness is not a necessary feature of the texts' resolutions. The ancestral vision occupies its spiritual places and mediates textual resolution. These places are often fractured rather than whole. The text resurrects an idea of ancestry dependent on the oracular divinations inherent to the processes of (re)memory.

Dana's loss of her left arm figuratively expresses her loss of the symbol-making, intuitive side of the feminine.[6] The imagery in this event recalls Toni Morrison's Eva (*Sula*) who has lost her left leg in some spiritually unrecoverable journey. Both events illustrate the physical forms that fracture can assume. Dana's lost arm is a loss of a spiritual energy that cannot be mended or replaced. Wholeness certainly is not the final portrait in these works.

It is my sense that the alternative spaces of Dixon's discussion need not be restricted to geographic spaces. They can also encompass the inflated provinces of the word and include the linguistic variations of song, dream, and memory. Because I see this kind of enlarged space with reference to the configuration of the word in women writers' works, I must argue against a thesis of wholeness. Instead, alternative spaces clarify the nature of spiritual and psychic fracture. The polysemic ramifications of fracture more precisely characterize the works of black women writers.

Consider Paule Marshall's *Praisesong for the Widow.*[7] The source of Avey's illness is within her lost spirit; but the spiritual distance which separates her self from her past is not mediated until she meets Lebert Joseph, whose eyes remind her of the spiritually knowing eyes of the Ibos (*le gain connaissance*) in the island's legendary past. Avey is taunted by overwhelming distortions in her vision, feeling as if she is "in the grip of a powerful hallucinogen—something that had dramatically expanded her vision, offering her a glimpse of things that were beyond her comprehension" during her last days on the ship (59). Before she can understand these experiences, the distortion in her sight expands to horrific proportions. She sees people as skeletons, understands friendly greetings as incipient attacks upon her person, and imagines herself being forcibly carried by a crowd whose voices seem a "sea of incomprehensible sound" (70). Paradoxically, at the same time these distortions are occurring, a vague sense of familiarity with the sounds, the scenes and the music of the folk on the wharf troubles her. (Recall that in *Kindred* Dana's quickly dissolving world is complicated by her sense of familiarity with fracture, expressed in her ability to handle the situation better than her white husband.) Because Avey cannot trust her vision and because the reflections she sees are distorted, the text relinquishes this level of story. In a reflexive recursion, the narrative wanders back in time to the early years of Avey's marriage to Jay Johnson. Marshall layers this narrative paradox in a manner faithful to the construction of the plurisignant text. She writes that Avey kept "seeing with mystifying clarity" (139). Her experiences and the textual explication illustrate the distinction between her shallow lifestyle and the deeper and more fragmented dimensions of the cultural history the textual recursion recovers.

The shifting back and forth between various dimensions of the past and the distorted dimensions of Avey's present eventually enables the narrative to sublimate successfully the distinctions between them. She begins to feel a kinship to the island folk who had once seemed so foreign to her. Significantly, her body's spiritual ground of being (her heart) and its physical link to creation (her navel) are the source of this reconnection. Marshall writes that she felt "what seemed to be hundreds of slender threads streaming out from her navel from the place where her heart was to enter those around her. . . . they felt as strong entering her as . . . lifelines. . . . The moment she began to founder those on shore would simply pull on the silken threads and haul her in" (190, 191). In a narrative act of recursion, Avey (re)members the threads that weave her back into the tapestry of her mythologies as the "silken, brightly colored threads" from her childhood—they were "those used in the embroidery on a summer dress." At the moment her eyes "screen over," her spirit takes over (191). Lebert Joseph, the incarnation of her ancient Ibo ancestors, acknowledges this spiritual reclamation and bows to her—an act of obeisance to the African goddesses she has recalled. Avey joins a ring dance, specific to her own West African clan. This is a textual acknowledgment of the spiritual history Avey has (re)membered.

Marshall's Avatara answers the imagery of the call in Gwendolyn Brooks's poem and becomes a teller.[8] In one sense, this imagery illustrates the degree of resolution found in the African-American woman-centered text. In another sense, although these resolutions feature a (re)membrance of spiritual history, the event is neither complete nor whole. Instead, the text merely contains a promise of wholeness. We are led to believe that Avey's resolve is strong but we are not told whether or not she is successful. The figurative imagery of this section even supports the notion that Avey has readied herself for death instead of for a kind of island retirement that seems to be the literal direction of the novel's concluding events.[9] At the novel's end, we can attest only to the fact that she is on the right spiritual course in her determination to return to the island of her childhood, to be "centered and sustained" and, "once restored to her proper axis," embody the ancestral presence (254).

In a similar mediation between history and memory, Toni Cade Bambara's *The Salt Eaters* (re)members goddesses, trickster figures, and various personae of the cultural diaspora.[10] Like Avey, the protagonist of this novel, Velma Henry (buried under the exacting politics of the civil rights movement), suffers the strain of her spiritual loss. The substance of her loss and its literary figures recall Marshall's images. In *The Salt Eaters*, "silvery tendrils that fluttered between her fingers extending out like tiny webs of invisible thread . . . [follow] from her to Minnie Ransom to faintly outlined witnesses by the windows." Velma, "caught up in the weave of the song Minnie was humming" (4), is woven into a tapestry similar to the one Paule Marshall weaves in order to moor Avatara's lost spirit.

The most significant mediation occurs in the final pages of *The Salt Eaters*. Here the reader learns of Velma's membership in the ancestral line of spiritual women that Minnie and Old Wife have incarnated in the text. One of the women in the group of healers is Velma's godmother Sophie, who has recognized Velma as being vulnerable to the mediation of the ancestral psychics. The network of women in this book deepens with Sophie's revelation. Velma's nexus is now a part of a community that is simultaneously present and past, temporal and detemporalized. The collective at the end of the book is a spiritual one and it is within this stronger and more sensible network of threads that the psychically lengthened lifelines will encourage the spirit's assertion.

The dislocation in Bambara's *The Salt Eaters* relates it structurally to Marshall's *Praisesong*. These works trace and interrelate patterns of spiritual, psychic, and cultural disruption. Initially, they descend into these ruptured spaces with a focus on an illness or injury suffered by the protagonist. In their simplest forms, Ursa's and Dana's are physical injuries. However, Velma's dilemma is probably one of the most specific explorations of subjective/objective discordance in the texts of this tradition. Her inability to locate a space that would center her fractured psyche leads to her suicide attempt and provokes the healing ministrations of Minnie Ransom and Old Wife. When Minnie asks Velma if she "wants to be well," she is really asking her if she is willing to replace her external world with a spiritual one (3). Her dementia results from the abusive agendas of the activists and revolutionaries who had populated her life. Like Marshall's Avey, Velma has sacrificed her cultural spirit. Still, this is a story that insists upon the primacy of the spirit and its means of salvaging a culture that faces erasure and invisibility. Her spiritual guide, the ancestor Old Wife, and the body of witnesses whose enclosure and metaphorical embrace is protective, gather together to divest her of her mask and save Velma Henry's soul.

Like Morrison's Sethe (Beloved), whose realization that "nothing ever dies" is a tactile (re)memory that can be counted upon for reference as the physical world dissolves around her, Old Wife reminds Min that "there is no death in age or spirit" (56). Velma's spiritual reclamation will come in a moment of translucence when, freed from "fire and water" she won't "drown in the air" (62). Ultimately, this realization propels Velma towards embracing the spiritual aura of the gathered witnesses. The chorus of patients in the clinic group is like a prayer group and similar to the women that Ella leads in her exorcism of the spirit-child in Morrison's Beloved.[11] Bambara writes of a woman like the historical Margaret Garner may have been (and certainly like the Sethe that Morrison imagined) when the narrator in The Salt-Eaters takes the time to define a person who:

> held on to sickness with a fiercesomeness that took twenty hard-praying folk to loosen. So used to being unwhole and unwell, one forgot what it was to walk upright and see clearly, breathe easily, think better than was taught, be better than one was programmed to believe—so concentration was necessary to help a neighbor experience the best of herself or himself. For people sometimes believed that it was safer to live with complaints, was necessary to cooperate with grief, was all right to become an accomplice in self-ambush (107).

Morrison's Sethe and Bambara's Velma are equally implicated in
a passage like this one. There are parallels as well to Avey's illness. Bambara foregrounds the idea of malady in a manner that
thickens the collusion of oppositional themes of the physical
and spiritual, the past and the present, and the individual and
the collective. A traumatic conflict ensues as each of these attempts to claim her as their center. Velma's inability to designate
or to name her own source freezes her inner action and motivates her suicidal attempt to kill the self that stood between her
and her spirit. Both physically and spiritually, Velma exists outside of these conflicts, swirling around and through the antag-
onism they generate. She is their nexus, but she has none of her
own. Instead, she's "off dancing . . . in the mud [that] seems to
belong to her ways" (43). Mired and thus entangled, the luminous freedom of light and air seems a distant and improbable
potential for this decentered "daughter of the yam."

In the narrative strategies of African-American women's
texts, dissonance precipitates the foregrounding of the inner
text. In *The Salt Eaters,* the inner story is an ancient one, removed by time and place from the contemporary events of Velma's political activism and her appearance in the clinic.
However, by reaching back and then forward, Min mediates between the ancient and intact wisdom that will do for Velma and
the fractured times of the novel's suprastructure. For Velma,
the direction of resurrection is wherever she might retrieve the
innervision of the mythic, spiritual selves that Old Wife and Min
represent. Bambara's trope is in making this place a psychiatric
clinic. Here the patients, perhaps the only really sane members
of this inverted civilization, accompany Velma as she is guided
toward her (re)membered self. Here, Bambara's story most
clearly shares the lineage of texts of black women's literature.

Loss is the substance of the history of women like Avey,
Velma, and Sethe. The mediative ways of (re)memory insist
themselves into previously unsuccessful and losing archival patterns. For women of the diaspora, artifice becomes a far more
spiritual than tangible dimension of cultural continuity. Morrison's Baby Suggs (*Beloved*) "ponders color" in the last days of
her life, an event I speak of in chapter eight as a careful, fragmented consideration of the pieces of light. This way of reconstruction (revision) is a way of shifting an alternative universe
into the place that history has poorly served. Because women's

cultures of the diaspora are fractured by history, the creative literature of African-American women has revised its form of documentation. Baby Suggs's pondering, Avey's dance, and Velma's surrender to the healer's hand and breath recenter their universe and allow a spiritual luminescence to replace their dimmed physical worlds.

Mediated Voices ▲

The idea of ancestry revises the histories that it reenacts through its intimate mediation of history and memory. In these texts, the privilege given the spoken word pushes women (who have not been included in historiography) and their oracular means of (re)membering into the foreground.

For example, although George, Cocoa's lover and husband in Naylor's *Mama Day,* recognizes how the spiritual history of the island is connected to the symbolic nature of language, he is unable to use this wisdom.[12] The way Cocoa speaks of her ancestor Sapphira puzzles him: "it was odd . . . the way you said it— she was the great, great, grand, Mother—as if you were listing the attributes of a goddess. The whole thing was . . . intriguing" (218). George's confusion works inversively to reveal the ancestral Sapphira as a reincarnated goddess, the embodiment of a powerful cultural icon. He is unable to connect the powerful implication of this revelation to his own behavior and systems of belief. As perceptive as George is in his intellectual recognition of the power in the voiced name of Cocoa's ancestor he is also spiritually disabled by his inability to understand and believe that the legacy is to be his potent reality—"if she really existed, there must be some record" (218). George's shallow spirit (for whom only the "present has potential") needed this record, these scripts of Western history (23). His spiritual blindness is eerily close to Ursa Corregidora's expressed doubt of the story her grandmother relates of their family's generation.

Early in Jones's *Corregidora,* Ursa confronts the question of accuracy that George raises. The hierarchical value of the written word over the spoken in Western historiography motivates this persistent concern. Ursa's grandmother slaps her when, after being told of the sadistic violence of the slaver Corregidora, Ursa responds by asking, "You telling the truth, Great

Gram?" Ursa's doubt provokes this response from her grand-mother: "When I'm *telling* you something don't you ever ask if I'm lying. Because they didn't want to leave no evidence of what they done—so it couldn't be held against them. . . . And I'm leaving evidence . . . we got to have evidence to hold up. That's why they burned all the papers, so there wouldn't be no evidence to hold up against them" (14; emphasis added). The disruption of historical record keeping prepares the text for its inversive alternative. Examples like this one dissemble Euro-American traditions that privilege writing. The assumption that this tradition's manner of documentation and records is the only historically acceptable evidence is necessarily disrupted.

The doubting generations that Gloria Naylor's George and Gayl Jones's Ursa represent are consistent characterizations. Paule Marshall features a similar episode in *Praisesong*. In a passage that confronts African mythologies with legends that are icons in the Christian mythic tradition, Avey (re)members her great-aunt's response to her childhood query about the walk-across-the-ocean Ibos, "'But how come they didn't drown?' . . . Slowly, standing on the consecrated ground her height almost matching her shadow which the afternoon sun had drawn out over the water at their feet, her great-aunt had turned and re-garded her in silence for the longest time" (39). The silence of her gaze replaces the words which had maintained the conse-crated ground where Cuney retells the story of the Ibos. Avey, whose doubt defiles this ground and undercuts both her aunt's spoken text and the stature of the myth, immediately under-stands the thoughtlessness of her careless question:

> If she could have reached up that day and snatched her question like a fly out of the air and swallowed it whole, she would have done so. And long after she had stopped going to Tatem and the old woman was dead, she was to catch herself flinching whenever she remembered the voice with the quietly dangerous note that had issued finally from under the wide hat brim.

Her aunt directly attacks the kind of records that Avatara and George seemed to value: "Did it say Jesus drowned when he went walking on the water in that Sunday School book your momma always sends with you?" (40). In Bambara's novel, Sophie expresses a similar concern about Velma's allegiance to Western values. Like George, Ursa, and Avey, Sophie suspected that Velma "would reject what could not be explained in terms of words, notes, numbers or those other systems whose roots had been driven far underground" (294). We are led to understand that Velma's healing would depend as much on Bambara's successful recentering of her spirit as it would depend on her own willingness to abandon the structural traps of the Western world.

George's incredulity personifies the fragile characterizations of Ursa, Avey, and Velma. Women's texts of this tradition draw attention to the disabling figures in a scriptocentric historicism and then shift toward the mediation of spoken evidence. Therefore, the story that Ursa's grandmother tells mediates the dishonesty and selectivity of written records. Although we are able to follow the focused sequence of events that follow Ursa's physical and spiritual recuperation, these events are specifically enabled by the accompanying subconscious dialogue she has with her past and her ancestors' pasts. Avey's memory of her Aunt Cuney's spoken (re)memory propels her toward her own spiritual recovery; but characters like George, whose generational continuity is irretrievable, lose their connection to this kind of memory and this kind of evidence. George's dependence on script inevitably leaves him vulnerable in a story where energy and power are invested in an ancient, spoken text.

Often, a subliminal voice—a murmur, a mutter, or an echo—enables the necessary spiritual mediation in these texts. For example, Avey's recovery begins when she notices "murmuring voices" that "set about divesting her of her troubling thoughts, quietly and deftly stripping her of them." The echo of these voices underscores the metaphorical emphasis of their recursive nature. Eventually, both the voices and their echoes pull the text towards a moment when the "pall over Avey Johnson's mind lifted . . . and she became dimly conscious" (197). "The necessaries had been done," Marshall's narrative notes (209). "The Old Parents, the Long-time People," witnesses like those who wait outside of the window for Bambara's Velma to heal, "would be pleased" (213).

Velma Henry also experiences the power of the mediated voice. Her redemption and healing become possible at the moment when she "mutter[s]" and feels "the warm breath of Minnie Ransom on her" (263, 264). In this instant the "Day of Restoration" is within Velma's grasp. The work of her elder, Minnie Ransom, and Minnie's guiding spiritual ancestor, the conjure woman known as Old Wife, help her to want some control over her spirit—to "want to be well." This is a translucent moment in an especially dense text. Bambara's work does not signal its linguistic diversions and spiritual dissolves by italicized structures like those in the works of Morrison, Marshall, or Naylor. Instead, "thick descriptions" prompted by the tangled webs of the political and social events of Velma's activist days occlude the dissipated spiritual self that Minnie and her ancestral guide attempt to recover.[13] Such thick descriptors as those employed by Bambara complicate the dimensions of this text. Its metaphorical and structural density holds both meaning and wholeness hostage. A consequence of the density is a certain obscurity that threatens to overwhelm the story of Velma's journey towards spiritual recovery.

The novel's opening question—"Are you sure, sweetheart, that you want to be well?"—poses the psychological dilemma of the story's events. However, in a typically recursive fashion, this question also pulls us into the underlying textual narrative—events that have led to Velma's psychic freeze and her "taut, dry and stiff" posture on a psychiatric clinic's stool (3). Her needs are clearly more ancient, deeper than and foreign to the psychologist's clinical experience. So the ritualized dimensions of Minnie's spiritual healing testify to her ability to reach the realms that Old Wife inhabits. As cultural artifact, the ways of healing, the language, the sounds, and the certain and specific touches are the manner in which the Geertzian thick descriptors mediate the modes of expression that revise traditional symbolic systems. Ritual is an important corollary to the distressed, inverted text. Cultural ritual is directly oppositional to the doctor's ineffectual presence. As an emblem of Western values, the clinic psychologist can only hover around the edges of Velma's healing (and the text itself), waiting for her release from Minnie's "first phase." At the novel's end he is totally disabled, an event that signifies the West's inability to heal cultural loss. Neither it nor he can address the dissonance of cultural pluralism. This is the territorial province of the Other.

The voices recovered in these works testify to the necromancy within the ancient word. They claim logocentrism and mythology as viable replacements for the scriptocentric dimensions of history. A result of this shift is the expansive nature of the spoken word. In *Mama Day*, it embraces the "part of our memory that we [don't] use to form words" (6). In consequence, sounds echo and resonate through this story, collapsing the legend of Sapphira, that "everybody knows but nobody talks about" into the events that form the story's text (5).

Dixon notes how "writers depict place and performance to set the narrative in motion and encourage reader participation" and that "the open-ended structure and ironic closure in many texts . . . invite readers to complete performances in and of the narrative." [14] Certainly Naylor's *Mama Day* encourages such participation. A narrative voice uses "we" and "ours" and "us" to retell the story of Willow Springs and involve the reader in its simultaneous recall of historical, spiritual, and physical events. The reader's voice is invited to join its community of tellers: "Think about it: ain't nobody really talking to you. . . . Really listen this time: the only voice is your own. . . . You done heard it the way we know it. . . . You done heard it without a single living soul really saying a word" (12). This voice—ancient, aware, and able to bridge the subjective and objective worlds and to match imagination with magic—connects the story's disparate events and maintains its presence over all of them. In addition, the ancestral narrative voices of the island's past and present generations as well as the personified island itself—its dust and purple flowers, the gardens and cemeteries, its abandoned houses and (re)membered rituals—gather to tell Naylor's story.

The ancestral voices in this story are primarily the voices of the island's generations. All of them mediate the text, bridging the events of Naylor's contemporary story of the lovers Cocoa and George with the haunting presence of Sapphira Wade, Cocoa's grandmother of five generations past, whose propensity for conjuring leaks into the present-day world. George is destined never to leave the island of Willow Springs and Mama Day readies him for the paradise for which Cocoa, perhaps because she has been geographically disengaged from her place in the island's history, could not prepare him.

Naylor's novel emphasizes how a collective revision of an ancient community substantively inserts a metaphorical language into the text. This language carries a symbol system more weighty than the individual word. For example, at one point in the story, Miranda tries to remember her ancestor's name. But her failure to do so is a "loss she can't describe" (279). Although she tries to use her psychic gift to discern the print on a damaged slip of paper where Sapphira's name is illegible, she can not read it. In her frustration, she falls asleep murmuring the names of women. It is the murmuring of the spoken text (rather than the effort to read) that enables Miranda finally to meet Sapphira Wade in her dreams. The importance of this oracular event is acknowledged at the point when Miranda is able to sense the being, the presence in this word: "Daughter." It is described as a "word [that] comes to cradle what has gone past weariness," and is the word that Miranda senses as the relational word of the oracular text (282). It also acknowledges the contradiction and paradox within the textures of this novel. There is enough metaphorical dislocation in *Mama Day* to contain the ambiguous histories of the spirit as well as the body. The text is implicated in this revision because the collection of tellers and listeners who organize its body and who include (in black women writers' texts) the reader as well, loses its alterity—its separation—at this juncture. In the same way that Miranda is cradled by the word that acknowledges her spiritual ancestor, the words of the text are incorporated into the generative spiritual body of Sapphira's linguistic acknowledgment.

Paule Marshall's *Praisesong* also relies on language and voice as a means of emphasizing the revisions in ways of knowing and experiencing the worlds in these works. Avey's husband Jay begins to lose things that are spiritually important to him, like music and his old blues records, at the same time he begins to value the *materia* of the Western world and its ethic. Jerome (a.k.a. Jay) shelves the songs and telling voices by which black women learn to manage their beings. He "abandoned [them] on the sidelines, out *of his line of vision*" (115; emphasis added).

A metaphorical vision of song, similar to the one Marshall

attaches to Jay's music, is found in Ntozake Shange's *Sassafrass, Cypress and Indigo*.[15] Shange's text recalls ancestral voices to assist her own obviously contemporary story. For example, when Sassafrass's living begins to echo a blues song, the text dissolves into italics and "from out of the closet came Billie . . . [and] The Lady sighed a familiar sigh" (80). Sassafrass herself enters the italicized narrative, signalling that there is no level of the story, no time or place in the story to which she is not privy. The lady who visits her psyche is not much different from the ladies who inhabit lakes in African women writers' stories. All are ladies (deities) who are responsible for creativity and generation. However, among the conflicts in this story is the encumbrance of Sassafrass's spiritual aura by the psychic and creative destructiveness of the abusive Mitch. Because of him she is unable to either write (Mitch admonishes her to "get into yourself and find out what's holding you back. You can create whole worlds, girl" [79]) or weave. When her creativity is held hostage, her dream/memory recalls the kind of procession of ladies that Brooks's Maud Martha revisions when her own creativity is threatened.[16] "The Lady turned to the doorway on her right and shouted, 'Come on, y'all,' and multitudes of brown-skinned dancing girls with ostrich-feather headpieces and tap shoes started doing the cake-walk all around Sassafrass, who was trying to figure out the stitching pattern on their embroidered dresses" (81).

These ladies come to instruct her and even more importantly, to displace Mitch, who had been "on her mind" (82). The mixture of images that Sassafrass learns to live with—the creation banner over the stove, the looms that recall her own growing up in her mother's home, her writing and her recipes—emphasize her fragmented spiritual energy, a resource she will need to rescue her self from the disabling presence of Mitch. The revision in this text is intimate and feminine. Its extensive metaphorical networks plunge through the traditions of African and African-American culture to (re)member the women's ways of knowing that allow a discovery of contemporary places and that reflect an ancient story. The symbolic networks of the novel travel across both dreams and memories without attention to either time or credible (i.e. Western) possibilities. The reader's attention is redirected to a level of text that privileges metaphorical words over the literal, and spiritual events over physical, and enjoins the syncopated rhythms of song, both jazz and blues, to articulate the praxis of a woman-centered ideology.

The poignancy in Shange's writing derives from her successful mingling of languages. Poetry and music exist in the same spaces as dialogue and dreams. The extreme sensitivity of her writing to extending women's creative spheres past the biological and into the spiritual realms testifies to her commitment to explore extensive dimensions of generation. Women's sharing of their most intimate and creative language is a significant feature of Shange's method. Part of this sharing is clearly evident in the recipes and letters from the sisters' mother, but it is also an important dimension of the lesbian relationships in this novel. Some of the most generative and thickest language surrounds Shange's descriptions of the women's dance collective, the Azure Bosum. Dense in color and texture, and full and round in shapes and forms, this imagery represents the deepest levels of this novel's stylistic effort. Here, the language is as full-bodied as the women's gender dance—"a dance of women discovering themselves in the universe." In the house Cypress shared with the dancers from the Azure Bosum, she "saw herself everywhere . . . nothing different from her in essence; no thing not woman" (138).

Shange attributes the textures of her story to a woman-centered ideology. Her opening lines—"Where there is a woman, there is magic [and] a woman with a moon falling from her mouth . . . is a consort of the spirits" immediately insist upon a relationship to the air and its spirits—a hallmark of the translucent text (3). In addition it specifies the way that the cultural tradition is gendered. Women are connected to necromancy and spirituality—the dimensions of text that center the black woman writer's tradition. In many ways, *Sassafrass, Cypress and Indigo* is a modern story that traces three sisters' coming-of-age outside of their mother's house. However, the internal irony is that none of them can spiritually leave their mother's presence (and the implicit symbolic presence of the more ancient cultural Mothers). This dimension of the text places Shange's work in the shared traditions of the African-American woman writer's canon.

The first glimmer of the plurisignance in this text occurs in an opening narrative that introduces the reader to the character

Indigo as a child "of the south" (3). This lyrical explanation of her persona dissolves and is replaced by the first of several variations of recipes and instructions that appear in the narrative. The first, an italicized passage that details how to manage a "Moon Journey," quickly returns to the regular type of the original text. The italics serve as the visual collocation for the series of instructions, recipes, dream sequences, and memories that flow into the pages of Shange's novel. Since the distinctiveness of the italic type collects these bits and pieces, some of the interpretive work is accomplished for the reader. Their visual appearance makes it clear that these dreamings are to be gathered together. Their sound makes it evident that these gathered words add their own voice to the story of the sisters and their mother.

Shange's layering of women's knowledge affirms a context for black women's experience in *Sassafrass*. Through these layers she assures that at least some of this information will be accessible to the community of women who are responsible for spiritual as well as physical generation. The text encourages the reader's perception of Cypress's newly discovered ability to "lay waste to the tunnels, caverns, and shadows of the other world" (the West) and to "draw upon memories of her own blood" (208). Male things, Western things, and material distractions are released in Shange's novel. What remains affirms womanspirit, an African imagination, and the ability of the spoken text to metaphorically assure these as the fertile grounds of a (re)membered generation.

(Re)membrance is also a lyrical accomplishment in Jones's *Corregidora*.[17] Yet there is a biting edge to Jones's narrative lyricism because the nature of the (historical) memory that must be recalled in order to be repelled is ugly and abusive. The ancestral voices in this text remind Ursa of her membership in the line of women who are related to a nineteenth-century slavemaster who was both father and grandfather to Ursa's grandmother. Like *Kindred*'s Dana, white slaveowners have compromised her cultural history, but old man Corregidora insisted on destroying the written records of his violent incest. The spiritual consequence of this event is that Ursa's recordkeeping has a history of abuse that is tied to her body. The opening event in the story details her miscarriage—the fault of her husband Mutt's violent anger. Ursa comes to understand that Mutt's violence and the violence of old Corregidora are pathetically linked. Jones's textual acquiescence to the weight of this memory echoes imagery in *Praisesong* and in *Sassafrass*. She makes the music of this text the haunting and sardonic tones of the blues.

The recursive strategy in *Corregidora* foregrounds memory and myth through the structural integrity of the blues line and the repetition that is inherent to this form. Repetition signals the early history of these worried lines. Significantly, blues not only repeats the lyric, but it repeats melody as well. This layering of recursive devices (like Shange's layers) propels *Corregidora* into several dimensions at once. Because the evidence of these women's lives is not enough to hold their terrifying history, and because the words of Ursa's songs may not by themselves convey the tragedy, their constant sound, illustrated in the litany of the text's recursive last lines, functions as additional insurance that this story will nurture rather than disable. On the final page of this novel, Ursa and Mutt engage in the sort of verbal dialectic that characterizes their relationship. It is at once a lyric and a melody. Keith Byerman's perceptive assessment of the story's final event interprets the embrace at the novel's end as "less a resolution of the issues raised than an acceptance of the need to live in a state of [dialectical] tension."[18] A more ideologically important implication of their embrace is that Ursa has pulled Mutt into her own dimension of living. His participation in her blues song is a triumph of form and substance. She has placed him into her way of record-keeping. The sounds of her living become Mutt's way of measuring the necessities of his own life:

> "I don't want a kind of woman that hurt you," he said.
> "Then you don't want me."
> "I don't want a kind of woman that hurt you.'
> "Then you don't want me."
> "I don't want a kind of woman that hurt you.'
> "Then you don't want me." . . . I fell against him crying. . . . He held me tight (185).

Her blues song implicates the textu[r]al structure of what Morrison calls "sounds older than words." It represents her effort to reclaim some unsullied form of creative generation.

Like other African-American women writers, Jones renders

Ursa's dreams and memories in italics. Ursa's effort to explain her way of living to her mother indicates that she is in touch with the spiritual (re)memories within the blues: "Yes, if you understood me, Mama, you'd see I was trying to explain it, in blues, without words, the explanation somewhere behind the words. To explain what will always be there. Soot crying out of my eyes" (66).

Ursa's singing is an affirmation of her creative force. It figuratively expresses the dimensions in her life. Yet because Mutt's violence threatens this creativity, Jones reconstructs this dilemma by closing her away from her music. Immediately following her miscarriage, she refuses to sing. However, when she has healed enough to want the expressiveness of song, the tone in her voice carries with it the dimensions of the loss she has suffered. Ursa's friend (a woman whose sense of language and sound the reader understands as more visceral than the sensibility with which males listen to Ursa) tells her that her voice "sounds like you been through something. Before it was beautiful . . . but you sound like you been through more now" (44). At this point the call of the blues voice, which by definition reaches out to enfold the listener into its ambivalent message of sorrow and strength, deepens. Its depth and its ability to allow listeners to feel her life become an ironic capstone to her talent.

The woman-centered ideology in African and African-American women's literature places with women's creative powers both the ability to create life and the ability to tell—to reveal the quality, dimensions, and history of living. This ideology assures that Ursa, having lost one aspect of this creativity, would experience a strengthening in the other. That this strength is also a definitive aspect of the blues tradition only makes it more appropriate that song should be a recourse for Ursa's spiritual fracture.

As both Morrison's Sethe (*Beloved*) and Ursa's abortive fertility indicate, generational fertility is vulnerable in an abusive culture. Jones's compensation for these losses is to foreground her textual strategy of inversion and call into use something Morrison's text calls "even older than words," and what Ursa has recognized as the "sound somewhere behind the word." The center of Jones's work is the indigenous sounds and music of the black artistic tradition. They serve as the devices of archival reclamation in this work.

In a consideration of the complexity in this literature, Cynthia Ward cites Jean-François Lyotard's comment that the fictional self "exists in a fabric of relations that is ... more complex and mobile than ever before." Ward uses Lyotard's frame to argue that it is not necessary to construct a "totalizing postmodern universe in order to account for textual resistance to resolution, in order to allow for the free play of conflicting realities or truths ... to speculate about decentered subjectivity." [19]

The spiritual presence of Sapphira Wade in Naylor's *Mama Day* illustrates the persistence of the decentered subject. The essence of her memory speaks to the tendency towards translucence in this tradition—a shift in the nature of the text towards complexity and away from clarity. In black women writers' texts, translucence is not a condition of sweetness and light. It is not weightless. Instead, translucence involves a hefty historical revisioning of black women's experience. This shift in vision pulls innervision, the realm of memory, into the history of the text. A movement in the air, a shimmering, a clarity, or a passage of shadows that accompanies a characters' impending (re)membrance are among the metaphorical figures that signal translucence. [20] For example, Avey's imminent conversion is signalled in a way that claims translucence as a device in Marshall's textual strategies: "Gradually, in the midst of the vertigo, she became aware of the cool dark current of air. . . . She felt it come to rest, like a soothing hand on her head, and it remained there, gently drawing away the heat and slowing down both her pulse and the whirling ring of harsh light behind her closed eyes" (158, 159). Only at this point is Avey able to understand the idea of ancestry embodied in the "Old Parents" and the "Long-time People" whom Lebert Joseph tells her are due the ritual of the yearly remembrance on island of Cariacou. Marshall's hyphenation of "Long-time People" is important. The hyphen relates the idea of longevity with time. These words modify each other and insist on the interpretation of time/aspect discussed in chapter five. An important mode of figuration in black women writers' texts is a shift in the way that time is represented and the way that it is mediated by the continuous/

contiguous presence of people unaffected by a Western valuation of time.

Cultural mythologies, once subliminated and/or unacknowledged by the traditional methods of reporting the past, are acknowledged when ancestral presences mediate the text.[21] In the privilege conferred by fiction and through the vision of a gendered and encultured text, these writers' works replace traditional historiography with a spiritual historicism. The result is a text where voices of both the present and the past texture the narrative structures of the novel and culminate in a resonant confusion of mythology and reality.

The archetype of the ancestor is an extended metaphor of cultural continuity within the black woman's diaspora through the insistent spirituality that characterizes these works. Marshall's *Praisesong* illustrates the numinous quality of these memories. Avatara is indeed the embodiment of the deities that Jay senses reside in her. They are ancient spirits who bridge the geographic and cultural diaspora and they are all women. These are deities whom Avey will eventually come to honor through her choice to become a teller and to pass on her ancestors' story in the final years of her life. Jay, who has displaced the music and words of his spirit in preference to his line of vision, is not quite certain how to "conduct himself" in the presence of the ancient women he sees in his wife: "the invisible forms of the deities . . . Erzulie with her jewels and gossamer veils, Yemoja to whom the rivers and seas are sacred; Oya, first wife of the thunder god and herself in charge of the winds and rains" (127).

In a similar vein, Shange's *Sassafrass* brings full circle the numinous promise of her dramatic choreopoem, *for colored girls*. The incarnate goddesses that Sassafrass and her sisters recover reflect the essence of their spiritual creativity. Shange explores the cultural regeneration of the goddess through a metonymical collection of Her creative dimensions—Sassafrass's weaving and writing, and Cypress's dance. Indigo comes to embody the powerful form of biological creativity. She becomes a midwife—a creatrix—emblematic of Shange's coalescence of the extended imaginative dimensions of the novel.

Because Indigo's vision functionally opens and closes the story, her perceptions frame the ancient contingencies and articulate her own fragile connections to the modern world. By mediating the myth of an African goddess and the history of her African-American ancestors, she forges an elemental link that embodies the qualities of air ("a moon in her mouth"), and earth ("earth blood, filled up with the geechees long gone"), and water ("and the sea") (3). The masculine element of fire is absent from her spiritual configuration—she is the only sister not confronted in this novel with the destructive auras of male egos and their physical aggression. At the end of the story, Indigo has come to embody the midwifery talents of her mentor, Aunt Haydee, and, in addition, has come to the place of this ancestor because more than having an "interest in folklore," Indigo "was the folks" (224).

A cultural relationship between the "folks" implicates the notion of generational continuity: the dimensions of relationships between women in these works are not merely biological. Instead, the shared gender and shared culture in the memories of these women who bridge the past and the present are the denominators which are most critical to their relationship and that form a spiritual kinship. For example, Minnie Ransom's qualities as the "*fabled* healer of the district" (emphasis added) in Bambara's *The Salt Eaters* are mythic, but it is the spiritual sisterhood between Minnie and Old Wife, the spirit-guide who mediates Bambara's story, that manages to center this unwieldy text and salvage Velma Henry's fractured soul. Ironically, despite the structural dissonance of the text, Velma hears Minnie's healing voice and accepts the ministrations offered to her.

Instead of surrendering meaning or form to a rigidly ideological and imposing Western tradition, these works successfully revise the nature of imagination. In terms of theory, they decenter the Western ethic and replace its operative aesthetic (which excludes them) with one that extends from a cultural tradition characterized by alterity. Because of this decentering, the text's responsibility is to itself rather than to an ideology. In consequence, its success depends on the artistry that the author uses to convey the voice of the central aesthetic. In terms of creativity, what appears behind the veil of the Western tradition is a shifted, alternative universe. In such works, the presuppositions of power in valor and maleness, accuracy in written records, and clarity in a temporal linearity are constantly dissembled.

The revision of Western literary hierarchies serves to distinguish the imaginative realms of black women's writing and to specify the oracular spaces it occupies.

Mediated Places ▲

One of the distinctive features of women's literature in the black tradition is how textual structures dissolve traditional historiography through a detailed collaboration between place, time, and event. For example, the setting of *Mama Day* is a fertile island where events have closer ties to the island's past than to the mainland's present. The space of this island is alternative because it has replaced the entire construct of *main*land with a chosen and minimalized place. Significantly, Willow Springs has no traditional historical locus; it does not even appear on the maps of the United States. These essential places allow the collaboration between language and voice where categories of culture and gender are expressively representational. In Shange's novel *Sassafrass, Cypress and Indigo*, for example, Indigo's conflict is centered around the uncertainty of her place. The reader is told quite early that she has "too much South" in her, an attestation that her dilemma has some relationship to specifying the appropriate place for her spirit. Her sisters share some dimension of this conflict, but what their mother calls experimental living destabilizes the places of their spirits. Because this novel's setting changes so frequently, both the textual structure and its content reflect Shange's emphasis on finding a spiritual mooring place. Until the sisters have recentered themselves spiritually, both experiments in living and life itself are doomed to failure.

Because ancestors are often the metaphorical mediation between the multiplied dimensions of time and place, the complicity between spiritual presences and the places of these spirits forms an important dimension of these works. Islands, dead-end ghetto streets, smoky nightclubs, and basements all share a figurative marginality. Their exteriority is a facet of the kind of decentering that pushes these texts towards plurisignance and rescues them from the utopic wholeness that Dixon would argue is the objective dimension of these alternative spaces.[22]

In Naylor's *Linden Hills*, subliminal places follow the lead of the subaltern as well as locate the ancestor.[23] In this novel, the frenzied search of a woman incarcerated in a basement reveals the ancestor. Willa Nedeed, whose imprisonment fuels her dementia, is a sardonic revisioning of the figure of the attic. Her dilemma functions as elliptical reference to the imagery of the basement in Ellison's *Invisible Man* and the subterranean passages in Richard Wright's short story "The Man Who Lived Underground." Here, however, the dead baby that Fred Daniels sees floating in the sewer in Wright's story is refigured as the dead child of Luther and Willa Nedeed. It is their understood (if not acknowledged) parenthood rather than anonymity that claims the tragedy in Naylor's second novel.

As different as Naylor's and Marshall's textual styles are, the cultural tradition that informs each of them is shared enough so that their texts are of the same canon. Island places are important to both of these authors. It is so important to Marshall, in *Praisesong*, that Avey is haunted by the memories of her childhood visits to Tatem Island well into the sixtieth year of her life. On the island, when she remembers her great-aunt Cuney (the ancestral presence of this novel who "resembled the trees in her straight, large-boned mass") a flash of memory recalls the flight motifs of Morrison's novels ("hands arched back like wings"). In a symbolic connection of her great-aunt's story and voice to the "distant yet powerful voice of the sea," Avey (re)members the story Cuney retold each summer of Ibo landing. In her (re)memory, both place and myth are intimately connected to the presence of this ancestor whose "mind was long gone with the Ibos" (32, 34, 37, 39).

The final pages of Marshall's story concretize the figurations in the African-American woman-centered text. In a rejection of conventional historiography, feelings are proven more durable and trustworthy than history. The reflective/reflexive text (re)members the sounds it had heard before as church bells, and voices collaborate to remind Avey of the mystifying time she spent on the wharf prior to her conversion.

Miranda, the present-day ancestor of Naylor's *Mama Day*, is a figurative as well as literal descendant of the historical/cultural line of Sapphira. She combines the mythic history of the island's past with the dangerous presence of this history in the contemporary memories of the island's residents. As a consequence, her particular vision reaches into all the layers of this text—the metaphorical scenes, the timeless characters, and the textured language. Naylor compels us to believe in Miranda's vision as accurate if not redemptive. She is able to coalesce the oppositions in the story's dense symbology and rephrase them into her own informed but contradictory presence. Miranda's vision of her place is mediated by her surety in her incarnate powers as much as it is informed by the spiritual presence of her ancestor.

> Miranda . . . turns her face to the sky. Gray. The color you'd get from blending a bridal dress and a funeral veil. A netted sheet of clouds is spreading up slowly from the southern horizon. Sorta like a web that she knows will get wider and thicker—and much more lower. . . . One time a wind's gonna come blow this old house down. That's when it's soaked up about as much sorrow as it can and ain't nothing left for it do but rot. . . . It's the early grieving for the loss that's bound to come to all her work (243).

The community of Willow Springs, the island place of this novel, is a way for Naylor to reach farther back, into "rhythms older than woman," to instantiate a connection between this island that borders Georgia and South Carolina and the (African) place further east and historically separated from it (140). The translucent presence of a metaphorical Africa survives on this island because of the intimate bonding between place and community. The ancestor sustains the figurative dimensions of the metaphorical and oracular textual language. In turn, this language sustains the intimacy between the past and the present. This mediative activity disables the space between objectivity and subjectivity and insists on a revisioned text that embraces the spiritual dissolves within its fractured places as the way towards meaning.

In both *The Women of Brewster Place* and *Linden Hills,* Naylor constructs communities whose historical sources generate the nature of their present. These works juxtapose images of time and place. "Dawn," the first section of *Brewster Place,* serves as an introduction to the history of street. Although the focus in this novel is on the memories of the women who are of this place, it is their spiritual dislocation that weds them to the sterile ghetto street. For this reason, when we learn in the last section of the novel ("Dusk") that Brewster Place waits "for death, which is a second behind the expiration of its spirit in the minds of its children . . . the colored daughters of Brewster [who] spread over the canvas of time, still wake up with their dreams misted on the edge of a yawn," we understand that its fate is theirs as well (192).

The narrative organization in Naylor's oeuvre supports her membership in the tradition of black women writers whose works are plurisignant—both ambivalent and ambiguous—and whose work echoes my earlier thesis of mythologies. The mythologies in Naylor's stories indiscriminately claim ambiguity, deconstructing its inherent polarities. Everything is simultaneous and real—the past and the present, the possible and barely imaginable, and the horrific potential of conjuring as well as its potential to mediate a calming reunion between Cocoa and George's spirit, fourteen years after his death, on the spot of land just past the island graveyard of her ancestors.

Miranda (Mama) Day, who has the ancient powers of her great grandmother Sapphira, must sacrifice George if she is to save her niece Cocoa. We have been warned that George's characteristically mainland disbelief leaves him vulnerable. Like Buchi Emecheta's character Aku-nna (*The Bride Price*), George's death may be intellectually reasoned (he had a weak heart and Aku-nna was anemic) or it may be accounted for in the novel's mythologies. In either case, the reader understands how all events in this novel, spiritual and physical, are vulnerable to the power of a natural world in which talking vines and whispering rocks and malevolent winds can sweep across the island and take hold just when Sapphira's children need to gather up that energy to save themselves.

A textual and cultural corollary to an even more ancient figuration is activated in the recovery of the spiritual metaphor of the ancestor as a topos in the canon of African-American women writers. These works make it clear that these ancestral women's lineage is inhabited by women of the African diaspora. There are both specific and subliminal references to Africa and her ancient women—whether in Paule Marshall's images of the returned Ibos, or in what Jay senses as Avey's "resident" goddesses, or in the knowledge from the "powers of the deep" that

Old Wife brings to Min's healing of a lost daughter of the yam, or in the "true" (i.e. "original") powers of Naylor's Sapphira Wade (*Mama Day*) who could "walk through a lightning storm without being touched; grab a bolt of lightning in the palm of her hand, . . . [turn] the moon into salve and . . . revise the meanings in words" (5).

The powerful creative presence that these (re)membered women exert on the black woman's text forces a theoretical consideration of the original mythologies that are at once responsible for their presence and characteristic of the tradition. Through the narrative activity of revision and recursion, texts of African-American women writers reinforce the ritualized behaviors of cultural memory, insisting on the relationship between the preserved (or recovered) myth, the creativity of women's language, and the place of necromancy in the voiced text. When speakerly texts are identifiable by the frames of a textual ritual that call into practice consistent figurations of language and voice, we must consider this persistence as definitive of both a tradition and a culture. Theoretical inquiry indicates the relationship between the themes of spiritual and cultural reclamation and the constructions within the woman-centered ideology they specify. In articulating a theory of these works, the previously tangential concern of a place of origin for what is essentially an idea of ancestry becomes more and more insistent. Following the ways of cultural memory in the black tradition means a passage across the middle waters—waters that may divide place but certainly have not disabled a memory. It is a memory of an original ancestor whose stature was assured by the mythic dimensions of her creative power and whose specified gender made her the legitimate ancestor of the women of Africa and the African diaspora.

7

▲▲▲▲▲▲▲▲▲▲▲▲▲▲▲▲▲▲▲▲▲▲▲▲▲▲▲▲▲▲▲

Visions of the Goddess:
West African Writers

> The Yorubas of Nigeria and the Ibos use the word
> "Mother" to mean best woman friend, a woman's sa-
> viour. My mother, my female friend, my female sa-
> viour . . . is here. Iyamide.
>
> Buchi Emecheta, *The Family*

The simultaneous appearance of both the ancestor and the deity in African creative literature argues convincingly for the literary kinship of these configurations to the ancestral metaphor
in African-American literature. In traditional religious paradigms of West Africa, deities and ancestors are dimensions of
the multifaceted concept of God, a conceptualization that E.
Bolaji Idowu notes "takes its . . . complexion from the sociological structure and climate."[1] Idowu places great emphasis on the
variations that exist within the religious concepts, practices, and
principles in traditional African religions. In the face of the
overwhelming body of critical study that treats Africa as if it
were one single continental culture, this is a critical point. My
references to the concepts of gods, goddesses, divinities, and
ancestors support the integrity of scholarship that acknowledges the plural cultures of West Africa. Although Idowu insists
on this critical multicultural perspective, he does argue for the
methodological validity in isolating patterns of belief that are
cross-cultural. He notes that identifying patterns in cultural
practices is an appropriate activity of literary criticism and
theory. The linguistic patterns of the metaphorical presence of

deity and ancestor establish the basis of my discussion in this chapter.

In "Structure and Reference: A Theory of African Folk Narrative," Gregory Shreve illustrates how Dahomean myths and legends (*hwenoho*) indicate a pattern of understanding history through the transference and cognitive style of myth and legend. A continued emphasis of my textual theory regards the revision of Western historiography in a consideration of texts whose narrative structures and imaginative domains affirm their cultural allegiance to the non-Western world. That the polarity of and oppositions between myth and history disappear outside of the West is an event that Shreve notes as well in his comments concerning the province of meaning in Dahomey. He writes:

> From the indigenous perspective, the narration of *hwenoho* and the reporting of history are identical processes. The narration of myth/legend amounts to a "reporting of events" even though these events have already transpired. . . . *No suspension of doubt* . . . is required in the world of myth and legend. . . . *The forms of the world of myth and legend will be forms belonging to those of everyday language*. . . . There is no basis for creating a separate list [because we] cannot show cause that its cognitive structure is separate from that of historical narration, or *even the relating of memories*. (Emphasis added.)[2]

Shreve's argument draws attention to a thesis in chapter five of this work—the critical parallel between the structures of telling in myths, traditions, and memory. The ritual relationship between myth, memory, and history reifies the presence of a spiritual deity and a human ancestor (see fig. 1). For example, both traditional ceremonies and mythic rituals figure strongly in Ghanaian playwright and poet Efua Sutherland's works. Because of the kind of stylization that these formalized structures project, the language in Sutherland's works functions as an agency of this stylization. The particular method of Sutherland, however, goes beyond the traditional dramatic presentation of language.

Sutherland's work illustrates how the realm of the ancestor establishes an important metaphorical base for the imaginative text. The (re)memory of ancestral words accompanies contemporary communities and mediates between linguistic patterns in their everyday lives and the metaphysical presence of their spiritual lives. Whether this presence is a deity of African writers or the ancestor of African-American works, the texts of these writers acknowledge memory as a creative pattern for the activity of their imaginations.

As both a literary feature and a linguistic device, recursion is a factor associated with the potency of the goddesses' images. She enables the text to be reflexive and reflective. In its looks inwards and backwards, textual patterns like repetition, sustained, persistent speech, and choral speech are emphasized.

Although an articulation of a sociopolitical feminine principle may be the result of the literary contextualizing of metaphors of spirit, community, and birth, that is not my focus. Instead, I explore how the ideology of a literary culture is enabled through the metaphorical articulation of its imagery and vision by authors who are women.

Like women writers of the African diaspora, West African women's texts sublimate event in preference to the density and richness of language. Ceremonies in words and rituals of language are as important as the dramatic, behavioral rituals they explicate. For example, because Sutherland invests language with a particular kind of creative energy, the dimensions of her work extend to enclose the activity of the word as well as the more traditional manifestations of dramatic action. The resulting text collects and shares emphasis between its linguistic structures. This kind of textual communion allows Sutherland's works to move between genres with ease. Because the story of her drama *Foriwa* is also the narrative of her short story "New Life at Kyerefaso," these two works provide an especially clear illustration of the parallels between linguistic and dramatic rituals.[3] In Sutherland's "New Life at Kyerefaso," the (pre)festival ceremonies mark the occasion where critical linguistic shifts occur in the narrative.

The events of both the drama and the story are centered on the activity of the village's Queen Mother, her daughter Foriwa, and Labaran, an outsider whose efforts to help the village revitalize itself are effectively rebuffed by everyone he meets except the Queen Mother and Foriwa. The drama focuses on the Queen Mother's decision to return the substance of spiritual power back to this disabled village (Kyerefaso) through an annual festival's ritual that honors the ancestors who founded the town on the banks of the River Kyerefa. There is, too, a symbolic dimension of this story that connects it even more intimately to the traditions it renews.

The shift of spiritual energy cannot occur until the Queen Mother herself accepts the challenge of her daughter whose reminder that "It's dawn again" signals the spiritual revolution of the text (8). Prior to her daughter's challenge, the Queen Mother had been so surrounded with the masculine imagery of the God tree (which is the village shrine) that she sees herself as its figural extension. She even dreams of this symbolic Other as promising her freedom from the village which has "rooted" her, "mounted like a gorgeous sacrifice to tradition" (8). However, Sutherland makes it quite clear that this disabling image is not her true spiritual essence. Her destiny is to remain in the village but as more than a "gorgeous sacrifice." Instead, she divests herself of the tree image and symbolizes renewed life. For this reason her essence is appropriately connected to the River Kyerefa, whose fertile, flowing imagery she more accurately personifies.

As the figure of the river, the Queen Mother represents the creative industry her ancestors had brought to the settlement by the river. The memory of their productive lives had been sullied by the deteriorating village life. It is foreshadowed then, when Labaran speculates that he hears the voice of the river accusing the townsfolk of carrying out empty rituals while their village is dying, that it will be the Queen Mother's voice which rises up in anger against this spiritual sacrilege (35). Lloyd Brown notes this passage as well in his discussion of this story. Curiously, he connects the voice of the river to a "river goddess" even though nowhere in Sutherland's drama is a "goddess" specifically mentioned.[4] The Queen Mother does exactly what Labaran says the river should do (disrupt the townsfolks' dangerous passivity by disrupting the festival to honor the ancestral spirits of/in the river)—an act that invests the Queen Mother with the spiritual

attributes of a deity. In the (pre)festival celebration, she challenges Kyerefaso to bring substance to the ritual. "I knew no
way of reaching my people better with such thoughts than to
use this ceremony of our festival as my interpreter. Kyerefaso
needs the new life of which we speak, and men to make it true"
(51). If this festival is "her interpreter," she is its mediator. As
the people come to "bathe in the coolness of [the] peaceful
stream" we understand that it is the waters of Kyerefa which the
Queen Mother represents, not the God tree. The men who "offer manliness to new life" (49), offer it at the feet of the Queen
Mother just as their ancestors settled on the banks of the river.
"The gun's rage is silenced in the stream" the Queen Mother
ritualistically replies to the men's ceremonial gesture. In taking
on the imagery of the festival, she assumes its figurative
dimension.[5]

The Queen Mother's revision of the ancient festival's ritual
language indicates her understanding that linguistic revision,
even of the "old languages," is within her purview. This revision
is not only her responsibility, but it represents a way of
(re)memory and a means of regathering the spirits (ancient and
actual) of the fractured village back to an effective dimension of
the village's contemporary existence. Once (re)membered, the
community, its ancestors, and its deities can dissipate the leth-
argy that has effectively arrested the village's livelihoods.

Ritual is not only a literal aspect of African women's literature, it is a textual strategy as well. Consider how the events in
Buchi Emecheta's *The Bride Price* collect into its carefully reticu-
lated, dense patterns. Because of the density of language, event,
and detail, the mythologies of this work ritualistically share this
distinctively gendered strategy with its African-American
counterparts.

In *The Bride Price*, the metaphorical (re)membrances (as fracturing as they may be for Aku-nna and her mother) are significant to the novel's textual events and Emecheta's telling. When
Aku-nna's mother goes to the village home "to placate their
Oboshi river goddess into giving her some babies" there is no
break in Emecheta's attentive, detailed prose. Whereas Flora
Nwapa's work is characterized by a preponderance of speech,
Emecheta's is characterized by a gradual but inevitably thick-
ening linguistic ritual between circumstance and event that

propels the work toward the destiny promised in the cultural mythologies.

There are no stunning moments of revelation, no especially gleaming sections of prose and no words of such distinction that they draw individual attention to themselves in Emecheta's work. Instead, her novels are characterized by the finest of balances—a careful, evenly weighted prose that weaves through the pages of her texts and collects figural energy as it proceeds. The result of such stylistic evenhandedness is a novel like *The Bride Price* that is luminous precisely because of its finely wrought crafting.

Ritual within this text is layered into ceremonies of death, marriage, fertility, and birth, and draws attention to the cultural patterns that frame the ways of telling these stories. Storytelling itself is important to Emecheta's characterization of Aku-nna, who recognizes in her Auntie Uzo's stories the parallels between her life and the lives of her ancestors. Emecheta writes that of all the storytelling Aku-nna heard in her village, her aunt's stories "attracted her most" (24). The reader discovers that this is a fatal attraction because it foreshadows Aku-nna's inability to separate herself from the tradition that these stories represent. She is bound to their texts because of her attraction to the cultural (re)membrances in her aunt's words. The "call" of her aunt's instructive stories, "intensely charged with philosophical lessons," was psychic bait for Aku-nna's spirit. Eventually, the conflict between Aku-nna's willing participation and enjoyment of ritual, and her efforts to extricate herself from its control, push the gathering elements of this novel toward its dramatic conclusion. Aku-nna's death at the end of *The Bride Price* represents a metaphorical response to her intimate connection to the village myth—a story that promises tragedy will overcome any girl for whom no bride price is paid.

In a discussion of another of Emecheta's works, *The Joys of Motherhood,* Cynthia Ward notes the author's interest in "telling the story of Nnu-Ego from many different angles, *as her mothers told her hers*" (emphasis added).[6] The exchange between the author, her characters, and their ancestral mentors complicates voice and underscores the multiple generations (both literal and figural) who are counted on to pattern (re)memory and who weave the ritual complex of voices in Emecheta's work. The collection of images recalls what I have labeled earlier in this text as an "absent/presence," and predicts the consistency of the spiritual presence of both deities and ancestors in this work.

The collected presences can be linked to the importance Emecheta's culture places on storytelling. In this regard, there are cultural parallels that Emecheta and Ama Ata Aidoo share. Aidoo also calls attention to the relationship between the stories she heard as a child from her grandmother and her development as a writer. In addition, her school training encouraged her to create oral performances as an accompaniment to all her written work. Both experiences heightened the creative skills she would eventually exploit between spoken and written texts.[7]

This factor of Aidoo's childhood illustrates the orchestration between literary and orate traditions that form the textual complexity in Aidoo's works. Women's voices conduct Aidoo's textual orchestra. The shiftiness of language—its flow from prose to poetry and its lapse from lecture to reverie to reflections—clarifies her successful literate (re)memberance of the oracular text. These linguistic revisions articulate a textual tradition we can recognize through the various weaves of voices and textures of an essentially oracular text.

Consider Aidoo's novel, *Our Sister Killjoy*.[8] To further involve textual structures in the collaboration between meaning and form, Aidoo weaves the voices between structures of verse and prose, and she exchanges the first and third person voices of the poetic and prosaic structures. In the way that Ntozake Shange and other African-American women writers privilege their textual dissolves with an italicized print, Aidoo features the oracular voice of these internal monologues in an emphasis on poetic structures. Poetry indicates an oracular source because of its relationship to song. The primary and spoken text of song expresses the figurative vision within Aidoo's style and characterizes the loneliness of the feminine imagination and the alienation of cultural loss (being away from home). Ironically, the initial pages of the novella primarily work to dissemble language. The pages alternate between prose and poetry, and between white spaces interrupted with a single word and pages so thick with prose that the contrasting visual image of these words with the mostly blank pages is striking.

Structurally, the initial chapters compose a series of shifts from poetry to prose, from pages with a single word on them to pages dense with the reflections of Aidoo's protagonist Sissie. In its epistle format, Aidoo's final chapter is dialogic. Here, Sissie's reflections exert a particular kind of control over the structural process. Even though the author and reader play prescribed roles in the communicative act that a letter requires, the pairing is dissembled when an epistle is the structure of a creative text. This deconstruction effaces the implicit pair and the text is left with Aidoo's dense lyricism to explain its content and structure. The love letter that initiates the closure of this novella immediately explicates the preceding pages. It opens with a declaration:

> My Precious Something,
>   First of all, there is this language. This language. . . . All that I was saying about language is that I wish you and I could share our hope, our fears, our fantasies, without feeling inhibited because we suspect that someone is listening (112, 115).

An inevitable complication of this text results when its listeners become tellers. Like Sissie, who insists on a name that recalls "an original concept" of an appellation given to a child when "there are not many girl babies in the family," the reader is both isolated and involved in the story's text (28). Even her letter's addressee is an ambiguous "something," an indication that Sissie cannot specify what her lover represents to her psyche. Because image and experience are so distancing, the collective assertion of Aidoo's thesis that "first of all, there is this language" is all that is left of the text. All "this language" follows the directive of Aidoo's first chapter title, "Into a Bad Dream." The dream chapter works quite specifically to dispense with any Western parameters. Time, distance, and place are all done away with in these early lines: "It is a long way home to Europe. A cruel past, a funny present, a major desert or two, a sea, an ocean, several different languages apart" (8). Note that both place and time are distanced in these lines. Although the semantic ambiguity seems to identify Europe as home, they instead allow for the interpretation that home is away from rather than toward Europe. Aidoo suggests that "time shrank" when the dream sequence begins in earnest. The connection between the opening dream and the closing letter is "this language" that attempts a restoration of the dissembled text. Although the language of the story seems oblique, actually it is the events of the story that are truly oblique and "this language" that centers the text. In this sense, Aidoo's work parallels Emecheta's.

Metaphors of the Spirit ▲

In Western ideologies, the coexistence of myth and memory (spiritual ancestors and contemporary villagers) is a traditionally competitive configuration. Their simultaneous existence in this literature testifies to what I have described as a dissolution of Western schisms between subjectivity and objectivity. A frame where synchronicity and unity emerge out of the dissolved spaces between polar oppositions reinforces the need to shift the interpretive vision in reference to Afrocentric texts. The presence of culturally specific metaphors is revealed by the systems of metaphysical signs within their texts. The signs of the goddess indicate the attention to these cultural metaphors.

In African-American women writers, the idea and presence of the ancestor indicate two important concepts: first, the textual perseverance of a primary (African) culture where the ancestor and the deity can inhabit the same metaphysical space, and second, the belief that a spiritual metaphor can center the metaphysics of a creative literature. Their dual presence in a literary cosmography of African spirituality establishes their relationship to each other and their importance to the creative and imaginative frameworks of the chosen text. The image of a goddess is a constant thread in the textual design and it enables, prompts, and reticulates the concerns of these chapters. Both as a concept and as a discrete figure, my attention to this image is a literary one. Insofar as she is a culturally sustaining and a gender-specified creative figure, her constancy in the literature of African women indicates its specific association with the creative traditions of women's literature.

At first, the Oboshi river goddess in *The Bride Price* is merely the impetus that prompts Ma Blackie's leave taking; but this goddess gradually comes to represent more than an excuse for Ma Blackie's absence. Although her presence certainly does not center the novel, her figural presence is felt during the ritual events we learn form an interpretive set of significant moments that mirror the themes of African-American women writers.

For example, Ezebona, one of the brother-in-law Okonkwo's wives, is called a "pretty woman, like a goddess" and is told that "a goddess who does not open her mouth too much will always be mysterious and beautiful." Here is a West African version of the African-American text of silence. A significant feature of the lessons from ancestors is the cultural/woman-centered mystique of the figure of the goddess. A conflict often involves the dilemma of women's power and voice and extends from the conflation of deities (who are empowered) and ancestors (whose voices assure generational continuity) and their juxtaposition to a male community that asserts itself over the spiritual. (Recall the incident from Paule Marshall's *Praisesong* that reveals Jay Johnson's discomfort when the presences of the goddesses in Avey become apparent to him. Jay "felt himself surrounded by a pantheon of the most ancient deities who had made their temple the tunneled darkness of his wife's flesh. And he held back, trembling . . . not quite knowing how to conduct himself in their presence" [127]).

Consider the juxtaposed imagery of deity and ancestor in Sutherland's "Queen Mother"—the spiritual leader of Kyerefaso. Her role had been merely titular, until she could "no longer agree to let them deck me up like a dead body for a funeral, with all that gold that has no power to dignify that which is already dead. And to be carried out there in procession" (25). She is finally angry enough to call upon her real weapon. Neither the gold, nor the title, nor her home compare to the power in her voice. "I have decided to speak" she declares to her daughter. Her voice is heard over that of the village elders and their representative, who is (ironically) the chief linguist. The Queen's behavior during the ceremony provokes him and he is considerably disturbed when the Queen's speech varies from the "customary question" (49). Her interruption destabilizes the established ritual speech, disturbs the males whose responsibility had been to direct this speech, and aggressively inserts her own voice as source and motivation for village behavior. Its new life would be linked to the annual ritual that the festival would celebrate but the Queen Mother would be the generative source of renewal and ceremony through her conscription of the (re)membered power in her voice. She becomes both titular and actual spiritual leader of Kyerefaso.

One of the important dimensions of this story is that Sutherland understands the contextual significance of the narrative. Because her creative visualization takes place both in the form of a prose narrative (the short story) and as a drama, she gives expression to the literary vehicle in each of the story's textual enclosures. "New Life" (the short story) opens with an epigraph that represents the ritual call to the community and clarifies the collective to whom the prose is directed. "Shall we say / Shall we put it this way" as epigraph is followed by a recursive line of text: "Shall we say [about] the maid of Kyerefaso, For[u]wa, that her voice in speech was like the murmur of a river quietly flowing beneath shadows of bamboo leaves" (283). Immediately, Foriwa's presence is linked to her spiritual ancestor through her qualities of voice. This connection indicates the interpretive significance of the link between the ancestral/spiritual voices that Sutherland technically acknowledges. Further, Sutherland makes it quite clear that it is the community whose attention to this relationship is significant.

The linguistic recursion of her title ("Queen Mother") reflects her (re)membrance of both an earth mother and river goddess. The leader of the ceremony calls to the community to "See how she stands waiting . . . to wash the dust from our brows in the coolness of her peaceful stream." The Queen Mother is so close in figural proximity to this stream that she may "be" (in the sense of representation) this water. In a similar way she metaphorically embodies the earth deity before whom the celebrants "spread the skins . . . the yield of the land . . . [and] the craft of [their] hands" (287). These interpretations of the Queen Mother indicate her figural plurisignance. In Sutherland's revision of the story as a drama, the river deity is an even more specific presence. However, in "New Life" she mediates the ritual festivals. In an inversive recursion, this ritual connects the village to its promising future by revising the substance of its symbolic traditions.

Although Lloyd Brown notes that one of the differences between Sutherland's *Edufa* and the Greek drama whose storyline it echoes is that "in Sutherland's play, death is not pronounced by an offended deity," his interpretation acknowledges a figurative level of this text that does specify a deity. This deity is symbolically folded into Sutherland's characterization of the wife Ampona who vows that she loves her husband Edufa more than her own life. This recurrent confluence, a parallel to the Queen Mother/river goddess blend, argues for its interpretive significance. Because Edufa needs a proxy for what he has been told is his impending death, this vow is also a curse. Brown, who notes that "in Ampona's personality [the] sense of tradition is a creative force" (69) attends to the quality of Ampona that makes her into a creative force and that metaphorically revisions her into a goddess figure.[9]

Adetokundo Pearce also likens Ampona's spirituality to the deity's, noting that Ampona is portrayed as "possessing almost divine sensibilities."[10] Sutherland's dialogue in *Edufa* consistently points to this reverence. For example, Edufa composes this song to Ampona:

> *Nne*
> *Nne Nne . . .*
> *If I find you*
> *Nne*
> *Nne Nne*
> *I'll have to worship you . . .*
> *I must adore you . . .*
> *She's wonderful . . .*
> *O, Mother. . . .* (41, 42)

As if she were a goddess to worship, revere, and adore, and further, as if Ampona were a primal Mother, Edufa agonizes in his effort to redeem himself for his selfish condemnation of his wife. Sutherland's dramatic tension develops through the character of Ampona, even though she is off stage during most of the drama. Figuratively invisible (like a deity) she gains stature outside of our vision until the moment of her staged entry. Then, she is treated with the delicate reverence that her endowed spirituality has earned her. The narrative directs Senchi (the poet) to speak "with profound admiration." Ampona herself is described as being in "a strange mood . . . frequently talk[ing] like one whose mind is straying" (49, 50). We sense that

she has more spiritual than physical essence at this point. The
choral voices that Lloyd Brown labels her "endorsement" are
the articulation of the community voice she has gained through
her metaphorical translucence.[11] Speaking for all women, as she
does, Sutherland makes Ampona's a collective rather than individual spirit and a sharp contrast given the communalism of her
generosity and thoughtfulness in the face of Edufa's selfish
carelessness. Through this contrast, Sutherland emphasizes the
different character of male and female voices. Abena, Edufa's
sister, is the other woman with symbolic voice in this drama. Her
opening poetic monologue that "begins slowly and sleepily"
awakens the play and then inversively propels it towards
dreaming.

> *Dreamlike views of mist rising*
> *Above too much water everywhere.*
> *I heard tonight,*
> *A voice stretched thin through the mist, calling.*
> *Heard in that calling, the quiver of Ampona's voice.* (1)

Ampona's qualities are water-like. A female's voice calls narrative attention to this symbolic connection. Abena's voice is
multiplied through the chorus of women until the climactic energy of the play itself is carried through the interplay of wom-
en's voices. Ampona represents a spiritual, deified voice. The
commentative chorus symbolizes the instructive ancestral voice,
and Abena represents the human community. This interwoven
text illustrates the symbolic figuration of spirituality within metaphor. Both dramas characterize a critical feature of the black
woman writer's tradition. The metaphorical spirit of Sutherland's works is carried through the imagery and voices of
women. Whether they are ancestral, living, or spiritual women,
Sutherland's method assures the context of spirituality as a significant dimension of her texts.

Similarly, whatever the temporal events of *The Bride Price,* a
spiritual level of text resides alongside the temporal. In a fashion similar to Sutherland's, this complicity emerges frequently
enough to remind the reader of its equally intense and reactive
presence. Aku-nna herself is pulled into a web of contradictory
cultural mythologies because she liked singing the praise songs

of the girls who had drowned—victims, it was said, of "the beautiful goddess of the river . . . only claiming back her own" (101). It is very early in the story where we actually learn of Aku-nna's effort to placate the contradictory traditions in her behavior. As a prepubescent child dreaming of marriage, her only goal was not to "let her father down." She planned to "have her marriage first of all solemnised by the beautiful goddess of Ibuza, then the Christians would sing . . . then her father Nna would call up the spirits of his great, great-grandparents to guide her" (10). Aku-nna's sense that she is protected by a gathering of cultural mythologies and Western religions is an ambivalent posture. The ambivalence expresses itself again when we learn that she would flaunt tradition in order to satisfy what she knows is right for her. Yet even the thought of indecision was frightening to her during her adolescence; and indecision was just as worrisome as the nagging fear that "she was beginning to feel that it was unjust that she was not to be allowed a say in her own life" (116).

Metaphors of Community ▲

My interest in the figurative goddess should not be read for its parallels to the (basically Euro-American feminist) predilection to perceive this cultural icon as "the" goddess—politically, socially, and anthropologically responsible for all gender-specific events from the creation of the world to the current politicization of the feminist agenda. Neither does my interest duplicate what I believe is the politically astute effort of Euro-American feminists to find historical evidence of positive images of women as goddesses or heroines, in order to contradict the traditional hierarchy that values maleness above femaleness. Whether or not powerful images of women as "creators of the universe, providers and teachers of law, possessors of ultimate wisdom [and] inventors of important cultural developments" were available to ancient women is not a concern especially relevant to a recovery of her literary imagery.[12]

The African deity imaged in black women's literature is very different from the highly romanticized versions of goddesses rediscovered by Western feminists. The African deity is a figure of both strength and tragedy—like the women whose lives echo hers (neither Efuru nor the lady of the lake knew joy in motherhood). Instead of looking to this goddess for indications about the communities of women whose lives she symbolically extends, the aesthetic interpretation of her image is achieved through her *being* in the culture, the myths, the religions and the art. Her literary being is neither decorative nor passive. Moreover, the patterns of her literary presence reveal attention to the same kind of feature that the ancestors underscore in African-American women writers' texts.

Ward calls attention to often contradictory angles in Emecheta's work. She makes particular reference to this vacillating perspective, noting that "Emecheta's subtle interweaving of often contradictory perspectives suggests a flexibility of social and cultural roles, rankings, and relationships that precludes any authoritative perspective or voice from telling us how to view the village, or indeed, read the novel."[13] Through this perspective, Ward acknowledges the critical role the audience plays in Emecheta's novels. They are the literal community in her work and this strategy links this writer to the African-American novelists who also encourage this structural attention to the reader. This shifting perspective argues for the conflation of the traditions of diaspora and West African literatures by women.

Like the methodology of mythologies, the metaphorical figures replicate the density in ancestral/spiritual presences. Images are meticulously layered upon each other by complications of voice, metaphor, and detail. Each is motivated by an attention to the importance of collectivity over individuality. In *The Bride Price*, Aku-nna's dilemma does not only concern the community's bias against her marrying Chike because he is a descendent of slaves but also concerns the community's determination that women are to be directed by the whim of males and traditions that belittle their personhood.

Political sociologist Halima Mohammed notes that postcolonial men's eagerness to point out the patrilineal nature of society indicates their regard of women as inferior. Heroic women in Nigerian history like the Hausaland leader, Queen Amina, and women who were prominent spiritual figures from Igboland and Nupeland who indicate women's important roles

in the lives of the communities, do not undermine the patrilineal system of those societies.[14] The historical presence of goddesses and/or heroines is not in itself powerful enough to
control the obvious sociocultural sexism in postcolonial Nigeria.
However, contemporary West African women writers suggest
that the roots of women's domination by male hierarchies are to
be found in both precolonialist and postcolonialist Africa.
Often, their works highlight very traditional structures of societies that prohibit women's wisdom from effectively determining the direction of women's social and cultural lives. Despite
the presence of Ana—an earth deity/mother of the Igbo and a
goddess who proclaims laws that are the "basis of all moral human behavior"—the tragic stories of writers like Emecheta and
Nwapa as well as the abuse women suffered in traditional, colonized, and decolonized Nigeria belie Her presence.[15] Although
Halima Mohammed places most of the blame for women's
oppression in Nigeria with the colonialists, she also recognizes
the need for attention to the gender-based spheres privileged
in novels like those by Buchi Emecheta. Mohammed identifies
gender and class stratification in precolonialist Nigeria as a potential vehicle for oppression and domination when social stratifications within the African community paralleled European
mores. West African literatures by women thematically emphasize the conflicts that ensue within the communities that do not
respect traditional over colonialized spheres of men's and wom-
en's power and the ancestral and mythic traditions that articulate the shared structures of these communities.

In Sutherland's "New Life," a collaboration between the female figures (the Queen Mother, the river goddess that she metaphorically represents, and her daughter) and the male figures
(Labaran, the masculine deity of the God tree, and the village
males) reestablish a traditional community balance and assure
the town's renewed fertility. An important symbolic acknowledgment of this empowered intimacy is indicated through the
peripheral action of the story that involves marriage rituals
(first, one of Foriwa's friends, finally Foriwa's own). The coop-
eration between the Queen Mother and her daughter articulates the necessary configuration of an empowered feminine
principle in a community. Although Labaran is certainly a significant part of the struggle to salvage the endangered commu-

nity, women reconstruct the ritual and, in this reinvestment in substantive cultural belief, enable the critical shift that this fractured community must experience. After all, Labaran had been in the village for months unable to initiate any behavior which would rescue it from its dangerous slide towards deterioration; but the Queen Mother does not individually rebirth her village's spirit.

Foriwa, too, revisions an ancient role in her contribution to this community salvation. She adjudicates the action of the play and the activity of ritual, determining that ritual behavior and ritual language will be properly enacted. Although the superficial events of this drama seem to concern a resolution of the oppositional ideologies between the indigenous past and the colonialized present, the internal action brings the past functionally into the present in ways that make its symbols meaningful, whole, and, most important, usable. The reclamation of a usable past is a kind of (re)membrance that is a part of a woman-centered ideology. When, during the ceremony, the Queen Mother's revised text of the traditional language accuses Kyerefaso's men of being weary of "parading in the ashes of their grandfathers' glorious deeds," she confronts them with the challenge of their ancestors' presence (49). As metaphors, the contrasting images of ashes and the river nullify each other. The threat of ashes foreshadows the community's loss of its collective memory.

The collective of the Queen Mother, her daughter Foriwa, and Labaran represent the ideal community—the goal of the re-visioned Kyerefaso. The generational figure of the mother and her fertile progeny (Foriwa and Labaran) assures this village of its new life. The festival of renewal gives credence to the old—a recursive reflection on the enabling continuity represented by the traditions of the ancestors and the traditional reverence extended to them. The community learns to use the ancient example in their contemporary lives in ways that will assure the generational continuity of their own spirits. In an acknowledgment that generation means the equitable and collective coexistence of the past and the present, the Queen Mother and her daughter are coconspirators in the salvation of Kyerefaso.

The idea of community is especially important to the West

African's history because of the fracture it experienced through colonialism. The metaphorical interest in this is analaogous to the diaspora metaphor of fracture extending from the slave trade. For example, as Paule Marshall's characters look across an ocean towards home, Aidoo's characters look back to an indigenous Africa. In *Our Sister Killjoy,* Aidoo renders this metaphor by merging the diaspora experience, the loneliness that Sissie feels for home, and the connection of gender between Sissie and the German woman Marija. Aidoo's central event concerns Sissie's journey away from and back to Ghana. Her reflections during this journey to Europe emphasize cultural alienation and the subsequent abandonment of a gendered collective that does reflect her culture. Sissie seems to want the intimacy that could extend from her physical bond to a West German woman, Marija, but the failure of this relationship underscores that gender cannot be abstracted from ethnicity.

Chapter titles acknowledge the association between ethnicity and gender as a key to Aidoo's text. "Into a Bad Dream," is the chapter that sends Sissie from Ghana to Germany. Her German experience is detailed in a chapter titled "The Plums"—a reference to the fruit that Marija offers Sissie. Sissie, who had no prior experience with this fruit, felt that she "had good reason to feel fascinated by the character of Marija's plums" (40, 41). The phrase "had good reason" is conceptually marked for recursion.[16] Reason is layered to mean both knowledge and intuition. It is recursive because the kind of knowledge Sissie will come to have about Marija will have a multiple character.

Sissie's relationship with Marija is juxtaposed, structurally and thematically, against the separation of continents and cultures. In Aidoo's work, gender is a cultural collective that cannot separate one from the other. Her textual organization emphasizes this thesis. Following the surreal dreaminess of the first chapter and the foreignness of the second, the third chapter is titled "From Our Sister Killjoy" and is written as a letter that contains Sissie's spiritual reveries.

After her separation from Marija, who gives her some plums as a parting gift, Sissie's reflections indicate her mistrust and sardonic awareness of the sterility in her European experiences. As a "black-eyed squint" she sees with greater depth and clarity. Because her perceptions are now reliably filtered through her ethnicity as well as her gender, the bad dream no longer claims her. The chapters that follow her separation from Marija share with her the "black-eyed squint" label.

Her visual acuity sees the tragic sterility endured by the Africans in London. This is the focus of the epistle that is the final chapter ("The Love Letter"). Here, Aidoo reveals how much of her story is about loss and letters—the language of spiritual reverie. The squint's reflectiveness is a paradigmatic example of reflective recursion—that which goes within as well as shows outwardly the spiritual dilemma of a fractured soul. The figural level of "The Love Letter" testifies to Sissie's love of her community.

Metaphors of Birth ▲

In "Ethics and Justice in Goddess Religion" Starhawk perceptively notes that "most writers on modern day Goddess religions, [or] womanspirit . . . cite the past to offer a historical basis for the present-day traditions." However, there is a significant potential for error inherent in such a perspective. Starhawk writes that "historical points are always arguable, and while the past may serve us with models and myths, we need not look to it to justify the reemergence of the feminine principle."[17] Indeed, if one compares the perspectives among African women writers of fiction and nonfiction concerning the background of women's oppression in contemporary Africa, what is noticeable is the contradiction among these perspectives. Writers of nonfiction often point to the introduction of colonialism in traditional Africa as the root of women's contemporary social status.[18]

In a discussion of the literary history of Negritude, Barbara Christian raises a point critical to the image of the African woman (both idealized, real, and spiritual). The hazard of becoming creatively "larger than life" was a political idealization that more often disabled rather than enabled a woman-centered principle. Christian explains that the tradition

idealized [the African woman] as mother earth, the source of all life, who in her traditional gendered sphere remained intact, untouched by the West. Revered as mother, powerful in her sphere of magic, she provided a source of cleansing for the men who had ventured out and were tainted by European education, religion, ideas, and money. Poetry, novels, treatises written by men who of course had access to writing (man's domain), stressed that image, embodying it sometimes in the realm of public policy.[19]

The Western tradition's connection of women to nature and mother earth makes this mythic imagery particularly subject to sociopolitical abuse. Nigerian sociologist/journalist Ayesha Imam points out that the "debunking of the 'nature' myth is particularly important" because of its paradigmatic power in the justification of men's behavior toward women and women's acceptance of their aggression as "natural."[20] Imam argues that the dangerous offshoot of such thinking is the fuel it provides for the arguments of sociobiologists like Desmond Morris, Robin Fox, and E. O. Wilson.

In linking the ideals of motherhood and womanhood to the idealization of an earth mother whose symbolically centered presence is characterized by an idyllic and transcendental beneficence, Negritude poets may have been responsible for as much literary sexism as sociobiologists have been responsible for the persistence of scientific racism. The romantic reveries that feature a primal and beneficent earth mother are about as far away from the characteristic experiences of African women's motherhood as one could imagine. However, this is not so much a condemnation of this genre as it is evidence for the relevance of gender as a facet of the interpretive critical frame when studying African literatures. What is particularly significant is that this same center in African women's creative literature prompts a distinct kind of symbology. Note, for example, the pregnant complexity in Aidoo's vision of motherhood as she links an image of the biological slavery of motherhood and the historical slavery of Africa's past in her drama, *Anowa*.[21]

I dreamt that I was a big, big woman. And from my insides were huge holes out of which poured men and women and children. And the sea was boiling hot and steaming. And as it boiled, it threw out . . . giant lobsters . . . each of whom . . . turned into a man or woman, but keeping its lobster head and claws. And they rushed to where I sat and seized the men and women as they poured out of me, and they tore them apart. . . . Since then, any time there is mention of a slave, I see a woman who is me and a bursting as of a ripe tomato or a swollen pod. (46, 47)

When controlled by the imagination and pens of women writers, the earth mother/goddess metaphor gains dimensionality. Rather than a flat center, her full and creative complexity illumine her plurisignance. This symbolic ambivalence becomes the figural challenge of her symbolism in women's writing.

Strategies of mothering and images of mothers in the creative literature of African women writers undercut the images of the Negritude poets insofar as their benign and passive idealizations have dominated the vision of the African mother. The imagery of motherhood in the creative literature of African women writers revises traditional understandings of what creativity and birth have meant for post-colonial African women. It is significant that although the image is indeed central to both male and female writers, as Carol Davies argues, the interpretation of the imagery rests with both the gender and the culture of the writer.[22] In noting that the spiritual center of women's lives in Africa is motherhood, Filomena Steady suggests that it is this difference which is "probably the most fundamental between the African woman and her Western counterpart."[23] Yet such centrism raises a critical question in terms of the generation of this imagery of motherhood and her creative figuration as a goddess responsible for procreation, fertility, and the kind of wisdom associated with mothering. Certainly acknowledgment of a goddess/earth mother is compelling mythology, especially for the creative writer. That women writers have chosen to weave her essence into the structural configurations of their literature testifies to the complex ambivalence of the imagery. Within a literature that attends to the dialectical components of this divinity and that uses the dissolution of this schism as a creative thesis, the imagery of the goddess is revisioned. Theologian Rosemary Ruether has suggested that an identifying factor of Western (and patriarchal) religions has been to "split apart the dialectical unities of mother religion into absolute dualism."[24] There is as important a factor, one that precedes the "absolute dualism" Ruether understands as the result of patriarchal religions—the traditionally dialectical nature of perception itself when it comes to the spiritual in the Western world.[25]

First, it is critical to acknowledge the history of gender abuse as tangential to the history of creative abuse. In *Second-Class Citizen,* Emecheta clearly attaches writing to her creative productivity, saying of writing that she felt "just as if it was another baby she had had . . . fulfilled."[26] In an ironic twist, Francis, the husband in that novel, tells his wife Adah that "You keep forgetting that you are a woman and that you are black . . . who [can] think of nothing except how to breast-feed her baby" (168). Precisely. In this novel, Adah's salvation is due to her ability to nourish her creative urge; her husband's frustration is that he is unable even to reach her figural level. Such impotence forces his limited perception that her only access to creativity resides within a biological sphere. The novel that Francis attempts to destroy in *Second-Class Citizen* is titled *The Bride Price.* In a paradigmatically recursive trope, Emecheta revisions the sustained generation of the West African woman's creative empowerment and access to the pen—the "white ink" of the feminist literati.

Although Aku-nna's mother Ma Blackie (*The Bride Price*) gains some measure of personal freedom at the time of her father's death, Aku-nna senses the ambivalence of this freedom because, according to tradition, her mother cannot remain unmarried. She must become one of the wives of her brother-in-law. Ma Blackie becomes pregnant by this new husband. However, rather than the gathering storm of events that threaten Aku-nna's growing sense of herself as a woman who is restricted by cultural traditions like the one that has imprisoned her mother, the textual complicity that places Emecheta's technique into the tradition of black women writers is the critical theoretical issue.

Susan Friedman notes that "cultural as well as biological resonances intensify the contradictory core of the . . . birth metaphor." Friedman makes this observation even though she claims that "woman's reclamation of the pregnant Word is itself a transcendence of historical prescription . . . that perfectly conjoins form and content."[27] African women writers are faced with articulating both sides of this contradiction not through the Euro-

American woman's loss of creative powers—the "pregnant word" is within their grasp—but through the loss of their generative powers. Their motherhood is abused by conditions within their cultures or within their cultural histories.

Consider the barely buried story of Ogea in Nwapa's *Efuru,* the girl-child who is given to Efuru for ten pounds in order to relieve her parents of their poverty and the difficulty in caring for this child. Ogea is just ten, and Nwapa claims the reader's sympathy with the confusion and loss she feels concerning her abandonment by her parents. Ogea "took a long time to settle down. . . . She did not know why her parents had brought her to the strange house. . . . Sometimes when . . . Ogonim . . . was crying . . . she cried with her." [28] Ogea's sorrow is a constant part of this story. She is abused by Ajanupu who has no patience with her. Upon the death of Efuru's daughter, Ogea's plaintive cry is heartrending. The poetic rhythms and repetitive language of her mournful cry indicate Nwapa's intent to draw attention to the interpretive significance that must be attached to this event—"Please don't put her in that coffin. . . . Please don't put her in that wretched coffin, put me instead. Oh, Ogonim you have killed me. Oh, Ogonim why did you decide to leave me. . . . You have killed me" (92). Rather than being the appropriate mourning cry that a woman is taught to express upon the death of a family member, Ogea's grievous weeping falls outside of the norm and the sympathizers who gather in Efuru's house hiss at her. Eventually, she is led away from the gravesite. Toward the end of this novel, Ogea is told that Efuru and Eneberi have agreed to marry her. Although she will, as the third wife, be Efuru's daughter, we know that there is little but further sorrow in store for her as a wife of the selfish Eneberi. Ogea's story reminds the reader of women's powerlessness in a community that in one sense supports them, but in another denies them power over the course of their own lives.

Aidoo's images in *Our Sister Killjoy* metaphorically acknowledge the sterility that results from an abusive generational history. Sissie's implicit intimacy with another woman assures that biological creativity will be neither at the center nor a product of this relationship. She is immediately compromised by a woman with fruit when she arrives in Germany, a symbolic promise of fertility; but her reflections reveal something quite different. Instead of fertility, Sissie is surrounded with sterility—an imagery that is contrasted by the cultural warmth and nurturing that Sissie mourns. Sissie decided that the Germans' cold food (nurture should be warm) "had something to do with [their] white skins, corn silk hair and very cold weather" (68). The contradictions in the imagery only underscore the sterile polarities in what Sissie finds in her sojourn: the implicitly lesbian relationship between Sissie and Marija; Sissie's dark skin and Marija's whiteness; Sissie's warm homeland and the cold European continent; fertility and sterility; and Marija's cold, white fingers on Sissie's (warm and brown) breast.

The principal narrator of "Certain Winds" anticipates trauma like Sissie's.[29] In that story, the conversion of the past and the present are clearly evident—and are also problematic. The narrator, M'ma Asana, sees the spirit of her deceased husband in her son-in-law. She senses the interruption of generational continuity, first by thinking through the ritual cycle as if to call it into being—"Pregnancy and birth and death and pain; and death again" (55). Then her thoughts articulate the story's thesis of dislocation: "When there are no more pregnancies, there are no more births and therefore, no more deaths. . . . Show me a fresh corpse my sister, so I can weep you old tears. The pit of her belly went cold, then her womb moved" (55, 56). The purely figurative movement in her empty womb acknowledges the kind of loss that Sissie experiences in her European trip and the emptiness that the relationship with Marija promises. The old woman of "Certain Winds," who recalls a time where ritual, even a tragic one, was reliable, shares with *Our Sister Killjoy*'s Sissie the confluence of seemingly contradictory imagery. Aidoo's artistry brings together the thematic dilemma shared by these two women. Her style is to use a dissembling linguistic manipulation to underscore themes that emphasize ambivalence in fertility and the vulnerability of women's places in traditional social structures.

In Nwapa's *Efuru,* the further that Efuru descends into the spirit of the goddess whom she has chosen to serve, the more her own presence is centered and Uhamiri's essence becomes the central metaphor. The goddess accompanies the dissembling ironies of the text's narrative inversion by claiming the center of the figurative revision. For example, at first the narrative structures of the text seem to support the notion that the physical activity of the village dominates the novel. Eventually we understand that this perspective is misleading. Consider the comfort offered Efuru when her daughter Ogonim dies. In a passage that seems to promise Efuru hope of another pregnancy and another child, she is offered the ambivalent solace of a village woman who tells of the eight conceptions she had experienced. She tells Efuru, in way of empathy, one would assume, that all of her children had died before they reached the age of one. One of these deaths, the last of her eight children, had been a daughter. She describes this child's dying in poignant detail, finally telling Efuru that even though she has never had another child, Efuru was young and should take some comfort in the fact that "it is still morning for you" (90, 91). Is it indeed "morning" or "mourning?" This woman offers her own tragedy to Efuru as a kind of convoluted evidence that Efuru's life will still include children. We are led to accept the sincerity of this telling of her personal tragedy as an offering of solace by Ajanupu, who directs us toward the hopefulness embedded in the mourner's expression of sympathy. Ajanupu insists that the neighbor speaks with wisdom and that her somewhat peculiar (to the reader, and probably to Efuru as well) expression of grief is exactly how one should "sympathize with a woman who has lost her only child" (91). It is clear that Ajanupu interprets the mourner's story as encouragement. But the underlying level of this comfort, which Efuru will come to realize, is that this empathetic outpouring will come to mean for her a promise of her own life. In *Beloved*, Morrison calls this Sethe's "own best thing" (273).

Because belief in divinity and belief in ancestors are both elements of traditional religion in Africa, the figurative presence of feminine deities (goddesses) in creative literatures by women indicates the creative relationship of this metaphor to the culture and gender of the author/artist. This imagery, used as archetypal sources within the literature, reflects the revision of this traditional cultural image when asserted by women's voices and controlled through women's vision. These deities are the source of gendered textual revision. Shifting narratives and language that exchanges poetic shapes for prosaic and textural dissonance for form are patterns that the spiritual presence of a goddess anticipates. (Re)membrance layers these texts because memory and history collapse into each other. An almost tangible, certainly translucent and obviously luminous mythology infuses the events of the story until time is less relevant than memory and the linear is less accurate than the circular. Through the weave of the imagery of a goddess into the textures of their works, spiritual metaphors are blended into these texts in ways that moor their works to a cultural and woman-centered ideology that specifies a black women writers' canon.

8

▲▲▲▲▲▲▲▲▲▲▲▲▲▲▲▲▲▲▲▲▲▲▲▲▲▲▲▲▲▲▲▲

Spirituals and Praisesongs:
Telling Testimonies

> It was in this world of woman speech, loud talk, angry words, women with tongues quick and sharp, tender sweet tongues, touching our world with their words, that I made speech my birthright . . . "talking back became for me a rite of initiation."
>
> bell hooks, *talking back*

The text of my argument concerning the literary sisterhood that African and African-American women writers share is bio-geographical and cultural. The text of my argument concerning the cultural experience is gender-based. My posture is deliberately recursive. Recursion is appropriate to this subject because no other women in the world have experienced a similarly shared and sundered historical connection like that between women of West Africa and women of the diaspora. We simply cannot ignore the lessons from cultural studies that indicate there are areas of intersection with the original culture that are always maintained when cultures are divided.[1] In beliefs and value systems, religion and language, echoes of the original culture persist. As a discrete figure of culture, gender must be figured into this schema as another point of intersection.

Because West African societies were clearly gender stratified, it is possible that this could continue to be a persistent line of demarcation in the experiences of women in the diaspora. The resonances between metaphors of West African women writers and the mediations within the texts of American writers are sustained through their cultural histories and their particular experiences of gender. Both women's cultures have been compromised by Western domination. As the "mule of the world" (the phrase is Hurston's) the black woman's experience with colonialism and slavery is intimately connected to the distinction of her gender.[2] Both the cultural construct of gender (the gender spheres that came along with growing up female in West Africa, the roles of women as "tellers" and cultural archivists, the lore of ladies of the lakes and deities), and the physical construct of gender (pregnancy, childbirth, and lactation) are implicated in the histories that have been revisioned in the imaginative texts of these writers. Both slavery and colonialism fractured these roles. The shared figurations in these writers' works reflect the intimacy between culture and the discrete constructs of gender that these women once shared.

My theoretical argument concerns the figurative relationship between the metaphors from the texts of West African writers and the ancestral mediation accomplished within the texts of African-American women writers. Within this perspective, mediation functions as the substance of metaphor; it places text into a resonant and sensuous relationship with its cultural and gender-based sources. In this chapter, two novels ground my theoretical perspective concerning the thematic exchange between mediation and metaphor. Toni Morrison's *Beloved* is a novel generated from the incidence of slavery, and Flora Nwapa's *Efuru* explores the creative dimensions of womanspirit in preference to the creative act of childbirth. Morrison's text has a resonance that extends from and encompasses the ancestral figure's history. If we were to read this novel merely as history, we would forego this intensity. Beloved's presence forces our acknowledgment of her spiritual depth. She mediates historical, contemporary, and spiritual spaces in Morrison's story. The intimacy Efuru shares with a goddess merges the sensual and spiritual in Nwapa's novel. This confluence indicates how the realm of the goddess is intimately connected to womanspirit. Both writers revise a traditional view of the relationship between story and the narrative spaces of real and contemporary events. The goddess Uhamiri's presence is a given in Nwapa's novel in the same way that the ghostly presence of Beloved is a given in Morrison's novel. In order to read these works, we must suspend the vision of reality in traditional historiography. These novels indicate the places where culture and memory converge in African and African-American women's texts. The ancestrally mediated places and voices, and the contradictions between childbirth and wholeness in Morrison's novel, are a recursive acknowledgment of the numinous metaphors in Nwapa's *Efuru.*

The sublimation of time and the privilege this extends places the recursion in Morrison's novel directly into the tradition of literature by black women. Like other works in this tradition, this novel's dependence on recursive structures argues that inversion can sustain an alternative reality. In a similarly inversive behavior, Nwapa's Efuru turns her life over to the goddess of the lake and replaces her reality with her spirit. In this novel, Nwapa juxtaposes the social circumstances that abuse women against cultural and communal memories that can save them. She imaginatively constructs a metaphorical realm of woman-spirit and uses the "childless" goddess Uhamiri as an embodiment of the figurative essence of spiritual womanhood.

Morrison's text replicates the shifted hierarchies that Nwapa's spiritual world proposes. This is an important reformulation of the Western ethic. *Beloved* proposes a paradigm for history that privileges the vision of its victims. Traditional processes of historiography are revised in this inversion. This is a critical posture for this novel to assume because slavery placed black women outside of the universe governed by the measure of history. Instead, the *aspect* of their being—the quality, nature, and presence of their state-of-being—becomes the appropriate measure of their reality. Morrison's novel claims black women's history as a history of absence because slavery denied them the right to nurture, the physical and psychic assurance of generation, and a promise of cultural and generational continuity.

Joan Kelly calls attention to the exclusion of women throughout historical time. Kelly clarifies how the activities of civilization have been determined by and are exclusive to males. In defining a feminist historiography that deconstructs male-centered constructions of historical periods, Kelly's argument is that history must be "rewritten and periodized" according to issues that affect women.[3] This is a perspective of a detemporalized history that deconstructs traditional eras. In black women's writing, time and history are simultaneously dissolved. Black women have lived in the universe Kelly academically discusses.

In *Beloved,* a history that reconstructs the story of Margaret Garner (an escaped slave who killed her child rather than see that daughter captured and returned to slavery), Morrison has restructured a difficult past. Her reclamation of this story from the scores of people who interviewed Margaret Garner shortly after she killed her child in 1855 constituted an act of recovery; but it has accomplished a mythic revisioning as well. Morrison refused to do further research on Garner beyond her review of the magazine article that recounted the astonishment of preachers and journalists who found Garner to be "very calm . . . very serene" after murdering her child.[4] The mythological aspects of Morrison's imaginative reconstruction of this event recall her earlier texts, rediscover the altered universe of the black diaspora, and challenge Western valuations of time and event (place and space).

Her narrative is a complex of voice, song, and imagery that insists upon its structural and thematic relationship to her earlier novels. It underscores how the past (even the literary past) is currently at work as the myth from which we construct the meaning and significance of our present. As Sethe practices holding back the past, and Beloved claims not only her own history but the histories of "sixty million and more," the vision of this novel becomes innervision, and is a cognitive reclamation of spiritual history.[5]

Sethe's experience with the spirit of her child is related to the trauma that Efuru experiences when she tries to maintain her community's sense that womanhood means motherhood no matter what the consequences. As long as Efuru is married to her physiology rather than her psyche, and as long as her efforts reflect a single-minded goal of finding joy only through motherhood, and peace and contentment only by way of marriage and service to her husbands, her spiritual essence will be unfulfilled. However, both Sethe and Efuru recover some form of spiritual essence (presence) in their radical departures from the community's norms. This confluence establishes the most important feature of their intertextuality.

Displacement of the traditional cultural values assigned to fertility and motherhood is Nwapa's thesis. The legacy of that displacement is Morrison's. In Nwapa's novel, the decentering of fertility and motherhood allows Efuru's spirituality to assert itself in their place. As the metaphorical center of this novel, womanspirit subverts the traditional, biological parameters of women's being. Beloved's existence in the temporal world is a revision similar to Efuru's displacement. The spirit of Sethe's dead child Beloved is at once the essence of spirituality as well as the embodiment of the contradictions implicit in biological motherhood for black women. Black women's experience with motherhood has not encouraged a romantic "life renewing itself" metaphor.

Creativity was a compromise of childbirth in the literature of the West. Susan Friedman writes that "facing constant challenges to their creativity, women writers often find their dilemma expressed in terms of the opposition between books and babies . . . for both material and ideological reasons, maternity and creativity have appeared to be mutually exclusive to women writers.[6] For black women, babies were often neither realistic nor a matter of choice, and black women writers have reconstructed the issue into the figurative dimensions of their literary texts. In their works, childbirth is often framed as a threat to survival rather than the (comparatively) benign worry that pregnancy will "sabotage their creative drive."[7] Consider how Aidoo's M'ma Asana ("Certain Winds") visualizes the experience that African women have had with birth: "Show me a fresh corpse my sister so I can weep you old tears;" or a childhood like that Nwapa's Ogea had to endure, or the absent presence of children that African-American mothers, mercilessly separated from their progeny, were forced to substitute for motherhood.

Perhaps it is this complication of generational continuity that leads to temporal displacement, a strategy that is central to the texts in this tradition. These are recursive literatures, they recover history and then subvert it; they assert the priority of time and then displace it; they offer the commonplace as reality and then assert the realm of the spirit as actuality. This is why Hurston's note that black folk think in glyphs rather than writing is not only an acknowledgment of another cosmology that permeates these texts, but an acknowledgment of the need to shift the paradigms we construct to understand thought.

Contemporary African-American literary structures facilitate the revision of the historical and cultural texts of black women's experiences. One of the most sustained examples of this process is Morrison's *Beloved.* In this novel, narrative structures are manipulated through a complicated interplay between implicit orature and the explicit structures of script. The novel's reclamation and revision of history function as both thematic emphasis and textual methodology. This persistence is strategized into the narrative structures of the text.

Morrison coalesces the known and unknown elements of slavery—the events, minuscule in significance to the captors but major disruptions of black folks' experience in nurturing, loving and being—and reconstructs them into a present incapacitated by its responsibility to carry and reformulate its horrific story. For Morrison, myth becomes a metaphorical abandonment of time. Because metaphor is represented as origin in myth, its instantiation in the place of history abandons the dissonance of time. Within this cosmology, the potential of Beloved's spirit is freed from history and threatens to consume her mother.

Efuru's acquiescence to the spirit Uhamiri does not contain the threatening potential of Sethe's behavior. Uhamiri will be Efuru's spiritual salvation rather than her condemnation. The question posed in the novel's closing lines, "She had never experienced the joy of motherhood. Why then did women worship her?" illustrates the recursive posture of the novel. Since both Morrison and Nwapa figuratively connect spirituality and motherhood, their novels illustrate the gender-based revision of this equation in black women's texts. The literature of this tradition acknowledges that motherhood has a history of *physical and spiritual* damage. Efuru knows, by the experiences documented in her community and by her own short-lived experience as a mother, that she must worry over its potential. Motherhood is not a middle-class choice for her. There is a community pressure for her to have children, but at what price? The novel's final question occurs in the context of one who slept soundly, not fitfully or with difficulty. Her dreams of the childless deity were comforting and soothing. Efuru's question regarding the nature of Uhamiri's divinity does not contain the kind of speculative doubt it may initally seem to express. Instead, it is a comment that confirms her *logical* intuition that spirituality need not be linked to motherhood. The wealth, beauty, peacefulness and honor that surround this goddess— qualities that Efuru lists quite explicitly—overwhelm Her endowment of biological motherhood. Efuru is absolutely right concerning her radical speculations on the nature of divinity. What she comes to celebrate and to embody as the goddesses' virtues have nothing whatsoever to do with biological fecundity. They have everything to do with a quiet and contented spirituality—the virtues that Efuru herself comes to represent in her community.

Spirit Voices ▲

When Zora Neale Hurston described dialect as the urge to adorn, an oral hieroglyph, she probably was not prefiguring the dimensions that Toni Morrison would bring to the glyph of black language. However, Hurston certainly recognized the potential in black language to dissolve the artificial constructs of time. Morrison's accomplishment with language is an act of liberation. Texts that seem to depend on script are revealed as texts that depend on oracy.[8] Walter Ong acknowledges this potential when he writes that orality is "[n]ever completely eradicable; reading a text oralizes it."[9] Morrison enriches Ong's observation. Her texts are a constant exchange between the assertive struggle of an implicit voice, and an explicit narrator inextricably bound to its spoken counterpoint.

As text, *Beloved* adds to the litany of Morrison's "talking books."[10] The collected callers and respondents in this work gather to tell a story that "seemed unwise to remember . . . It was not a story to pass on. . . . This is not a story to pass on" (274, 275). Like the repetitive litany frequently used as a narrative device in black women's literature, the novel's closing phrases echo with contradiction. The phrase "pass on" becomes a directive that assures the story's telling. Morrison revisions "pass on," and inverts it to mean "go on—continue—tell," in defiance of the logic of its seeming "unwise to remember." This directive illustrates what I see as a contrapuntal interplay between implicitly orate and explicitly literate structures. This behavior dominates Morrison's novel and mediates speech and narrative in the same way that Beloved's presence mediates the spiritual and physical realms.

In a dialogue with Hélène Cixous about the nature of their discourse in *The Newly Born Woman,* Catherine Clément accepts that "there can be two women in the same space who are *differently* engaged, speaking of almost exactly the *same things* investing in two or three different kinds of discourse and going from one to the other and then on to the spoken exchange." Cixous replies that she "distrust[s] the identification of a subject with a single discourse.[11]

The narrative of *Beloved* is not entrusted to the single discourse of any of the three women implicated in the myth. Neither is it left to only one dimension. Instead, a collective telling validates the literate text. Each of the voices of the three women in this novel, Denver, Sethe and Beloved, is distinct—a different kind of discourse, even though the women are all in the same dissolved space of Beloved's ephemeral presence. Consider the moment when Sethe finally acknowledges Beloved as the spirit of her dead child. Here, Sethe's narrative is a dense structure complicated with smells, touches, and colors—the only remaining frames of her reality. Hers is a vibrant and redolent discourse, almost as if the vitality of her telling would defy the dying and killing she acknowledges with her wintry declaration that "Beloved, she my daughter" (200).

Denver's discourse, in the same space as Sethe's, represents the "differently engaged" but "same things" that Cixous and Clément discuss. Morrison highlights this "same difference" with repetition and recursion. Denver's first words, "Beloved is my sister," take us back to Sethe's (205). Her narrative recollects her first memories, propels her into the dilemma that challenges Beloved's kinship to her, and (re)members her sister's death from a variety of perspectives, each of which complicates the temporal spaces in which they occurred. Her memory collapses action into physical and sensorial responses. Finally, her opening and somewhat tentative claim of Beloved as "my sister"

is repeated in a resonant and conclusive acknowledgment—
"She's mine, Beloved. She's mine" (209).

In this section, Beloved's discourse is the trace element that
dislocates the narrative structure of Sethe's and Denver's
thoughts. Her discourse also supports the narrative because this
dissembling quality underscores her own disruptive nature.
Her assertion, "I am Beloved and she is mine," is the last structure syntactically marked as a sentence (210).

Nwapa's novel also uses the strategies of collective discourse
to metaphysically extend the text into a spirit realm. Talk is her
artifice. The transformations of voice in *Efuru* are based on the
effective accumulation of a community of tellers whose message
is radically different from what they intend it to be. For example, recall how the mourner's recitation of her still-born and
dead children, which is intended to promise Efuru that she will
have more children, is revisioned as an assurance that Efuru will
birth a spiritual self.[12] Like Morrison's text, Nwapa's novel gradually turns itself over to the spiritual realm and relinquishes its
energy to the spiritual guidance of the goddess Uhamiri, the
Woman of the Lake. The textual consequence of this guidance
is that spirituality is constantly reminded of the corresponding
presence of mortality. The goddess, a metaphysical presence
rather than a visual one, is only revealed through Her complicitous involvement in Efuru's life and through Efuru's speculations concerning the ways in which Her watery presence
ambivalently represents fertility and motherhood: "She had
never experienced the joy of motherhood. Why then did
women worship her?" (281).

Even though events dominate the physical text, and womanspirit centers the figural text, *talk* collects both of these into its
own elliptical and ambivalent structures. Language (literally, the
voice of Nwapa's work) is the structural event of her stories. Lul-
labies and praisesongs are woven through this novel. A village
storyteller narrates a folkstory dense with song and verse about
a girl who marries a spirit and is rescued by her sister. Efuru is
constantly counseled by women in and away from her village. A
preponderance of talk folds Nwapa's text into structures that
enable her to direct the mythologies in the text. Ancestors and
goddesses are a part of these stories and their dialogues.

Because of their constancy, we are forced to underscore the ways in which talk enables the spirituality of the novel. Through the contradictory and multiple presence of competing advice and tradition—the message of the folkstories versus the lives of the villagers; comforting village life itself as compared to the upheavals in the large market of Onitsha—talk gathers the disparate elements of this story and directs the reader towards its textural plurisignance.

As in *Efuru, Beloved*'s blend of word and text also allows a figural collapse of the narrative that reveals an introspective textual dimension. The story is folded into the enriched realm of spirit and voice. As an example, consider how the text prefigures the narrative streams of Sethe, Denver, and Beloved that begin with their acknowledgment of Beloved as daughter, sister, and self.

The three are ice-skating in a place where "the sky above them was another country." At this moment, when the "peace of winter stars seemed permanent," Beloved sings the song that fulfills her mother's intimation that this is indeed her daughter. Morrison allows Sethe this bittersweet realization through a construction familiar to black women writers' texts. Memory is returned through song. "'I made that song up,' said Sethe. . . . 'Nobody knows that song but me and my children.'" Beloved turned to look at Sethe. "'I know it,' she said" (176). Once Sethe understands that the woman-child who has appeared in her house is the manifestation of the spirit whose life she took, she offers it back the only life she has—her own.

Morrison acknowledges the recursion in Beloved's knowledge (Is Beloved saying that she knows the song or that she knows that only Sethe and her children know that song?) by forcing the text into the spiritual places that her knowledge presumes. Sethe's response is to tell her daughters it is "time to sleep." The text layers this metaphor. They "stumbled over the snow, but" (and Morrison uses the following recursive structure three times) "nobody saw them falling" (174). In this way, the text prepares itself, the reader, and these three women for its temporal lapse. The chapter just prior to Sethe's discursive monologue ends with "the thoughts of the women of 124, unspeakable thoughts, unspoken" (199); but they are spoken, for the next voice is Sethe's. Her first statement is in dialect, a sign that the text is about to embrace recursion and signify upon itself: "Beloved, she my daughter. She mine" (200).

Using a similar emphasis on recursion, Nwapa's mortal woman, who agrees to become a worshipper of Uhamiri, embodies the goddess' metaphorical presence. Efuru is unfailingly good and selfless. She is long-suffering and patient—a "remarkable woman" we learn on the very first page of this story. Her quiet beauty is as spiritual as it is evidenced physically. Efuru herself has the qualities that the textual events and linguistic structures of the novel evidence. When her daughter Ogonim dies, the narrative pulls us relentlessly into the sorrow of that moment. We feel, with Efuru, that the occasion will surely be the end of her. Yet, she gathers her spiritual energy and forces herself out of her depression, moving closer to intimacy with the goddess. It is Efuru who is called upon to help the sick and to give advice. She becomes the center of the women's community in the way that the goddess centers the community's indigenous spiritual lives. At this point, Efuru's decision to dedicate herself to the service of this goddess, even in the midst of her marriage to Gilbert (Eneberi), articulates her intense dedication to the centering womanspirit that the childless goddess represents. Both the Lady and Efuru were happy, wealthy, beautiful, and childless. But Efuru's understanding that the goddess could not assure her children (because She "has not got children herself") marks her dependence on the womanspirit she has nurtured and developed throughout her life (208).

At the point that she disconnects the goddess from her wishful thinking about motherhood, Efuru decides that "she was growing logical in her reasoning. She thought it unusual for women to be logical. Usually, intuition did their reasoning for them" (208). Ironically, her intuition warns her on the occasion of their daughter's birth that the experience would be radically different from her expectations. So this display of re-visioned logic is related to her intuitive dream of Uhamiri. In this dream, Efuru "had never seen [H]er look so beautiful before." The beauty of Efuru's now logical intuition (her spirit) is reinforced by her dream of the goddess' loveliness. Each becomes the other's spiritual/physical Other. As the representative of the best aspects of the spiritual Uhamiri and as an ideal of modern womanhood, *Efuru* as a praisesong raises a dimension of creativity rarely revealed in West African literature critical of women's lives.

Because, like the language of *Efuru,* the language of *Beloved* is song, dialogue, monologue, incantation, and prayer, both novels create a chorus of black voices. In *Beloved,* Ella leads a gathering of women whose merged voices become "just sound"—a purity that enables the incantatory words in this work to gain meaning, power, and form. As a spiritual, *Beloved* is emblematic of the antithetical call of those early African-American songs that have their origins in the praisesongs of Africa.

Sethe, whose name ironically is like "Lethe," the river of forgetfulness, is the teller of this story.[13] She is forced to remember her daughter's death in a cruel recursion—her grief comes to have form and dangerous presence. Some comfort comes from her mother-in-law, Baby Suggs, whose own frustrated procreation (her sons have been unaccounted for after slavery, her grandchildren tragically killed or left) Morrison symbolically renders her grief as a frustrated and fractured creativity. Baby Sugg's final months are spent "pondering color"—a careful, fragmented consideration of the pieces of light (4). Understanding that death is "anything but forgetfulness," she prepares herself for the memory that the spirit-child Beloved suffers (4). When Baby Suggs dies, Sethe and her daughter Denver are alone with the presence of Beloved, until Paul D. from Sweet Home arrives and challenges the ephemeral spirit into its powerful and eventually malevolent manifestation.

Because origin and source are thematic issues in this novel, we must acknowledge the interpretive significance of Beloved as not only Sethe's dead daughter returned, but the return of all the (African) faces, all the drowned, (re)membered faces of mothers and their children who lost their being because of the force of Euro-American slave history. Beloved becomes a cultural mooring place, a moment for reclamation and for naming. Morrison's epigraph to her novel recalls the text of the Old Testament: "I will call her Beloved who was not Beloved." Beloved insists that she needs "to find a place to be." Her being depended on not losing her self again. "Call me my name," she insists to Paul D. She demands to be removed from her nothingness, to be "called," to be specified (117).

Mothering and Wholeness ▲

In Nwapa's *Idu*, there is a reflection on the issue of motherhood and birth. Idu suspects that "when a woman is good, God, our ancestors, and the Woman of the Lake all look at her stomach, not at her head, but at her stomach" (42). Consider the psychic fracture this separation underscores. Idu feels that her entire cultural community dissects her. Wholeness is the sacrifice of motherhood.

This sense of fracture informs Nwapa's creative revisioning of motherhood. The contradictory, layered, and plurisignant tones of her first novel (*Efuru*) lead to the literary climax of *Idu*, her second novel.[14] Even though Nwapa's struggle to assert the vitality of the truly engaged feminine principle of creativity is the essence of *Efuru*, Idu's reflection and resolution testify to the overwhelming significance of biological motherhood in all aspects of African traditional life. The important deities, the ancestors, and the supreme god all look at a woman's stomach as a means of rewarding goodness. Idu's lament, that they ignore her knowledge (her head), articulates her frustration over the consequences of childbirth and motherhood in her community. The ambivalence is clear in the themes of *Idu* and *Efuru*; but *Idu* speaks directly to the dire consequences of womanspirit denied. The novel's conclusion specifies the pathos of its thesis. It is also an illustration of a recursive text. Idu tragically summons her spiritual energy, wills herself dead and follows the husband to whom she had devoted her life to the spirit realm. Only her child Ijoma is left. She decides that the child she is carrying will not be born, which is a declaration of control over the childbirth issue. Finally in control of her spiritual life, Idu chooses death and relinquishes motherhood in a pitiful claim of self-determination.

In a reflection on the metaphors of birth like those figured in *Idu* and *Efuru*, Morrison has labeled mother-love as "a killer." In a *New York Times* essay where she discussed the writing of *Beloved*, she noted how mother-love displaces the self: "The precious interior, the loved self, whatever that is, whatever vocabulary you ascribe to it, is suppressed or displaced and put someplace else. . . . It's always something other that is more valuable, more beautiful, more wonderful than the self—that's too bad, but that's the horns of that dilemma." [15] Thwarted by something like slavery, mother-love is daemonic.

In *Beloved*, Morrison has written a tragedy of mother-love denied and has revealed its consequence. Sethe, who has lost one daughter to infanticide and whose sons have run away (afraid of the ghostly presence that haunts their house), is vulnerable to the killing spirit of her dead daughter. It is a tragedy complicated by history, and Morrison's claiming the language of that intangible memory dissolves her narrative into the voices of the three women whose stories connect and sustain each other's living and dying. Sethe's monologue claims that she can "sleep like the drowned," but sleep allows the "sixty million and more" access. Beloved, who is full of the memory of those millions of faces that are like hers, fights not to "lose her [mother] again." Chewing and swallowing, she is devoured and re-membered by the strength of Sethe's insistent, killing mother-love (215). Denver is afraid that the event that seemed to suspend "ethical" conduct and that allowed her mother to kill her sister could again threaten them. Or worse, that perhaps there is something else in their world "terrible enough to make her do it again." She is torn between love and survival which are mutually exclusive in her decentered universe because she is the daughter of a slave.

Wholeness is an irrelevancy in these lives. Love and survival simply cannot exist on the same plane in this alternative universe. Consider how the reproductive effort of women in West Africa collects cultural experiences like the pain of a clitoridectomy; the loneliness of being given away (or giving away one's daughter) as a servant to a family of greater means; and the acquiescence to the nearly disabling notion that a child is likely to die before she reaches her first birthday. These are the kinds of tragedies Nwapa's women experience—sometimes with disarming casualness. Nwapa nonetheless refuses her reader this casual distance. In her insistence that talk dominate the text, the reader's implicit dialogic involvement makes us complicitous with the fragmented worlds of her literary mothers.

In a pre-vision of the issue of Morrison's *Beloved*, where a devouring mother-love eats away at a mother's own "best-self" (her individual spirit), Nwapa's work reflects the spiritual costliness of motherhood—the most significant standard by which Efuru's traditional Igbo community measures success. In deference to this implacable measure, motherhood is the only position which Efuru does not achieve. Even though her community does envy her idyllic marriage with Gilbert, her financial success, her beauty, and her (seeming) contentment, their admiration is always accompanied by the ultimate qualifier—she is no one's mother. We almost suspect that if she were, the wholeness that seems to govern her life would be disrupted and the community's women could better identify with her as their comrade in the everyday trauma their mothering endures. However, Efuru has had some experience with the world she simply chooses to abandon. The death of her daughter, Ogonim, realizes her pre-vision on the occasion of her daughter's birth that she has not really had a child at all, but that she is instead enmeshed in some sort of dream. In an effort to suggest that her intuitive judgment (her head) may indeed have more potential than the biological event, Nwapa rewards her intuition by designating Efuru as the extension of this Woman of the Lake, the goddess the villagers revere across generations and regardless of Her maternity.

Worship, reverence, and respect are earned by the thoughtful, empathetic ministrations of Efuru to everyone in need throughout the story. Whether or not the tangential theme of her marrying, becoming pregnant, and losing both the child and her two husbands dominates the events of this text, the constant thread that organizes these events is the development of Efuru's generous spirit and the subsequent respect that all who meet her come to feel for her consistent caring and magnaminity. Ironically, Efuru's mothering of the sick, the village children, and the poor is never perceived as being equivalent to the biological motherhood it represents; but Ajanupu does call her a "woman among women" and her elevated status and spiritual loveliness represent the significant achievement of Nwapa's novel (107).

In a recursive acquiescence to the theme of motherhood, the Woman of the Lake, who has no children, has Efuru as her child; and Efuru, who has no child, evolves into the community's mothering spirit. Not until the end of this story do we appreciate the implicit revision of Efuru's spiritual beauty. Neither she nor the goddess is childless because each has birthed a creative extension that testifies to the creative and communal essence of gendered spirituality. She and the goddess are head children, the reformulated women whose stomach no longer centers their being or determines whether or not they are good.

In a tactic that dissembles the text, Nwapa makes the issue of contradicting complexities the single most important situation of the linguistic episodes that collect the events of this story. Morrison's style also privileges this episodic structure. The streaming linguistic madness of Pecola's monologue with herself in *The Bluest Eye* is like the eddying recollection of Beloved's monologue with her spiritual history. The symbols in color, the legacy of names enclosed and worn close to a body, the textural dependence on scents, food, and flowering trees are recalled to this story that alternates between Margaret Garner's historic presence and Toni Morrison's reconstruction of that presence. Because their lives are likely to be disabled by their (re)memories of their histories, or their lost, killed children, these are a fragile people.

Ironically, as disruptive of the illusory wholeness the community of newly freed slaves tries to maintain in Morrison's novel is, mediation sustains the text and rescues it from the formlessness of illusion. Even the historic present in *Beloved* masks the story, making it seem as if it will be a survival story. The traditions of shift and inversion in the black text warn us of this mask.[16] The fact that the story centers on spiritual *presence* rather than the historic *present* is critical to the construction and perception of this story. The participants themselves are (or should be) suspect. What kind of community can be formed by a mother who cannot account for the sons she birthed during slavery, a daughter-in-law who has killed one of her children, various slaves from a plantation sardonically named "Sweet Home" and newly freed slaves from other plantations? The constructs of community—children, homes, stability and potential—are all brittle here. These fragmented gatherers carry with them the grievous loads of their (re)memories. Ghosts run rampant throughout this community and become what they are supposed to be—spirits who embody the legacies of all those who have preceded them and who are weighted with the burdens of the destructive history of slavery.

Places of the Spirit ▲

In "Toward the Solstice," Adrienne Rich questions the language she should use to speak to "the spirits that claim a place" in her house. These spirits ("tenants") pull her into their places until she experiences their essence. The experience results in her feeling "ghosted" by their ephemeral presence.[17] When spirits "claim a place," there is a simultaneous disruption of the spaces occupied by others. This kind of spiritual sharing is almost an act of effacement because their essence dissolves into the Other until their shared nature characterizes them. When Morrison's spirit-child claims her space, it is not only the dimensions of being that Beloved inhabits, it is dimensionality itself.

Because history disables human potential, then assertiveness, the ghostly insistence that Rich writes of in "Solstice," comes from outside of history. Beloved's existence is liminal. Between worlds, without a past or a present, she is a confrontation of a killing history and a disabling present. Since neither aspect allows the kind of life a post-emancipation black community would have imagined for itself (because at the very least, "not a house in the county ain't packed to the rafters with some dead Negro's grief"), *Beloved* is a text that collects textures of living and dying (5). Morrison has written novels marked by seasons (*The Bluest Eye*) and years (*Sula*), but this story is marked by the shifting presence of a house, number 124 on Bluestone Road— introduced in book one as "spiteful," in book two as "loud," and in book three, finally, as "quiet." This shift allows the focus of the novel to ignore the possible frames of time. Neither distance nor years mattered to the place on Bluestone Road where Beloved insisted herself back into reality. For Sethe, "the future was a matter of keeping the past at bay" (42). Since this story (not a story to "pass on") demystifies time, allowing it to be where/whenever it must be, we prepare for absence—neither future nor present exists in the woman who walked fully dressed out of the water. The community she enters is already constantly threatened by the psychological and spiritual accompaniment of its history. When it materializes before them, in the form of Beloved, the weight is unbearable.

There is a similar form of memory in *Efuru*. Here, the villagers are responsible for the culture's stories (although they often abrogate this responsibility), assuring their reflection in the culture's values. No words in Nwapa's text are more prophetic than those spoken by the anonymous voices of the village farmers. Ironically, they predict the revision that asserts the feminine principle of the text. "You would think the woman of the lake is her mother" is a villager's assessment of Efuru's presence (8). Yet not one of them is willing to graciously affirm the value of this relationship.

In much the same way that Hurston's Janie serves to illumine her friend Phoeby's uneventful life, Nwapa's Efuru acts as a vessel that gathers up all the community's best hopes and most satisfied dreams and mirrors them in the potential of her own life.[18] In these works, attentiveness to one's self as a way of strenthening the community is synonymous with accepting one's innerspirit as a personal commitment of a communal myth. Because Efuru willingly assumes this commitment, it is incorrect to interpret her questions regarding the source of the reverence and respect directed towards Uhamiri as an indication of her doubt regarding the choice she has made. After all, they are essentially no different from the warnings that the village gossip Omirima expresses to Efuru's mother-in-law, Ajanupu. Upon hearing this gossip, Ajanupu laments that Efuru has "spoilt everything. How many women in this town who worship Uhamiri have children?" (203). Since it is clear to everyone in the village that women who have devoted themselves to this goddess cease having children or have no children at all, Efuru cannot have made an uninformed choice. In addition, her mother-in-law reveals that "she was not consulted" in Efuru's decision to accept the call of the deity. Such a betrayal of custom—failure to consult elders in a choice that is of such social importance—further argues for the deliberateness in Efuru's decision to pull her life in a direction away from motherhood.

Place is not merely the geographic space that the community inhabits, but place, as both Morrison's and Nwapa's novels indicate, can be the places of the spirit. When this is so, the community in these works has a specific role in voicing the traditions that may be challenged by the text. There is a great deal of attention focused on cultural traditions in black women's texts. It is almost as if this collocation of mores will serve to contrast whatever the spirit challenges. In *Efuru,* the story's drama reaches a metaphysical peak as we understand Nwapa's interest in revealing the complexity of women's lives. Variously confronted with the expectations of traditional beliefs—("I washed Ogonim's corpse and dressed her . . . If I don't wash my hands very well, I shall forget things easily" [93]); of customary practice ("we don't ask people how may children they have. It is not done" [34]); of the reality of encroaching modernism on village life (Onitsha market, once an area where social and moral norms could be reinforced, had become a terrible place); of the conflict of biological motherhood versus other kinds of blessings ("We are not going to eat happy marriage. Marriage must be fruitful. . . . Of what use is it if your husband licks your body, worships you and buys everything . . . for you and you are not productive?" [171]); and of the omnipresent spiritual and ancestral worlds and their traditions—the text indicates how Efuru's choice is at least partially due to the thickness of her role as a woman in an Igbo community. In order to indicate this density, structures characteristic of shift are foregrounded and rearrange two critical dimensions of Efuru's life—her motherhood and her spirituality.

Because of the contrast between spiritual and geographic places, and cultural and gendered spheres, Beloved's insistence on a space for her essence rather than a presence in the temporal life and death cycle is a critical indicator of the literature in this tradition. Beloved insists "I am not dead. I am not . . . I am where she told me." It is as if Sethe's telling, her voice, has assured Beloved her essence. Death loses its permanence in such a voiced universe. The essence of Beloved's presence is Sethe's (re)membrance of her.

The struggle of the community to assert its place in the days following emancipation is filtered through the experiences of Sethe, Denver, and Beloved. Like Efuru, Sethe experiences ostracism—the unspeakable act that frames her entrance into their tenuously structured community fractures the semblance of normalcy they strive to maintain. Her daughter is also on the fringes of the community, and of sanity. Denver seeks shelter throughout the novel because she cannot endure the fluctuating presence of a house whose spite, noise, and calm nurture the spirit of her dead sister. She uses the "emerald closet" of the woods as her escape (she "smelled like bark in the day and leaves at night" [19]). The bower of trees she looks to for escape is unlike the chokecherry-like sketch of scars on her mother's back from the slaver's whip, but is like the ancient serene daisy trees on Isle des Chevaliers (*Tar Baby*) or the willowy Pilate (*Song of Solomon*) whose connection to things past is protective and sheltering. What finally shelters Denver, however, what finally saves them all from the life-draining power of Beloved's insistent spirit, is the shelter she seeks from the women in the community.

Ella's gathering of women uses a collective belief to go "back to a beginning of sound" and send the aberrant spirit-child back to its own (261). Sethe and Beloved, who are in the house, are startled to find the community's women gathered in the road. There are thirty of them, who are either gazing at the sky or have their eyes closed. Sight and vision are sublimated for this moment when the sound of their voices must heal the malevolence that threatens their community: "The voices of women searched for the right combination, the key, the code, the sound that broke the back of words. Building voice upon voice until they found it . . . a wave of sound wide enough to sound deep water . . . broke over Sethe and she trembled like the baptized in its wash" (261).

Although a gathering of women in these works testifies to the strength of traditions, the appropriateness of certain behaviors and the strict limitations of women's roles, it is also evidence of their lack of control over the dimensions of their own lives. In this way, Nwapa's talking books are subversive texts. The preponderance of talk in her works overwhelms the reader with the chorus of claims that women rightfully have about the abuse and decentering of their spirits. A single voice could not have accomplished this. A tragically tainted individual voice that bewailed women's place could not have had the same effect as the collected voice of the "people" who shout to Efuru telling her "Kneel down, kneel down, you are a woman" during the ritual drinking of palm wine to celebrate the giving of bride price (23). The layered voices of aunts, mothers, sisters, friends, and neighbors—the significant others of *Efuru*—testify with overwhelming evidence to the lack of control women have at the very moments they feel they are assertive and decisive. This recursive text reaches its spiritual dimension through the juxtaposition of choral voices and the tragedies they specify.

With the emphasis on collectivity, Nwapa's focus on her title character seems to be an aberration. It is not. Lloyd Brown perceptively anticipates that the Western reader's reaction to texts with "name titles" may be to expect a "study of the individual." Instead, Brown argues that *Efuru,* like other African novels, is a "reenactment of the relationship between individual and community. . . . the Nwapa heroine is . . . crucial as the main focus of her community's attention." [19] Nwapa's re-visioned folkstory overwhelmingly emphasizes Efuru's empathy and goodness in the face of the tragic loss of her daughter and the physical and emotional desertion of her two husbands. It is a consequence of Nwapa's vision that Efuru's told story would be a praisesong—a communal celebration of womanspirit in the most literal sense of this word.

The effort that Denver makes in Morrison's *Beloved* to wrest control of her life back into a tangible dimension is equally indicative of the effort that moors the metaphorical dimensions of black women's texts. Denver tells what Beloved is, knowing that "nobody was going to help her unless she told it" (253). She chooses to tell her story to a woman both who understood the rage that prompted Sethe's violent choice and who resented the invasion of this killing as an act that sucks away at the effort of life. Ella gathers the community's women outside of Sethe's house in response to Denver's attestation. Telling was a means of enabling the creative convention of women's voices who gathered on Bluestone Road. Just as important, telling is testimony that recenters the spirits of women, mythic and ancestral, into places where their passionate articulation assures them that neither geography nor history can separate them from the integrity of the essential Word.

▲▲▲▲▲▲▲▲▲▲▲▲▲▲▲▲▲▲▲▲▲▲▲▲▲▲▲▲▲▲▲▲▲▲▲▲▲▲▲

Notes

Introduction. Cultural Moorings and Spiritual Metaphors

1. Ntozake Shange, *for colored girls who have considered suicide/when the rainbow is enuf* (New York: Macmillan, 1977), 36.

2. In this book I limit my discussion of African women writers to contemporary writers of West Africa. The history of the slave trade makes it more likely that these countries would share cultural metaphors with the women of the diaspora. The similarity between their selection and use of the metaphor of the goddess and the ancestral metaphor used by black women writers of the diaspora is significant to literary and cultural studies.

3. The literary significance of the call and response tradition in black orature has received much attention. See, e.g., Keith Byerman's discussion of the folk basis of this tradition and its literary reconfigurations in his book, *Fingering the Jagged Grain: Tradition and Form in Recent Black Fiction* (Athens: University of Georgia Press, 1985); and John Callahan, *In the African-American Grain: The Pursuit of Voice in Twentieth-Century Black Fiction* (Urbana: University of Illinois Press, 1988). Callahan's work benefits from the earlier and more theoretical work of Robert Stepto, *From Behind the Veil: A Study of Afro-American Narrative* (Urbana: University of Illinois Press, 1979).

4. D. G. Ritchie and Jefferson Davis are quoted in Sidney Wilhelm, "Racism in the Age of Equality: The Constitutional Dimension," in *Assessment of the Status of African-Americans,* ed. Wornie L. Reed (Boston: William Monroe Trotter Institute/University of Massachusetts, 1989), 64.

5. For a critique of the language and methodology of criticism, see Barbara Christian, "The Race for Theory," *Feminist Studies* 14, no. 1 (Spring 1988): 67–80; and Barbara Smith, "Toward a Black Feminist Criticism," and Deborah McDowell, "New Directions for Black Feminist Criticism," both in *The New Feminist Criticism: Essays on Women, Literature, and Theory*, ed. Elaine Showalter (New York: Pantheon, 1985), 168–185, esp. 174, and 186–199, esp. 187, respectively.

6. A debate concerning the language of contemporary criticism and the membership of the interpretive community can be found in *New Literary History* 18, no. 2 (Winter 1987); e.g. essays by Joyce Ann Joyce, "The Black Canon: Reconstructing Black American Literary Criticism" (335–344) and "Who the Cap Fit: Unconsciousness and Unconscionableness in the Criticism of Houston Baker and Henry Louis Gates" (371–383); Henry Louis Gates, Jr., "What's Love Got to Do with It?" (345–362); and Houston Baker, "In Dubious Battle" (363–369). Kwame Anthony Appiah explores the racialist politics that instigate debates like the ones between Gates, Baker, and Joyce in "The Conservation of 'Race,'" *Black American Literature Forum* 23, no. 1 (Spring 1989): 37–60.

7. Smith, 174.

8. See Mary Helen Washington, ed., *Midnight Birds: Stories of Contemporary Black Women Writers* (New York: Anchor/Doubleday, 1980); Hortense Spillers, "The Politics of Intimacy: A Discussion," in *Sturdy Black Bridges: Visions of Black Women in Literature*, ed. Roseann P. Bell et al. (New York: Anchor/Doubleday, 1979), 88; Dianne Sadoff, "Black Matrilineage: The Case of Alice Walker and Zora Neale Hurston," *Signs* 11, no. 1 (Autumn 1985): 4–26; and Mae Gwendolyn Henderson, "Speaking in Tongues: Dialogics, Dialectics, and the Black Woman Writer's Literary Tradition," in *Changing Our Own Words: Essays on Criticism, Theory, and Writing by Black Women*, ed. Cheryl Wall (New Brunswick, N. J.: Rutgers University Press, 1989), 16–37.

9. Chinua Achebe, *Things Fall Apart* (London: Heinemann, 1958).

10. Wole Soyinka, *Season of Anomy* (London: Rex Collings, 1973).

11. Al Young, *Seduction by Light* (New York: Dell, 1988).

12. Ibid., 211, 212.

13. Richard Perry, *Montgomery's Children* (New York: New American Library, 1984), 208.

14. Ernest Gaines, *In My Father's House* (New York: Norton, 1978); and Ayi Kwei Armah, *Why Are We So Blest?* (London: Heinemann, 1974).

15. Wole Soyinka, *The Interpreters* (London: Heinemann, 1974), 9.

16. Leroi Jones, *The System of Dante's Hell* (New York: Grove, 1965), 7.

17. James Baldwin, *Go Tell It on the Mountain* (New York: Alfred A. Knopf, 1953).

18. James Baldwin, *The Fire Next Time* (New York: Dial, 1963), 30.

19. David Bradley, *The Chaneysville Incident* (New York: Avon, 1981).

20. For a cogent and thorough discussion of this novel, see Klaus Ensslen, "Fictionalizing History: David Bradley's *The Chaneysville Incident*," *Callaloo* 11, no. 2 (Spring 1988): 289–296, esp. 286.

21. Bradley, 450.

Chapter 1. Voice, Gender, and Culture

1. Ntozake Shange, *Sassafrass, Cypress and Indigo* (New York: St. Martin's Press, 1982).

2. Ibid., 3.

3. See, for example, Morgan Dalphinis, *Caribbean and African Languages: Social History, Language, Literature, and Education* (London: Karia Press, 1985); J. L. Dillard, *Black English: Its History and Usage in the United States* (New York: Random House, 1972); and Uriel Weinreich, *Languages in Contact* (The Hague, Netherlands: Mouton and Co., 1968).

4. Lawrence Lipking, "Aristotle's Sister: A Poetics of Abandonment," in *Abandoned Women and the Poetic Tradition* (Chicago: University of Chicago Press, 1988), 209–228, esp. 210, 211.

5. Henry Louis Gates, Jr., "Criticism in the Jungle," in *Black Literature and Literary Theory* (New York: London, 1984), 4.

6. The majority of texts published in this area are anthologies of edited essays and do not attempt theoretical cohesiveness. These works underscore the serious interest in collecting essays on black women's literature but they are also a telling indication that sustained, book-length, theoretical inquiry does not (yet) characterize the study of this literature. A recent exception to this trend is Houston Baker's *Workings of the Spirit: The Poetics of Afro-American Women's Writing* (Chicago: University of Chicago Press, 1991). As Baker's work indicates, a change in the way scholars study black women's literature will occur over time. First, however, the industry that has opened the margins of published discourse in bits and pieces must allow academic and scholarly objectives to gain a hold over the gerrymandered spaces of critical inquiry. For a cogent and stunning presentation of this argument, see W. Lawrence Hogue, *Discourse and the Other: The Production of the African-American Text* (Durham, N. C.: Duke University Press, 1986).

Among recently edited collections are: Houston Baker, ed., *Black Literature in the 1990s* (Chicago: University of Chicago Press, 1990); Joanne Braxton and Andrée McLaughlin, eds., *Wild Women in the Whirlwind: Afra-American Culture and the Contemporary Literary Renaissance* (New Brunswick, N. J.: Rutgers University Press, 1989); and Wall, ed. (intro., n. 8 above). See also Barbara Christian, *Black Feminist Criticism* (New York: Pergamon, 1985); Mari Evans, ed., *Black Women Writers 1950–1980: The Development of a Tradition* (New York: Anchor Press, 1984); Carol Boyce Davies and Anne Adams Graves, eds., *Ngambika: Studies of Women in African Literature* (New York: Africa World Press, 1986); and Lloyd Brown, *Women Writers in Black Africa* (Westport, Conn.: Greenwood Press, 1981).

7. Ishmael Reed, "Can a Metronome Know the Thunder or Summon a God?" in *The Black Aesthetic*, ed. Addison Gayle, Jr. (Garden City, N.Y.: Anchor Books, 1972), 382.

8. Benvenuto Cellini, from *The Autobiography*, in *Renaissance*, ed. Edward Weatherly (New York: Dell, 1962), 246–249.

9. In traditional Africa, women preserved ancestry through their verbal archives. For example, praisesongs, eulogies, ballads, and myths were all part

of women's verbal litanies of their cultures. See, e.g., Deirdre La Pin, "Women in African Literature," in *African Women South of the Sahara,* ed. Margaret Jean Hay and Sharon Stichter (New York: Longman, 1984), 102–118; and Ruth Finnegan, *Oral Literature in Africa* (New York: Oxford University Press, 1970).

10. See Gates's discussion in his *Figures in Black* (New York: Oxford University Press, 1987), esp. 249. I discuss the "speakerly text" in chapter 4, "The Word Assumes its Raiment," of Karla F. C. Holloway, *The Character of the Word: The Texts of Zora Neale Hurston* (Westport, Conn.: Greenwood Press, 1987), 47–73.

11. Gates, *Figures in Black,* 249.

12. Gates, "Criticism in the Jungle," 12.

13. Eshu was a linguist for the sky god, Olorun, an orisha of Yoruban mythology. His linguistic capability is more extensive and significant than that of translator, for he was also a mischievous orisha of chance and unpredictability. Gates has settled upon this character (Esu) as "the metaphor for the critical activity of interpretation" in the black text. Although I defer to the excellence of his choosing a linguistic trickster as a critical metaphor, it is a signifyin(g) choice as well because Eshu, whom Gates understates as a "phallic god of generation and fecundity," is known to stir up some significant mess because of his sexual misconduct. One Yoruba legend explains that he has been exiled from people's houses because of his "propensity for sexual exploits, for creating chaos, and for generally offending social sensibilities." See Harold Courlander, *Tales of Yoruba Gods and Heroes* (New York: Crown Publishers, 1973), 181–182. Gates's *The Signifying Monkey: A Theory of Afro-American Literary Criticism* (New York: Oxford University Press, 1988), does deal with the sexuality of Es(h)u; see esp. 26–30 on Es(h)u as a "copulating copula."

14. See Julia Kristeva, "Revolution in Poetic Language," in *The Kristeva Reader,* ed. Toril Moi (New York: Columbia University Press, 1986), 90–136.

15. Toni Morrison, *Beloved* (New York: Alfred A. Knopf, 1987), 16, 17.

16. See Hélène Cixous, "The Laugh of the Medusa," in *New French Feminisms: An Anthology,* ed. E. Marks and I. de Courtivron (New York: Schocken, 1981), 245, 256; Luce Irigaray, *This Sex Which Is Not One,* trans. Catherine Porter with Caroline Burke (Ithaca, N.Y.: Cornell University Press, 1985); and Hélène Cixous and Catherine Clément, *The Newly Born Woman,* trans. Betsy Wing (Minneapolis: University of Minnesota Press, 1986).

17. Mary Poovey, "Feminism and Deconstruction," *Feminist Studies* 14, no. 1 (Spring 1988): 51–66, esp. 56.

18. Christian's discussion in "African Women Writers vs. Illich," in her work *Black Feminist Criticism* (n. 6 above), 124, is largely political theory rather than literary theory possibly because it was initially written for a symposium that addressed Ivan Illich's conclusions about women's place in society and his concepts of gender. Her critical posture in this essay addresses women's literature as sociopolitical empowerment. A facet of her argument that is relevant to the discussion of feminist criticism and the African woman writer is her comment that there are versions of Western feminism that are ethnocentric (147).

19. Alice Walker, *The Color Purple* (New York: Harcourt Brace Jovanovich, 1982), 3. Some (representative) essays and reviews that excoriated Walker and her book are: Richard Barksdale, "Castration Symbolism in Recent Black American Fiction," *College Language Association Journal* 29, no. 4 (June 1986): 400–413; E. R. Shipp, "Blacks in Heated Debate over 'The Color Purple,'" *New York Times* (January 27, 1986); and David Bradley, "Telling the Black Woman's Story," *New York Times Magazine* (January 1984), 34.

The attacks on this book (and the film) relate to the efforts to control the image of black males in American society. They are a response to the negative images that permeate the public domain. I cannot argue against the evidence that black males are among the most vulnerable to the institutions of racism in this country. However, I believe that the agenda of control (and the consequential anger when the image is out-of-control) is a remnant of the 1960s civil rights movement when black males did exert their control both over the vision this country had of blackness and over women in the movement who were to stand (silently) alongside the revolutionary brother-leaders. Realism in portraiture is not the current issue now any more than it was then. Black women's vocal assertiveness threatens to remove the veil over intrafamilial struggle, to draw attention to women in order to regather the fractured women's community, and to rearticulate the place of the black community in America *through women's words*. Each of these behaviors flaunts the ethical legacy of the 1960s revolution: to protect the community's integrity by masking the community's identity, to define the community as indivisible, and to take the English word "spokesmen" quite literally. My sense is that the remnants of this subliminal ethic instigate the attack on black women writers' voices as if they were a threat to community.

20. Carol Boyce Davies, "Motherhood in the Works of Male and Female Igbo Writers: Achebe, Emecheta, Nwapa, and Nzekwu," in Davies and Graves, eds. (n. 6 above), 243.

21. Buchi Emecheta, *The Joys of Motherhood* (New York: George Braziller, 1979), 222; Toni Morrison, *The Bluest Eye* (New York: Washington Square Press, 1970); Zora Neale Hurston, *Their Eyes Were Watching God* (1937; reprint, Urbana: University of Illinois Press, 1978), 92, 286.

22. Davies, "Introduction," in Davies and Graves, eds., 16.

23. James A. Snead, "Repetition as a Figure of Black Culture," in *Black Literature and Literary Theory*, ed. Henry L. Gates, Jr. (New York: Methuen, 1984), 59–79, cites Hegel's "first and still most penetratingly systematic definition by a European of the 'African character'" in order to indicate how the distinctions by which Hegel "had seemed to define [African cultures'] nonexistence . . . may now be valued as positive terms, given a revised metaphysics of rupture and opening" (62–63).

24. Gabriel Setiloane, *African Theology* (Johannesburg: Skotaville Publishers, 1986), 9.

25. See Dalphinis's discussion of audience participation in oral literature (n. 3 above). Zora Neale Hurston gives examples of formulaic story structures in *Mules and Men* (Bloomington: Indiana University Press, 1978).

26. Buchi Emecheta, *The Rape of Shavi* (New York: George Braziller, 1985).

27. Jean Miller, *Toward a New Psychology of Women* (Boston: Beacon Press, 1976), 83.

28. Poovey, 60.

29. Davies, "Motherhood" (n. 20 above), 252.

30. Davies's discussion of a distinction between personhood and mother-hood is uncomfortably close to Western notions of feminist individuation. Her argument in the Introduction to Davies and Graves, eds. (n. 6 above), about the preoccupation of motherhood in African women writers' texts, is a clue that there may be some need to reevaluate this somewhat pejorative use of "preoccupation" and to look at existence and motherhood outside of the valuations of Western feminism.

31. Flora Nwapa, *Efuru* (London: Heinemann, 1966), 281.

32. Toni Cade Bambara, "Commitment," in Bell et al., eds. (intro., n. 8), 236.

33. Toni Morrison, *Song of Solomon* (New York: Alfred A. Knopf, 1977), 337.

34. Gwendolyn Brooks, *Maud Martha,* in her *Blacks* (Chicago: David Co., 1987), 141–322, esp. 200.

35. Mary Helen Washington, "Taming All That Anger Down," in Gates, ed., *Black Literature and Literary Theory* (n. 5 above), 252.

36. Hurston, *Their Eyes Were Watching God* (n. 21 above), 119.

37. Ibid., 286.

38. Gayl Jones, *Corregidora* (1975; reprint, Boston: Beacon Press, 1986).

39. Holloway (n. 10 above).

40. Barbara Johnson, "Thresholds of Difference," in *"Race," Writing and Difference,* ed. Henry Louis Gates, Jr. (Chicago: University of Chicago Press, 1986), 328.

41. Ibid., 328. See also my discussion in chapter five of *The Character of the Word* on resolving the seeming structural dissimilarities of *Their Eyes Were Watching God.*

42. Jean Toomer, *Cane* (New York: Boni and Liveright, 1923).

Chapter 2. Novel Politics of Literary Interpretation

1. Milan Kundera, *The Art of the Novel* (New York: Grove Press, 1986), 120–153, esp. 122.

2. Appiah (intro., n. 6), 38.

3. Octavia Butler, *Adulthood Rites* (New York: Warner Books, 1989).

4. Appiah, 56.

5. Stanley Fish, "Change," *South Atlantic Quarterly* 86, no. 4 (Fall 1987): 424–425.

6. Mikhail Bakhtin, *Problems of Dostoevsky's Poetics,* trans. R. W. Rotsel (Ann Arbor, Mich.: Ardis, 1973), 150–151. Bakhtin, in noting that the juxtaposition of words in a polyphonic text (such as Dostoevsky's or the multiplied and

layered texts of African and African-American writers) insists that "the dialogical angle cannot be measured by means of purely linguistic criteria. . . .
dialogical relationships are, then, extra-linguistic phenomena. But they must
not be separated from the province of the word" (150–151).

7. Caryl Emerson, "Outer Word and Inner Speech," in *Bakhtin: Essays and
Dialogues on His Work*, ed. Gary Saul Morson (Chicago: University of Chicago
Press, 1981), 23.

8. Bakhtin, 72. Bakhtin's view of the word calls into consideration the
premises of a theory of the communal rather than the individuated word.
Bakhtin's commentary here (on Dostoevsky) notes that the idea is "not a subjective individual-psychological formulation. . . . The idea is interindividual
and intersubjective. The sphere of its existence is not the individual consciousness, but the dialogical intercourse between consciousnesses" (72). Because
the idea is related to the word, this formulation is another expression of the
multivocalic (polyphonic) text.

9. The double vision of the black text is an African dimension of the text,
historically related to the multiple voices of the tradition of orature in African
literatures, specifically the tradition of call and response. This aspect of the
black text is further evidence of its intimacy with the spirit of a community.
The text's communal voice is a pattern that is present in black musical traditions as well as black literary traditions.

10. Françoise Lionnet, *Autobiographical Voices: Race, Gender, and Self-
Portraiture* (Ithaca, N. Y.: Cornell University Press, 1989), 8, 29.

11. Toni Morrison, *Sula* (New York: Alfred A. Knopf, 1974), 93.

12. As quoted in Kimberly Benston, "Facing Tradition: Revisionary Scenes
in African American Literature," *PMLA* 105, no. 1 (January 1990): 98–109,
esp. 106.

13. Ibid., 107.

14. Tina McElroy Ansa, *Baby of the Family* (New York: Harcourt Brace Jovanovich, 1989), 38, 9.

15. Alice Walker, *The Temple of My Familiar* (New York: Harcourt Brace Jovanovich, 1989).

16. Buchi Emecheta, *Head Above Water* (London: Fontana, 1986), 6.

17. Morrison, *Song of Solomon* (chap. 1, n. 33), 312.

18. Alice Walker, *The Color Purple* (chap. 1, n. 19).

19. Benston, 105.

20. Terry Eagleton, *Literary Theory* (Minneapolis: University of Minnesota
Press, 1983), 215.

21. Jacques Derrida, as quoted in Michael Ryan, *Marxism and Deconstruction*
(Baltimore: Johns Hopkins University Press, 1982), 14.

22. Ngugi wa Thiong'o, *Decolonizing the Mind: The Politics of Language in
African Literature* (London: James Currey, 1986).

23. Rand Bishop, *African Literature, African Critics* (Westport, Conn.:
Greenwood, 1989), 60, 61.

24. Ibid.

25. See Henry Louis Gates, Jr., "Writing 'Race' and the Difference It
Makes," in *"Race," Writing and Difference* (chap. 1, n. 40), 1–20. His comment

was included as a personal aside in this essay: "I once thought it our [critics of black literature] most important gesture to master the canon of criticism, to imitate and apply it, but I now believe that we must turn to the black tradition itself to develop theories of criticism indigenous to our literatures" (13).

26. Christopher Miller, "Ethnicity and Ethics," *South Atlantic Quarterly* 87, no. 1 (Winter 1988): 75–108, esp. 78, 79. I am indebted here to Miller's dicussion because it has forced me to look more critically at the use of the term, "community." In the critical vocabulary of a black literary theory, community raises the issue of ethnicity, and therefore, generally acknowledges an ethic different from one easily supported by Western critical theory. This sense of a communal sharing of value and history is significantly different from a Marxist notion of class consciousness—one that denies cultural specificity and that labels anthropological (cultural) concerns as inappropriate to this sense of community. Interestingly, Miller notes that "from the perspective of anthropologically oriented criticism, the Marxist approach tends to project a Eurocentric paradigm onto Africa" (76). This tendency is sufficient rationale for distancing the anthropologists' query from a study of Third World literatures as well as introducing critical questions about Marxist readings of literatures of the Third World.

27. Morrison, "Rootedness: The Ancestor as Foundation," in Evans, ed. (chap. 1, n. 6), 344–345.

28. Joan Kelly, *Women, History, and Theory* (Chicago: University of Chicago Press, 1984), 61.

29. As quoted in Ryan, 72.

30. Lionnet, 30.

Chapter 3. Revision and (Re)membrance in Literature

1. See chapter four for a linguistic (and syntactically based) explanation. The distinction between syntactic and literary recursion is one of place. Although both are phenomena of linguistic deep structures, the locus for syntactic recursion lies within the grammatical structure of the text. Literary recursion resides in the interpretive (semantic) levels of the text.

2. I urge the reader to attend carefully to the distinction between a process of reflection (which projects an identical image) and a reflexive, mediative posture which has a depth and resonance not possible with mere reflection. Reflection is like the superficial image that Toni Morrison's Jadine (*Tar Baby* [New York: Alfred A. Knopf, 1981]) attempts to convey as she models the behaviors she has assumed from her Euro-American education. However, the reflexive posture that Jade attempts to avoid disturbs her dreams throughout the novel. Taunting, critical women—her cultural ancestors—permeate the depths of the cultural and gendered identity Jade neglects. The combination of these permits a text that is at once emblematic and interpretive of the culture it describes.

3. I use the term "plurisignation" in an effort to distinguish the idea of

multiple meanings from a text that is simply ambiguous. Rather than meaning only one or the other of these terms, plurisignance signals the simultaneous appearance of both multiple and ambiguous meanings in a text.

4. Gates, *Figures in Black* (chap. 1, no. 10), 128, 129.

5. Sandra Gilbert and Susan Gubar, *The Madwoman in the Attic: The Woman Writer and the Nineteenth-Century Literary Imagination* (New Haven, Conn.: Yale University Press, 1979), 50; and Addison Gayle, *The Black Aesthetic* (New York: Doubleday, 1972), 42. The question of identity (definition) is a central problematic to the interpretation of the aesthetic that monitors the canon. Gayle and feminist critics share a recognition of the hegemony of ethnocentrism and phallocentrism in narrowing the critical vision of literary canons.

6. One illustration of these assigned spaces is the space that seemed to be slotted for Valerie Smith's essay, "Gender and Afro-Americanist Literary Theory and Criticism," in Elaine Showalter's essay collection, *Speaking of Gender* (Boston: Routledge, Chapman and Hall, 1989). Smith's essay is the only one of fourteen that specifically addresses the issue of race and ethnicity (also the only one of the group not previously published in another journal or collection).

I am aware of the argument (see Henry Louis Gates, Jr. "Tell Me, Sir, . . . What is 'Black' Literature?" *PMLA* 105, no. 1 [January 1990]: 11–22) that the feminist movement has in fact assured a significant audience for black women authors and that women's studies has incorporated the "work and lives of black women as their subject matter in a manner unprecedented in the American academy" (Gates, 14). However, considering the history of silence and absence that existed in the academy before the women's studies publishing and research surge, establishing a precedent in the study of black women writers need not involve a massive movement in order to contrast with the energy directed toward this work by other segments of the academy. My sense is that women's studies still must be critical of its own tendency towards token acknowledgment of Third World women's cultures.

7. See Christopher Norris's essay, "Theory of Language and the Language of Literature," *Journal of Literary Semantics* 7, no. 2 (1978): 90–98, for a particularly cogent assessment of the complicated relationship between linguistics and literary criticism—a relationship that would force the issues of text toward concerns of discourse and grammar as well as meaning. Norris suggests that "literary language . . . throws a paradox into the received notions of normative grammar. Literature is thus transformed . . . to a central informative role in the more open, more speculative but at the same time more empirically adequate theory of language" (91).

8. Wahneema Lubiano, "Constructing and Reconstructing Afro-American Texts: The Critic as Ambassador and Referee," *American Literary History*, 1, no. 2 (Summer 1989): 432–447, 433.

9. Shange, *Sassafrass, Cypress, and Indigo* (chap. 1, no. 1), 81.

10. Brooks, *Maud Martha* (chap. 1, no. 34), 200–201.

11. Toni Morrison, *Beloved* (chap. 1, n. 15), 274.

12. Brooks, 212, 213.

13. Gloria Naylor, *The Women of Brewster Place* (New York: Penguin Books,

1983), 103. Interestingly, luminous moments in African-American women writers' texts are often accompanied by a visual translucence such that the textual language itself is a factor in the shimmering quality of the metaphorical intent. See chapter five for further textual illustrations of translucence that blend the rhetorical and metaphorical levels of text.

14. Flora Nwapa, *One Is Enough* (Enugu, Nigeria: Tana Press, 1984), 132.

15. Zora Neale Hurston, *Their Eyes Were Watching God* (chap. 1, n. 21); Efua Sutherland, "Edufa" (London: Longman, 1967); and Ama Ata Aidoo, *Our Sister Killjoy: Or, Reflections of a Black-Eyed Squint* (London: Longman, 1966). See chapter six for further discussion of this dimension of black women's writing.

16. This issue needs to be fully and thoroughly researched. The most basic parameters of the discussion, which are the only specifics I will raise here, seem to involve the privileged considerations of *act* (as opposed to *word*) in the works of black males. The result of such a concentration seems to be an emphasis on a visualization of behavior and being in their works rather than the emphasis on language and telling found in the works of women writers of the canon. See my comments in the introduction of "Cultural Moorings . . ." relevant to this difference.

17. Nwapa, *One Is Enough*, 107.

18. Christian (intro., n. 5), 68. Christian's essay bewails the lack of clarity in the critical enterprise. She argues that current analysis reveals a central inattentiveness to text. In addition she argues that this criticism is as "hegemonic as the world it attacks" (71). Christian's comments reduce valuable critical activity to a practical criticism and undermine the theoretical because it "has silenced many of us to the extent that some of us feel we can no longer discuss our own literature" (69). Ironically, Christian's protest against writers whose criticism ignored the Third World and continued to exert control over the Western world supports the argument for a textual exploration of the origins that frame and are identified by the literature of African and African-American women writers.

19. Christian, 68; Zora Neale Hurston, "Characteristics of Negro Expression," in *Negro: An Anthology*, ed. Nancy Cunard (New York: Frederick Ungar, 1934), 31.

20. Buchi Emecheta, *The Joys of Motherhood* (New York: George Braziller, 1979); and Chinua Achebe, *Things Fall Apart* (London: Heinemann, 1958).

21. Paul Ricoeur, "Hermeneutics: The Approaches to Symbol," in *Existential Phenomenology to Structuralism*, ed. Vernon Gras (New York: Dell, 1973), 88.

22. Byerman, (intro., n. 3), 276.

23. Morrison, *Beloved* (chap. 1, n. 15), 35–36.

24. Claudia Tate, "Reshuffling the Deck: Or, (Re)Reading Race and Gender in Black Women's Writing," *Tulsa Studies in Women's Literature* 7, no. 1 (Spring 1988): 119–132.

25. Ibid., 120.

26. Lillian Robinson, "Canon Fathers and Myth Universe," *New Literary History* 19, no. 1 (Autumn 1987): 23–35, esp. 32.

27. Ibid., 34.

28. Christoper Miller, "Theories of Africans: The Question of Literary Anthropology," in Gates, ed., *"Race," Writing, and Difference* (chap. 1, no. 40), 281–300, esp. 300.

Chapter 4. Revision and (Re)membrance in Language

1. Dalphinis (chap. 1, n. 3 above), 8.

2. Bonnie Barthold, *Black Time: Fiction of Africa, the Caribbean, and the United States* (New Haven, Conn.: Yale University Press, 1981), 10, 11.

3. Jonathan Culler, *On Deconstruction: Theory and Criticism after Structuralism* (Ithaca, N. Y.: Cornell University Press, 1982), 128, 129.

4. Alton Becker, "Language in Particular: A Lecture," in *Linguistics in Context: Connecting Observation and Understanding,* ed. Deborah Tannen (Norwood, N. J.: Ablex, 1988), 20.

5. Ama Ata Aidoo, "A Gift from Somewhere," in her *No Sweetness Here* (New York: Doubleday, 1970), 65–88, esp. 65. Note the second sentence's inversion of the adverbial phrase—"a long time ago."

6. Ibid., 88.

7. Benjamin Whorf, "A Hopi Consideration of the Universe," in *Language, Thought, and Reality: Selected Writings of Benjamin Lee Whorf,* ed. J. B. Carroll (Cambridge, Mass.: MIT Press, 1956).

8. See Gates, *Figures in Black* (chap. 1, n. 10), 242–245. Gates's discussion concerns the structures of signifying. These he explains as revisionist structures, but they can also be seen as structures of replication. Revision and repetition are, in the black literary tradition, not only complementary strategies, but interactive and self-referential.

9. The Western goal of achieving independence (individuation), is certainly antithetical to the African concept of communal responsibility and sense of belonging to a group. The individualistic and particularistic universe is a worldview generally not privileged within Third World cultures. However, it is a dominant view of correct or "normal" behavioral patterns in the Western world—even to the point of its imposition on Third World cultures that exist within the Western world. Gabriel Setiloane writes (chap. 1, n. 24) that "it needs to be stated clearly that the African sense of community extends far beyond the family, the clan or the tribe. Exclusion . . . is a foreign Western importation. It is this principle of inclusion rather than separation which accounts for the life together in community" (10).

10. Gates, *Figures in Black,* 178.

11. See Setiloane, 9–11.

12. Susan Willis, *Specifying: Black Women Writing the American Experience* (Madison: University of Wisconsin Press, 1987), 38.

13. See Holloway (chap. 1, n. 10).

14. See, e.g., the chapter seven discussion of the narrative directive in Morrison's *Beloved,* "this was not a story to pass on" (chap. 1, n. 15, 274–275).

15. Linguists and folklorists have a rich resource in the body of text emerg-

ing from rap music within black communities in the United States. The linguistic structuring of these poetic forms is very specific and obviously linked to the forms represented in ballads, praisesongs and archival records. Folklorists must examine the poetics of rap music for its connection to traditional constructs—aphorism and hero-making—of African-American poetry.

16. I am indebted to Abena Busia's discussion of logocentric vs. scriptocentric traditions in her essay, "Words Whispered over Voids: A Context for Black Women's Rebellious Voices in the Novel of the African Diaspora," in *Studies in Black American Literature: III*, ed. Joe Weixlmann and Houston A. Baker (Greenwood, Fla.: Penkevill Publishing Co., 1988), 1–41.

17. The word "say" is used as a recursive metaphor in *The Color Purple*. It represents the activity of talking; it signals declaration; it is an active verb in a text where women's activity is frustrated or denied.

18. See chapter six in Holloway for an extended discussion of this shift. Note that it has been mostly misunderstood in the critical commentary relevant to Hurston's *Their Eyes Were Watching God*, including that by Hurston's biographer, R. Hemenway.

19. As quoted in Susan Stewart, "Bakhtin's Anti-Linguistics," in Morson, ed. (chap. 2, n. 7), 53.

20. Ibid., 53.

21. Brown (chap. 1, n. 6), 137.

22. Buchi Emecheta, *Second-Class Citizen* (New York: George Braziller, 1973), 31.

23. Ibid.

24. Cixous and Clément (chap. 1, n. 16), 145.

25. Gayatri Spivak writes in the Foreword to her translation of the Bengali short story, "Draupadi," by Mahasveta Devi (*Writing and Sexual Difference*, ed. Elizabeth A. Abel [University of Chicago Press, 1982], 262): " I have suggested elsewhere that, when we wander out of our own academic and First World enclosure we share something like a relationship with [the village villain] Senanayak's doublethink. When we speak for ourselves, we urge with conviction: the personal is also political. For the rest of the world's women, the sense of whose personal micrology is difficult (though not impossible) for us to acquire, we fall back on a colonialist theory of most efficient information retrieval. We will not be able to speak to the women out there if we depend completely on conferences and anthologies by Western-trained informants. As I see their photographs in women's studies journals or on book jackets— indeed, as I look in the glass—it is Senanayak with his anti-Facist paperback that I behold. In inextricably mingling historico-political specificity with the sexual differential in a literary discourse, [the author] Mahasveta Devi invites us to begin effacing that image."

26. Bakhtin (chap. 2, n. 5), 88.

Chapter 5. Mythologies

1. Buchi Emecheta, *The Bride Price* (New York: George Braziller, 1976), 7, 168.

2. Gloria Naylor, *Mama Day* (New York: Ticknor and Fields, 1988), 5.

3. See Claude Lévi-Strauss, "The Structural Study of Myth," in *European Literary Theory and Practice,* ed. Vernon Gras (New York: Delta Publishing Co., 1973), 288–316.

4. Ibid., 293.

5. Alice Walker, "Everyday Use," in *In Love and Trouble: Stories of Black Women,* ed. Alice Walker (New York: Harcourt, 1973), 47–59.

6. See Northrup Frye, "Theory of Myths, " in his *Anatomy of Criticism* (New Brunswick, N. J.: Princeton University Press, 1957), esp. 161–162.

7. Paule Marshall, *Praisesong for the Widow* (New York: E. P. Dutton, 1983), 209.

8. Casting doubt on the teller, or otherwise devaluing oral testimony, has been a historical device that has marginalized the experiences of women. Texts such as Marshall's seek to place memory and myth in the same psychic space, an activity that reasserts black women's control over their words and their visions in their words. Lévi-Strauss writes that "myth is the part of language where the formula *traduttore, tradittore* reaches its lowest truth value" (Lévi-Strauss, 293).

9. Marshall, 209.

10. Willis (chap. 4, n. 12), 53–82.

11. Setiloane ([chap. 1, n. 24], 41) discusses religion in terms of consciousness of self and communities and of a divinity that is a "cause of being." Instead of the Western sense of religion as something acquired, Setiloane suggests that one of the key distinctions between Africa and the West is that "religion, a sense of a Power other than self, at work and determining existence, its origins and vicissitudes . . . is as old as being human itself; it is of the human's very nature. Hence the difference between Africa and the West in their attitude toward religion. There is actually no African word to translate 'religion.' At best it is translated as 'a people's ways' or 'customs' (*mekgwa/amasiko*) something lived and practised, not discussed and discoursed about."

12. Lévi-Strauss ([n. 3 above], 203, 204) describes myth using a linguistic vocabulary that identifies constituent units ("mythemes") that are useful in identifying "bundles of relations" within mythology.

13. Frye, "Theories of Myths," 135.

14. Northrup Frye, *Fables of Identity* (New York: Harcourt, Brace and World, 1963).

15. See Roland Barthes, *Mythologies,* trans. Antoinette Lavers (New York: Hill and Wang, 1972).

16. Zora Neale Hurston, *Moses, Man of the Mountain* (1939; reprint, Urbana: University of Illinois Press, 1984).

17. Setiloane (chap. 1, n. 24).

18. Harold Courlander, *Tales of Yoruba Gods and Heroes* (New York: Crown, 1973), 7.

19. Hurston, *Moses,* 103, 104.

20. Zora Neale Hurston, *Mules and Men* (1938; reprint, Bloomington: Indiana University Press, 1978), 193.

21. Hurston, *Their Eyes Were Watching God* (chap. 1, n. 21); Zora Neale Hurston, *Jonah's Gourd Vine* (1934; reprint, Philadelphia: J. B. Lippincott, 1971), and *Seraph on the Suwannee* (New York: Charles Scribner's Sons, 1948).

22. Victor Turner, "Myth and Symbol," as quoted in Houston Baker, *Blues, Ideology and Afro-American Literature: A Vernacular Theory* (Chicago: University of Chicago Press, 1985), 114, 115, 116.

23. Baker, ibid., 118.

24. Joan Kelly, *Women, History, and Theory* (Chicago: University of Chicago Press, 1984), 2.

25. Baker, *Blues*, 122. Baker's proposition that there is a distinction between myth and literature is borne out as he continues his discussion of the freedom of mythic discourse. In contrast to this view see Gates on the "speakerly text" in *Figures in Black* (chap. 1, n. 10). The privilege or the liminality of voice is the crucial proposition in a theory of African-American literature.

26. Joseph Adjaye, "Time, Calendar, and History among the Akan of Ghana," *Journal of Ethnic Studies* 15, no. 1 (Fall 1987): 71–99, esp. 95.

27. Frye (n. 6 above), 134.

28. Baker, *Blues*, 122.

29. Ibid., 121.

30. Toni Cade Bambara, *The Salt Eaters* (New York: Vintage, 1980), 7.

31. Gayl Jones, *Corregidora* (1975; reprint Boston: Beacon Press, 1986), 14.

32. Buchi Emecheta, *Second-Class Citizen* (New York: George Braziller, 1975), 166; and Hélène Cixous, "The Laugh of the Medusa: Viewpoint," trans. Keith Cohen and Paula Cohen, *Signs* 1, no. 4 (Summer 1976): 875–893.

33. Poovey (chap. 1, n. 17), 62.

34. Mary Helen Washington, *Invented Lives: Narratives of Black Women 1860–1960* (New York: Anchor Press, 1987), xv: Washington perceptively labels the *Negro Digest* essay as "an act of sabotage"—an important and appropriate indictment of this kind of marginalizing discourse that too often has been excused as critical license.

35. See Gates, "Writing 'Race and the Difference in Makes,'" in Gates, ed., "*Race*," *Writing, and Difference* (chap. 1, n. 37), esp. 7–9: Gates "imagine[s] the scene" of Phillis Wheatley's command performance before a group of "the most respectable characters in Boston" where she was interrogated as to the authorship of her own work. It was an occasion that was to assure her a publisher but at the same time an occasion that would be repeated countless times in black letters especially when women writers were concerned. Authorship, competency, and "daring to tell" have been the constant external and thematic challenges of black women's literature.

36. Fish (chap. 2, n. 5), 443.

37. Poovey (chap. 1, n. 17), 63.

Chapter 6. The Idea of Ancestry

1. Octavia Butler, *Kindred* (Boston: Beacon Press, 1971), 261, 9.

2. Compare ambivalence and collisions in Butler to the implicit tension of Hurston's attempts to straddle subjective/objective selves in her work.

3. See Clifford Geertz, "From the Native's Point of View: On the Nature of Anthropological Understanding," in his *Local Knowledge* (New York: Basic Books, 1983), 70.

4. Lionnet (chap. 2, n. 10), 131–132, 166.

5. Melvin Dixon, *Ride Out the Wilderness: Geography and Identity in Afro-American Literature* (Urbana: University of Illinois Press, 1987). See also Byerman (intro., n. 3), 276–278: I believe that Byerman's allegiance to a Western vision of wholeness allows his thesis of spiritual "health, creativity, and wholeness" to assert itself over texts where the dissolution of these elements is often a feature of the concluding events. Inclusion, which Byerman presents as the goal of community membership, must be understood as thematically distinct from "wholeness."

6. See Stephanie Demetrakopoulos's essay, "*Sula* and the Primacy of Woman-to-Woman Bonds," in *New Dimensions of Spirituality*, ed. K.F.C. Holloway and S. Demetrakopoulos (Westport, Conn.: Greenwood Press, 1987), 55–56.

7. Marshall (chap. 5, n. 7).

8. Gwendolyn Brooks, "One wants a Teller in a time like this" from "Notes from the Childhood and the Girlhood" in *Blacks* (chap. 1, n. 34), 132.

9. I am indebted to Julie Elizabeth Moody, a North Carolina State University graduate student in English, for this insight.

10. Bambara, *The Salt Eaters* (chap. 5, n. 30).

11. Morrison, *Beloved* (chap. 1, n. 15), 255–262.

12. Naylor, *Mama Day* (chap. 5, n. 2).

13. See Clifford Geertz, "Thick Description: Toward an Interpretive Theory of Culture," in his *Interpretation of Cultures* (New York: Basic Books, 1973), 3–32. Using a phrase he borrows from philosopher Gilbert Ryle, Geertz discusses the "intellectual effort" towards "thick description"—a "multiplicity of complex conceptual structures . . . superimposed or knotted into one another, which are at once strange, irregular, and inexplicit" (10). Such a creative effort towards thickness characterizes the language of dense texts such as Bambara's.

14. Dixon, 5.

15. Shange, *Sassafrass, Cypress and Indigo* (chap. 1, n. 1).

16. Brooks, *Maud Martha* (chap. 1, n. 34). Maud sees a procession of women who "strode down her imagination" (200–201).

17. Gayl Jones (chap. 5, n. 31).

18. Byerman (intro., n. 3), 181.

19. Jean-François Lyotard, *The Postmodern Condition: A Report on Knowledge*, as quoted in Cynthia Ward, "What They Told Buchi Emecheta: Oral Subjectivity and the Joys of 'Otherhood,'" *PMLA* 105, no. 1 (January 1990): 83–97. Ward makes this argument in the context of questioning the defining of African literature "entirely in terms of 'not European.'" According to Ward, this

definition suppresses cultural differences within the Third World as it searches for some utopic unity. A "not European" definition also argues that African literatures "written in English are motivated by and directed toward the non-African, the colonizer" (86–87).

20. See chapter three for a discussion of the translucent text.

21. Traditional methods of reporting history and the Western notion of civilization privilege the written text while devaluing the legitimacy and accuracy of the voiced text. Western methodology and systems of privilege are historically responsible for preserving theories that associate disability with cultures for whom the spoken text is an original and preserved method of record keeping.

22. Dixon's (n. 5 above) acquiescence to the reader's role in completing the textual thesis supports my notion that the text by itself does not achieve a wholeness or completion in its resolution.

23. Gloria Naylor, *Linden Hills* (New York: Penguin, 1986).

Chapter 7. Visions of the Goddess

1. E. Bolaji Idowu, *African Traditional Religion* (London: SCM Press, 1973), 149.

2. Gregory A. Shreve, "Structure and Reference: A Theory of African Folk Narrative," in *Phenomenology in Modern African Studies,* ed. Sunday Anozie (New York: Conch Magazine, 1982), 42.

3. Efua Sutherland, *Foriwa* (Ghana: Ghana Publishing Corp., 1967), *Edufa* (London: Longman Drumbeat, 1967), and "New Life at Kyerefaso," in *Nommo: An Anthology of Modern Black African and Black American Literature,* ed. William H. Robinson (New York: Macmillan, 1972), 283–287. In "New Life," the protagonist's name is spelled "Foruwa."

4. Brown (chap. 1, n. 6), 74.

5. Ibid.

6. Ward (chap. 6, n. 19), 93.

7. An interview with Ama Ata Aidoo, in Oladele Taiwo, *Female Novelists of Modern Africa* (New York: St. Martin's Press, 1984). Taiwo writes that Emecheta was influenced by "stories told by the women in moonlight sessions in the villages when she was young" and that "her grandmother, whom she much admired, was a keen storyteller and succeeded in getting her to recognise storytelling as an important cultural event" (100).

8. Ama Ata Aidoo, *Our Sister Killjoy: Or Reflections from a Black-eyed Squint* (London: Longman, 1966).

9. Brown (chap. 1, n. 6), 69.

10. Adetokundo Pearce, "The Didactic Essence of Efua Sutherland's Plays," in *Women in African Literature Today,* ed. Eldred D. Jones (Trenton, N.J.: Africa World Press, 1987), 74.

11. Brown, 69.

12. Merlin Stone, *Ancient Mirrors of Womanhood* (Boston: Beacon Press, 1970), 8, 9. Note, however, that if a sociopolitical agenda were the point here, it would be important to clarify that although goddess reverence (acknowl-

edgment) may have been a factor of social structures in West Africa, this reverence was not necessarily beneficial to the role or status of women within those ancient communities, nor have they assured direct benefits to women's status in contemporary communities.

13. Ward (chap. 6, n. 19), 92–93.

14. Halima Mohammed, "Women in Nigerian History: Examples from Borno Empire, Nupeland, and Igboland," *Women in Nigeria Today*, ed. S. Bappa et al. (London: Zed Publishers, 1985), 45.

15. Stone, 8, 9.

16. See chapters three and four for a discussion of recursive structures.

17. Starhawk, "Ethics and Justice in Goddess Religion," *Anima: An Experimental Journal* 7 (Fall Equinox 1980).

18. See Gloria Emeagwali, "Women in Pre-capitalist, Socio-economic Formations in Nigeria," in Bappa et al., eds., and Mohammed.

19. Christian (chap. 1, n. 6), 147.

20. Ayesha Imam, "Toward an Adequate Analysis of the Position of Women in Society," in Bappa et al., eds. (n. 14 above), 15, 16.

21. Ama Ata Aidoo, *Anowa* (London: Longman, 1970), 46, 47.

22. Davies, "Introduction," in Davies and Graves, eds. (chap. 1, n. 6), 17.

23. Filomena Steady, "The Black Woman Cross-Culturally," as quoted in Davies, "Motherhood in the Works of Male and Female Igbo Writers," in Davies and Graves, eds., 243.

24. Rosemary Ruether, *New Woman/New Earth: Sexist Ideologies and Human Liberation* (New York: Seabury, 1975), 194, 195.

25. Although Reuther's discussion does not support this view, it is my sense that perceiving mother religions as having a dialectical unity is a Western mode of thought. My argument, were I to engage this thesis in any detail, would be that the kind of interpretation which Reuther herself brings to the discussion of mother religions presupposes a dialectic—a reflection of her own Western perceptions. The first question ought to be whether or not a dialectic itself is Western and therefore as much an anomaly in mother religions as the split of unity that Reuther identifies in these religions.

26. Emecheta, *Second-Class Citizen* (chap. 5, no. 32), 166.

27. Susan Stanford Friedman, "Creativity and the Childbirth Metaphor," in Showalter, ed., *Speaking of Gender* (chap. 3, n. 6), 73–100, esp. 80.

28. Nwapa, *Efuru* (chap. 1, n. 31), 45.

29. Ama Ata Aidoo, "Certain Winds from the South," in *Aidoo* (chap. 4, n. 5), 55–64.

Chapter 8. Spirituals and Praisesongs

1. See Weinreich (chap. 1, n. 3 above).

2. The phrase is from Zora Neale Hurston, *Their Eyes Were Watching God* (chap. 1, n. 21), 29. Janie's grandmother tells her that black women are the least in the world—the mule—labor driven and poorly rewarded for their hard labors.

3. Kelly (chap. 5, n. 24), 6: It is especially telling that when Kelly mentions

black women in her discussion, it is to "help us [I presume she means white feminists] appreciate the social formation of 'femininity' as an internalization of ascribed inferiority which serves, at the same time, to manipulate those who have the authority women lack." Such use of black women's experience in feminist scholarship reflects unflatteringly on the politics of this academic movement.

4. Mervyn Rothstein, "Morrison Discusses New Novel," *New York Times* (August 26, 1987).

5. Morrison, *Beloved* (chap. 1, n. 15). The epigraph to this novel, "Sixty million and more," is a reference to the captured Africans who did not survive the middle passage.

6. Friedman (chap. 7, n. 27), 75.

7. Ibid., 89.

8. Gates's term is "free indirect discourse" for this narrative technique. One of his many discussions on this strategy occurs in *Figures in Black* (chap. 1, n. 10), where he notes that Hurston's "oral hieroglyph" is a "spoken or mimetic voice masking as a diegetic voice, but also a diegetic voice masking as a mimetic one . . . a free narrative of division" (243). The masking that Gates describes is equivalent to what I see as the shift in the elliptical interplay between implicit structures of orature and explicit structures of literature.

9. Walter Ong, *Orality and Literacy: The Technologizing of the World* (New York: Methuen, 1983), 175.

10. See Gates, *Figures in Black*.

11. Cixous and Clément, (chap. 1, n. 16), 136. Although my coauthor and I experienced a similar sharing of discursive space in our creation of *New Dimensions* (chap. 6, n. 6), it was clear to us that when women do not share cultural origins, the sharing of narrative space can create artistic tensions. This conflict worked for us in *New Dimensions* because the nature of our enterprise was to reveal alternative cultural facets of the reading act. There is a noticeable lack of tension in the discourse of Sethe, Denver, and Beloved (Morrison, *Beloved*) because they are spiritually linked, one to the other.

12. This event from Nwapa's *Efuru* (chap. 1, n. 31) is discussed in chapter seven.

13. "Sethe" is phonologically and semantically similar to "Lethe," the name of the river of forgetfulness in Hades. Its similarity to forgetfulness and oblivion becomes especially significant in a later chapter where Sethe urges her daughters to sleep so that their dream-like (re)membrances can assert themselves in the text. For further discussion on names and their significance in Morrison, see Ruth Rosenburg, "And the Children May Know Their Names," *Literary Onomastics Studies* 8 (1981), 195–219.

14. Flora Nwapa, *Idu* (London: Heinemann, 1970).

15. Rothstein (n. 4 above).

16. Black literary theory's interest in the nature of inversion in the African-American text provides some rich critical discussion and speculation. See, e.g., *Blues* (chap. 5, n. 22), 122. The dissolution of normalcy would seem to predict the inversive cognitive and narrative strategies of *Beloved*. However, the importance of inversion in signalling subversion in black women's writing

is the dimension that is distinct to a woman-centered ideology. Gates identifies the "mystery type of narrative discourse" as one "characterized by plot inversions" (*Signifying Monkey* [chap. 1, n. 13], 229). He notes that these function as temporal inversions. Gates's point is that Ishmael Reed's texts contain a sort of indeterminacy that predicates the use of inversion as textual impediment. Impediment is somewhat closer to the subversion I describe, but it implies a blockage that is not a feature in black woman writers' use of this technique.

17. Adrienne Rich, "Toward the Solstice," *The Dream of a Common Language: Poems 1974–1977* (New York: Norton, 1979), 69.

18. Phoeby, whose name means "like the moon," reflects the poetic light of Janie's experience; however, she has no light of her own.

19. Brown (chap. 1, n. 6), 136.

Index